Feminism, National Identity and European Integration in Modern Spain

Feminism, National Identity and European Integration in Modern Spain

Defining a Democracy, 1960–Present

Kathryn L. Mahaney

BLOOMSBURY ACADEMIC
LONDON • NEW YORK • OXFORD • NEW DELHI • SYDNEY

BLOOMSBURY ACADEMIC

Bloomsbury Publishing Plc, 50 Bedford Square, London, WC1B 3DP, UK
Bloomsbury Publishing Inc, 1359 Broadway, New York, NY 10018, USA
Bloomsbury Publishing Ireland, 29 Earlsfort Terrace, Dublin 2, D02 AY28, Ireland

BLOOMSBURY, BLOOMSBURY ACADEMIC and the Diana logo are
trademarks of Bloomsbury Publishing Plc

First published in Great Britain 2024
Paperback edition published 2026

Copyright © Kathryn L. Mahaney, 2024

Kathryn L. Mahaney has asserted her right under the Copyright, Designs and
Patents Act, 1988, to be identified as Author of this work.

For legal purposes the Acknowledgments on pp. viii–x constitute an extension of this
copyright page.

Cover image © Astrolounge / Getty Images

All rights reserved. No part of this publication may be: i) reproduced or transmitted in
any form, electronic or mechanical, including photocopying, recording or by means of
any information storage or retrieval system without prior permission in writing from the
publishers; or ii) used or reproduced in any way for the training, development or operation
of artificial intelligence (AI) technologies, including generative AI technologies. The rights
holders expressly reserve this publication from the text and data mining exception as
per Article 4(3) of the Digital Single Market Directive (EU) 2019/790.

Bloomsbury Publishing Plc does not have any control over, or responsibility for, any
third-party websites referred to or in this book. All internet addresses given in this
book were correct at the time of going to press. The author and publisher regret
any inconvenience caused if addresses have changed or sites have ceased
to exist, but can accept no responsibility for any such changes.

Every effort has been made to trace the copyright holders and obtain permission
to reproduce the copyright material. Please do get in touch with any enquiries or
any information relating to such material or the rights holder. We would be
pleased to rectify any omissions in subsequent editions of this publication
should they be drawn to our attention.

A catalogue record for this book is available from the British Library.

A catalog record for this book is available from the Library of Congress.

ISBN:	HB:	978-1-3501-9510-3
	PB:	978-1-3501-9511-0
	ePDF:	978-1-3501-9512-7
	eBook:	978-1-3501-9513-4

Typeset by Integra Software Services Pvt. Ltd.

For product safety related questions contact productsafety@bloomsbury.com.

To find out more about our authors and books visit www.bloomsbury.com
and sign up for our newsletters.

To my three biggest loves: Cesc, Joan, and Alex

Contents

Acknowledgments   viii

Introduction   1

1   Female Sentinels of Occident: The *Sección Femenina*, Women's Rights, and Francoist Spain's Search for International Acceptance in Postwar Western Europe   21

2   "What We Want is For Each Woman to Be Her Own Protagonist": Re-examining the Feminist "Triumphs" of Transition-Era Spain   51

3   Transnationalizing the Transition and Beyond: How Domestic Feminist Conflict and Global Feminist Networks Affected Late Twentieth-Century Spanish Politics   85

4   Violent Inequalities: Debates on Intimate Partner Violence, Gender Equality, and the Ongoing Struggle to Define Post-Francoist Democratic Spain   113

5   Conclusions: "La Lucha Continúa," the Struggle Continues   139

Notes   155
Bibliography   195
Index   205

Acknowledgments

This book is based on my dissertation and so I remain indebted to my incredible advisor, Dagmar Herzog, for her support both while I was in graduate school and still today. She has always believed in me, has always been honest with me, and has, perhaps most importantly, always been kind. I am grateful for her mentorship. Similarly, Helena Rosenblatt and Mary Gibson offered critique of the dissertation that has been very helpful as I crafted the book manuscript; thank you to both of them for pushing me to think more critically.

I must also thank some scholars in my field. Temma Kaplan has been an invaluable resource for broadening my research, which she did by gifting me with an extensive, decades-in-the-making personal collection of newspaper clippings and feminist memorabilia, and for reading and correcting early drafts of several chapters. Julia Hudson-Richards also read early drafts and offered suggestions for re-framing and strengthening my Chapter 1 argument, and in addition pointed me to some sources I may not have otherwise found. Louie Dean Valencia consulted with me about how best to describe some of my feminist comic book pamphlets. Lastly, I owe an immense debt to Aurora Morcillo who is no longer with us but was always so kind, generous, and encouraging. I cannot believe that I can no longer rely on her guidance and keen insight. I have missed her every time I sat down to write.

Of course, I am also grateful for the assistance of several archivists and researchers who helped me uncover my archival documents. I would like to thank the archivists at the United Nations Archives in New York City as well as the National Libraries of Catalonia and of Spain for their guidance as I conducted my research. Likewise, I would like to thank my colleagues Suzanne Dunai and Matt Erlich, who tracked down sources for me during their research years in Madrid when I'm sure they could have found a better use for their time. Pedro Ochoa similarly allowed me to take advantage of his proximity to the Biblioteca Nacional de España during Covid when I needed more materials but could not travel to do my own research. Javier Tébar at the Fundació Cipriano García Arxiu Històric de CCOO de Catalunya pulled every feminist and tangentially feminist record he could think of for me when he heard the scope of my project, and these sources added depth to my analysis. And I owe much to the women of Ca la Dona and its Centre de Documentació in Barcelona who went far beyond their job descriptions while helping me navigate their archives. Mercè Otero Vidal and Mireia Bofill in particular provided invaluable commentary on sources I was studying, gave me books for my personal library, brought memorabilia from their homes to show me, and rearranged their personal schedules to ensure that I had sufficient time in the archives.

I would be remiss if I neglected to acknowledge that none of this would have been possible without my colleagues, friends, and family. Jess Davidson and fellow scholars in the ASPHS, thank you for your collegiality and for making me feel at home in the field of Spanish history. The community I've found in the Thistle Class Association, especially Mike McBride, Kimberly Pasley, Larry Liggett, and Alex Liggett, has provided me with a world beyond academia while consistently reminding me that other things in my life are also of immense value. Arnout van der Meer, Joke van Oers, Annie DeVries, Elizabeth Churchich—I am 1,000 percent happy to have met you in graduate school.

I moved to Finland in 2018 and finished this book while forging a new life in a foreign-to-me place. Thank you to the Faculty of Social Sciences at the University of Helsinki for making me and Alex feel so welcome, but particularly to Jari Eloranta and Hanna Kuusi. I'm also incredibly grateful to have Seona Candy, Lisa Gemmel, and Måns Magnusson in my life—the friendship and community they've offered have been beyond compare.

My mother and father, Jack and Colleen Mahaney, and sister and brother-in-law, Kristin Mahaney and Matt Gaines, have all somehow tolerated me throughout this process, even on those days when I was too busy reading, writing, or simply agonizing over the project to pick up the phone or to return their texts. It's a miracle that I remain in their good graces, and I am so lucky to have a family who believes in me unconditionally.

Finally, I have to thank my husband, Alex Gomez-del-Moral, who has stood with me since the beginning of our respective graduate careers. There is so much I could say, but I'll just leave it at this: I feel blessed to have found a partner who is also a colleague, and who has been willing to switch hats as needed—sometimes providing me with ego-stroking and validation that I almost certainly didn't deserve, other times being as brutally critical as any anonymous reviewer. I needed both. I am also grateful for a partner willing to go all-in, without prompting, on co-parenting and sharing the drudgery of household management; completing a dissertation and then a book while raising small children would have been impossible without Alex's commitment to ensuring that he pulled his weight and often much of mine as well. This book is dedicated to the lights of my life, Cesc and Joan, but, most of all to Alex, who gave me those beautiful boys but who also gave me the love and support necessary so I could have much, much more in my life besides.

Introduction

In Barcelona, 2007 was a year that ended in scandal. Three years before, the socialists of the *Partido Socialista Obrero Español* (Spanish Socialist Worker's Party, henceforth PSOE) had swept into power following a general election that had been disastrous for the center-right *Partido Popular* (Popular Party, henceforth PP), which had governed Spain since 1996. Almost immediately, the PSOE and their leader, newly elected Spanish president José Luis Rodríguez Zapatero, had found themselves embroiled in a culture war with conservative activists and politicians determined to stop the party's efforts to promote gender equality. From their perspective, conservatives had reason for alarm: Zapatero had run his 2004 campaign on a platform that included women's rights as a central issue, and before the year was out, his administration made passage of a seminal law that established unprecedented protections for victims of gender violence, the *Ley Orgánica de Medidas de Protección Integral contra la Violencia de Género* (Organic Law for Integral Protection Measures against Gender Violence, or LOMPIVG), its first significant legislative achievement.

Against this backdrop, in December 2007 Barcelona authorities arrested fourteen people alleged to have provided or obtained illegal abortions—Spanish abortion restrictions were among the strictest in Western Europe—including several psychologists and psychiatrists accused of falsifying medical records to afford perfectly healthy women access abortions on mental health grounds. Conservative media in Spain as well as abroad were quickly in uproar: the national newspaper *El Mundo* described the incident as the dismantling of a thirty-year-old "abortion ring" headed by "abortion tycoon" Dr. Carlos Morín; right-wing news organ *La Razón* denounced Spain having become an "illegal abortion Mecca"; and in the wake of the arrests, conservative TV network *Intereconomía* aired incendiary abortion footage it had taken covertly at a clinic in Madrid—the first time such footage had ever aired on Spanish national television, American anti-abortion news service LifeSite.com reported.[1] Rather than shrinking from the controversy, though, and in a move influenced by legislation in other European nations as well as Spanish feminists' demands, Zapatero seized the moment as an opportunity to revisit Spain's stance on abortions. At a December 17 meeting with PSOE leadership, the Spanish president called on his party to weigh whether a reform of the country's abortion laws—a loosening of restrictions possibly to be modeled after other European abortion codes—was called for. The PSOE formally announced its intention to reopen debate on abortion's legality in 2008, and two years later a new law went into effect that guaranteed abortion on demand up to the fourteenth week of pregnancy.[2]

Unsurprisingly, the outrage among abortion foes in Spain rose to a fever pitch. Between 2008 when the PSOE declared its intentions on abortion reform and the resulting law's passage in 2010, Catholic Church officials and independent anti-abortion activists developed and disseminated their position that abortion was not a "human right" in need of defense. Spain, they argued, was already free of exploitation and discrimination, and new laws seeking new, imagined rights for minorities were unnecessary. "There are laws that prevent [these things], older than Zapatero himself," stressed Gádor Joya, the spokesperson for Right to Life. As such, he continued,

> Mr. Zapatero is late to promote the dignity of workers, immigrants, and all people whatever their sexual orientation, race, or religion ... His contribution to Spanish life is quite another thing. He has divided society around a supposed right to violently end the life of a human being that cannot defend itself. That is Zapatero's struggle for the dignity of the person.[3]

Joya articulated his organization's belief that Zapatero might claim to work for equality but his support of abortion reform belied a disregard for human life—and conservative Spaniards broadly shared this view, with the unaffiliated but similarly minded organization *Hazte Oir* (Speak Up!), for instance, disseminating Joya's statement to its wide-ranging internet network. That organization's president, Ignacio Arsuaga, denounced Zapatero even more forcefully, arguing that the socialist leader's reforms not only divided society as Joya had claimed, but were also of a "totalitarian nature." Arsuaga called on *Hazte Oir*'s supporters to "resist this nightmare society ... [and] stop the deterioration of institutions and democratic freedoms" that would follow from abortion's legalization.[4] In his view, Zapatero's legalization of abortion could destroy democracy itself—the very foundation of Spaniards' civil rights, and indeed of human rights—instead of protecting it.

Ghosts of Repression: Historicizing Francoism's Long Shadow

Arsuaga's claims were neither random nor ill-considered. The *Hazte Oir* president must have known the terrible and all-too-fresh nature of the specters his words, and the threat of totalitarianism, raised in the minds of countless Spanish citizens. Less than half a century earlier, as the countercultural 1960s dawned in Western Europe, Spain had entered its third decade of dictatorship under the rule of Generalissimo Francisco Franco. The Franco regime (1936–75), the memory and legacies of which remain deeply divisive in Spain, was more than the simple domain of a political strongman. Rather, the regime had from its inception sought to reengineer Spanish society. In the founding mythology on which the Francoist imaginary was built, Spain was an exceptional nation, divinely blessed with unique spiritual and cultural gifts and thus destined for global moral as well as social and political leadership. In this vein, the regime continually relegitimated its hegemony through dissemination and frequent commemoration of a carefully curated official version of the bloody conflict—the Spanish Civil War (1936–9)—that had brought Franco to power. This narrative cast the war as having saved Spain from the disastrous Second Republic, which the regime painted as a failed democracy that had threatened to tear Spanish society apart and destroy the nation's traditions and culture. Indeed, as historian Sandie Holguín has argued, Franco and his Nationalist forces began to construct this official memory of the Spanish Civil War while it still raged, shepherding tourists around active battlefields on tours that

> played a critical role in creating and consecrating a series of narratives that the Franco regime would repeat obsessively until its demise in 1975, and helped to fashion a Francoist vision of national identity that—the Nationalists claimed—had temporarily been stolen by the architects of the Second Republic. On these tours, the Nationalists depicted the war as both a Crusade and a new Reconquista, thereby exalting a Nationalist heroism that depended on complete humiliation of the 'Red' enemy.[5]

Francoist officials thereby sought to cement the legitimacy of their newly established Catholic moral and social order, with Spain's homegrown counterpart to the various fascist parties that had emerged in Interwar Europe, the *Falange Española*, at the center of the regime's political organization, Franco's *Movimiento Nacional* (National Movement). Franco's new order included a rejection of democratic politics, criminalization of all political parties save the National Movement and its subsidiary ideological camps, and revival of archaic legal structures that in many cases dated to the Napoleonic *Code Civil* introduced when French forces occupied Spain in 1808, or earlier still. As part of this, the regime harshly imposed a legal and social subordination of women both to their male relations and to the patriarchal designs of the regime as a whole. Authorities accomplished this especially through the complicity of the Spanish Catholic Church, which preached a deeply conservative and nationalistic brand of religion termed "National-Catholicism," as well as with help from the *Sección Femenina* (SF), the official Women's Section of the Falange.[6]

Under this new National-Catholic social order Spanish women found their access to the public sphere severely curtailed. National-Catholicism's gender hierarchy stressed domestic life—more specifically, the roles of wife, mother, and homemaker—as women's divinely ordained and thus highest calling. The Franco regime committed itself quite early to this ideology, evident in its wartime *Fuero del Trabajo* ("Labor Charter") of 1938, which would serve a cornerstone for subsequent Francoist legality and which spoke of "free[ing] married women from the workshop and factory."[7] In line with this mission, both the regime's own legal edifice and the full weight of Franco-era society's expectations conspired to drive women from the workplace and into caregiving roles in the home.

A second Francoist policy dating from 1938 explicitly prohibited married women's work if authorities judged the male breadwinner's salary sufficient, and otherwise still required wives to obtain written permission from their husbands in order to secure legal employment (or to engage in commercial activities, hold a passport, or open a bank account).[8] Regardless of their marital status women were furthermore barred from entry to certain professions—most notably, the legal field—and were subject to the absolute authority of their head of household, whose permission they likewise needed even to take a trip of any length.[9] All of these controls stemmed from National-Catholic authorities' dread that unrestricted exposure to the opposite sex would inevitably lead to temptation and sin, a fear that also moved the regime to impose a ban on coeducation past the age of six; to establish a puritanical censorial regime that, for instance, retouched inappropriately racy posters for films such as the 1949 Cecil B. DeMille epic *Samson and Delilah*; and to require that swimsuit-clad beachgoers (including children) don modest ankle-length robes whenever unsubmerged.[10]

Sección Femenina was thoroughly complicit in the imposition of this gendered order. Throughout the 1940s and 1950s, women's magazines published by SF disseminated a domestic, submissive, and pious feminine model in keeping with the group's eighteen-point creed, which exhorted Spain's women to, for instance, "let the man in your life be the best patriot," "obey, and by your example teach others to obey," and "try always to be the wheel of the cart and let the one guiding it be in control."[11] Also, by law, women could only avail themselves of their already-limited right to work, or attend university, or even get a passport, with proof of having performed (or having received an exemption from performing) a period of "national service" in the SF's *Servicio Social* ("Social Service"), which trained participants in domestic and caregiving skills while inculcating them with National-Catholic gender notions. Nearly 825,000 women spent time in this system between 1938 and 1961, and as many as 1.2 million had done so by the time the program ended in 1978.[12]

Meanwhile, Franco sought to legitimize his regime in foreign eyes, particularly after the fall of his earliest allies, Nazi Germany and Fascist Italy. Despite the repression that characterized his dictatorship, Franco aspired to a place among the globe's elite nations. Toward this end, from the late 1940s onward, he sought to cultivate Spain's ties with leading nations in the Cold War-era Western bloc and he took steps to improve his regime's foreign image enough to make such diplomacy possible. In 1953, for example, Franco negotiated a partnership with American President Dwight D. Eisenhower allowing the United States to establish strategically advantageous military bases in several Spanish cities. Spain gained United Nations membership in 1955, after a decade of rejection, in part as a result of this alliance. Franco's actions as a UN member further demonstrate his concern about Spain's reputation: he signed several UN conventions he had no intention of complying with because, as scholar Lynn Savery has argued, Franco wanted Spain to be "part of the international community on paper if not in practice."[13]

The Franco regime also never wavered in its ambition to raise Spain to a position of global leadership, rather than simply become part of an international global elite. In its infancy, the Franco regime had touted its new Spain as a "spiritual sentinel of the West"—a beacon of Christian morality relighted in an age of spiritual decadence.[14] This conceit never disappeared (and in fact would underlay *Sección Femenina*'s aspirations to global leadership on women's rights in the late 1960s), but during the 1950s and especially the 1960s, a period when Spain possessed one of the world's fastest-growing economies, it shifted in focus beyond moral leadership and toward the aim of establishing the nation as a leading trade power in Europe and the world. Hence, Franco's repeated efforts to establish economic as well as diplomatic ties with his European neighbors as well as with the United States, particularly after the launch of the European Economic Community (EEC) in 1958.[15]

Despite Franco's efforts, and some notable successes, his authoritarian Spain never did manage to fully sell itself as a typical, prosperous Western European capitalist nation. For example, Eisenhower met with Franco in Madrid in 1959, becoming the first sitting US President to visit Spain under the dictatorship—yet when Franco's regime applied for membership to the fledgling EEC in 1962, hoping to build on this diplomatic success and extend Spanish influence, the application was rejected. Amid an international press campaign opposing Spain's admission, the Congress of the European Movement decreed that "only democratic nations could join the European Community."[16] Clearly, "democratic" was something they did not consider Spain to be. This was hardly surprising, as memory of the world wars and the commitment to liberal democratic values that the EEC claimed to champion left that body unwilling to partner too closely with a regime that many considered a fascist relic. Preferential economic affiliation, negotiated in 1970, was the most they were willing to offer.[17] UN leaders on occasion showed similar unease: in September 1975 for instance, General Secretary Kurt Waldheim criticized Spain's reliance on terror and lobbied the government to release political prisoners and stay executions.[18]

Nor did lived conditions in Spain ever come to resemble any sort of Western European normalcy. The nation, thanks to the transformative economic Stabilization Plan implemented by regime officials in 1959, possessed the second-fastest growing economy in the world throughout the 1960s. Yet throughout, Spaniards remained plagued by anxiety over what they perceived to be their nation's continued backwardness by comparison with the rest of Western Europe.[19] The nation's repeated rejection from EEC membership, coupled with the businessmen's and officials' fears of Spanish exclusion from the European "Common Market," did nothing to mitigate this sentiment. Western notions of Francoism's comparative anachronistic conservatism on social issues underscored the continued differences that set Franco's Spain apart from its neighbors, even as Franco's desire for international connection grew and manifested in his ultimately unsuccessful pursuit of EEC membership.

There was, moreover, substance to Spain's fears of its own backwardness: as historians Antonio Cazorla and Inbal Ofer have noted, pockets of abject poverty persisted alongside spectacles of mass consumption even in Spain's most prosperous cities, with outlying areas like Madrid's Orcasitas neighborhood lacking running water into the 1970s.[20] Similarly, while Spain seemed to make strides toward expanding women's legal and economic rights—several *Sección Femenina*-backed reforms enacted by the regime in the late 1950s and 1960s put some Spanish women's rights on par with, if not ahead of, the norm in Western Europe—these advances had a limited impact on those women who remained banned from the legal profession and any trade involving machinery deemed "dangerous." This was even more the case for those whose spouses simply denied them the still legally indispensable permission to work or beat them with impunity in the absence of any law criminalizing such abuse.[21]

What's in a Label?: Struggles over Defining Spanish Feminism

Franco's death in 1975 did little to dispel these problems. The EEC expressed doubt that Spain would or could pursue sociopolitical reforms in the post-Franco era. Partly in response to these doubts, Spanish politicians and activists battled over how best to define the nation's new democracy and, more specifically, how as well as whether to create policies on gender equality. Contemporaneously, Spanish feminist organizations, which had formed and operated clandestinely during the last decade of the Franco regime, began to publicly demand legislation on issues such as decriminalization of adultery and abortion, and legalization of divorce. At the same time, politicians who in 1977 began to draft a new democratic constitution for post-Francoist Spain did so fully aware that international observers expected the new democracy to protect women's rights. The resulting document consequently included a clause that proclaimed Spanish women full and equal citizens—this guarantee, the framers hoped, would convince the global community of the nation's liberalizing intentions, and at last win Spain international acceptance and EEC membership.[22] Meanwhile, the simultaneity of the Constitution's historic new protections for Spanish women and the visibility of feminist protest in Spain led contemporaries and historians alike to interpret the document's final form as a feminist triumph—when in fact, as this book shows, these activists had little direct voice in crafting the constitution, whose architects were driven less by feminist pressures than their own desire (long felt by the Franco regime, too) to combat Spain's lingering political notoriety abroad.

Spain's feminists were hardly well-positioned to exert any such influence: they struggled to agree about what "feminism" was, and who as well as what policy positions qualified as "feminist." Indeed, these categories remained slippery throughout the period examined here, and so require some measure of explanation before proceeding further.

As used in most discourse circulating during much of the Franco era, "feminist" (the Spanish word was *feminista*) amounted to little more than an ill-defined slur used to discredit women deemed troublesome by Francoist society for behaving counter to the regime's hegemonic gender norms. Thus, for instance, correspondents covering Britain's 1966 parliamentary election for *ABC* argued that gender-bending "boyish" feminists were to blame for that year's decreased number of female candidates for parliament. They also blamed these "feminists" for male hippies' effeminacy and for the bikini's emergence, a garment they believed women wore to provoke shows of masculinity from men like the hippies even though such display of female flesh was, according to National-Catholic norms, vulgar.[23]

Though *Sección Femenina* fought to expand women's legal and economic rights, the organization's leadership was among those using "feminist" as a pejorative term. In a speech celebrating the passage of a major law on women's rights in 1961, SF founder Pilar Primo de Rivera underlined that "this legislation is not in the least way feminist ... we do not seek to make men and women the same ... this law, rather than being feminist, is to the contrary support that men give to women as the weaker sex in order to simplify their lives."[24] Indeed, the consensus among Spanish historians is that, despite its support for some expanded rights for women, SF was neither feminist nor had feminist aspirations. Historian Aurora Morcillo, a leading authority on the organization, theorized the distinction between women's rights activists like those in the *Sección Femenina* and those feminists (she called them cultural) who believe that whatever differences may exist between the sexes are no bar to equality: "Right-wing women celebrate the distinction between the sexes, but whereas cultural feminists challenge patriarchal privilege, right-wing women call themselves antifeminist and seek protection within patriarchy."[25] This book agrees with Morcillo's explanation and does not challenge the consensus of Spanish historians that SF cannot be considered feminist, despite arguing that the organization's periodic calls for reform ultimately helped place Spain's women's rights policies on par with what the rest of Western Europe promoted. In relation to neighboring countries, the *Sección Femenina*'s activism was progressive—defined here as genuinely supportive of some degree of emancipatory social and political reform, or "progress," by contrast with immobilist or reactionary stances—but its motivations were emphatically not.

As of the mid-1960s and especially a decade later, as Franco lay dying, the term "feminism" became more acceptable, but often even less easily defined. SF continued to disavow all notions of feminism in its work to preserve traditional feminine subservience and domesticity, but other conservatives were increasingly willing to define *as* "feminism" a limited vision of women's legal equality with men. In general use, these conservatives described as "feminists" a subset of respectable women who promoted a tepid form of women's rights advocacy similar to SF's, even as conservatives, along with SF, rejected the feminist activists and politics emerging from clandestine organizations in the late 1970s.

Even traditionally regime-aligned camps such as the Spanish Catholic clergy became willing to contest what was "feminist" and what wasn't. The Church, for instance, embraced a tightly circumscribed "christian" feminism that largely reinforced rather than challenged Franco-era gender relations. Between 1963 and 1967 multiple *ABC* articles featured author Lili Álvarez advocating this kind of "purified" and "feminine" feminism that stressed piety, sexual purity, and humility alongside support for SF's conception of women's rights.[26] Likewise, following an August 1975 speech in which Pope Paul VI advocated a feminism grounded in women's divinely ordained destiny as "daughter, virgin, wife, mother, and widow," prominent Spanish journalist and Sevillan cathedral canon Juan Ordóñez Márquez called for a "Marian" feminism following the example of the Virgin Mary, which he deemed "in flagrant contradiction with the feminist promotion efforts of [the time]."[27]

Yet while these as well as *Sección Femenina*'s positions could be described as falling within a larger category of activism for women's rights and might also in some cases be termed "progressive," it is a more complex matter—and in the case of *Sección Femenina*, would be inappropriate—to label them "feminist," a slippery term that covered a variety of reformist as well as revolutionary ideologies. This is only further complicated by the pattern, illustrated throughout this book, of male politicians claiming the mantle of "feminist" and instituting "feminist" policies and legislation without female input or approval—a pattern continued steadily through the remainder of the century.

As "feminism" became a more widely used term in the late Franco years, both self-identified feminists in the clandestine feminist movement and their conservative critics often rejected their political foes' versions of feminism. Thus, for example, conservative critics rejected their opponents not for being feminist—the term was, depending on who wielded it and in which context, not necessarily a damning slur—but rather for being the wrong *kind* of feminist. Significantly, moreover, the self-identified feminists emerging from clandestine organizations did so not as a unified force, but as activists who themselves had different beliefs and priorities. Though these activists all rejected conservatives' idea of respectable and limited "feminism," they also disagreed amongst themselves about how to define their own feminism and its demands and they rejected those who believed differently as insufficiently feminist or as wrongheaded about what feminism and its goals were.

Generally speaking, feminists emerging from clandestine movements and opposing Francoist conservatives broke down into two camps: double militants and single militants. The two differed somewhat on what they felt constituted equality with men, but they differed far more on how they thought women ought to achieve the aim of equality. Double militants believed that feminist activism ought to take place within as well as outside the political parties seeking to effect broad-ranging social change in Spain and, during the framing of the 1978 Constitution, supported this document's ratification and the political order it established notwithstanding their exclusion from its creation. Single militants, by contrast, considered this constitutional order irredeemably tainted by its overwhelmingly male and often conservative and cynical authorship, in which Franco-era political elites had figured far too much. For them, true feminist progress could only come through a fundamental break with the preexisting order, and militancy should take place exclusively within feminist organizations not tied to Spain's ideologically compromised party politics.

These differences only ossified over time. In the early 1970s, single and double militants had attempted to find common ground even as they critiqued others whose ideas conflicted with theirs. A decade later, however, in 1983, the establishment of a national *Instituto de la Mujer* (Women's Bureau, or *Instituto*) irrevocably divided single and double militants into two distinct and non-overlapping ideological camps, with double militants populating the *Instituto* and becoming involved within political parties and ensconced in government administration and single militants choosing to remain outside government structures and continue their grassroots activism. Each condemned the other, though single militants did so most vociferously, for being either not truly feminist or for being the wrong kind of feminist.

In this book, I use the terms "single militant" and "double militant" to refer to these groups before the formation of the *Instituto*. After its formation, the terms "independent feminist" and "institutional feminist" are perhaps more useful descriptors. "Independent feminists," those who chose to continue grassroots work, refers to the single militants who remained in organizations separate from political and government structures and were critical of their government-affiliated counterparts; "institutional feminists" signifies those double militants who became part of the Spanish government by joining and working within political parties, government administration, and, of course, the *Instituto*. In general, independent feminists had politics that both institutional feminists and the Spanish public perceived as "radical," and so I also occasionally refer to independent feminists as radical when doing so might be helpful. Lastly, even though there were stark ideological divisions between feminists, it is sometimes useful to highlight points of common ground or common action and, in these instances I simply refer to "feminists" and intend it to be a very general descriptor of women who participated in or allied with the different branches of the feminist movement.

Though the groups shared a mutual disdain, the disdain they felt for each other was not necessarily equally great. Institutional feminists voiced less public criticism of independent feminists than vice-versa, likely because the government-funded feminists of the *Instituto* had the satisfaction of access to comparatively greater (albeit still limited) political leverage. They also enjoyed more positive public perception. Throughout the end of the twentieth century and the beginning of the twenty-first, Spanish society was sympathetic to institutional feminists and their demands: institutional feminism was the new "acceptable," mainstream form of feminism and independent feminism, to which critics now applied the pejorative label "radical," was either dismissed as populated by man-haters or mocked and belittled in other ways. With the dawn of the new millennium, conservative public figures in Spain muddied the rhetorical waters still further as, in a perverse turn of events, they began to use institutional "feminist" rhetoric to argue against feminist ideals and pursue the repeal of legislation that had during the intervening decades markedly increased the scope of women's rights in Spain, most notably expanded access to abortion and protections for victims of intimate partner violence.

Feminism—A Window into Forty Years of Fighting over the Soul of Spanish Democracy

This book suggests that the semantic confusion and oftentimes tense ideological conflict that marked Spanish feminism during and following the birth of Spain's current democracy point to larger truths about the forging and character of post-Franco Spanish political culture. In the years leading up to the constitution's framing, and even more so in the decades that followed, debates within and about feminism—in particular the battles to define what constituted women's rights and to delineate how women could best lay claim to those rights—are in large part how Spaniards wrestled with anxieties about their nation's perceived backwardness within Western Europe and uncertainties about the shape that the nation's identity would take after Francoism. These debates consumed the rest of the twentieth century as feminists, politicians, international organizations, and ordinary citizens alike fought protracted battles over adultery, divorce, abortion, and intimate partner violence legislation. However, I show, the debates also played out as a composition of theme and variations: Spaniards' anxieties evolved as the nation gained a respected position in Western Europe and as its citizens embraced the nation's liberalization. My book tracks these variations and this evolution.

This book also argues that even as debates about women's rights played a central role in defining and refining Spain's democracy, feminism and feminist activists had less political leverage than historians and activists have supposed. Indeed, there remains much concerning the nature of modern Spanish feminism and its relationship to contemporary Spain's society and political culture that scholars have yet to explore, have examined with an insufficiently critical eye, or that stems from (often partisan) popular as well as scholarly assumptions about women's movements in Spain under and after Franco. As such, this study first aims to expand our understanding of the structure of and trajectory followed by Spain's feminist movement and organizations: when and where, it asks, did feminism emerge, how did its female champions organize themselves, what were their demands, and to what degree were these internally diverse and even contradictory? Answers to these questions abound in scholarship on Spanish women, but they are far from complete. While the basic narrative of feminism during the late Franco years and the Spanish transition to democracy is fairly well understood, many of those accounts date from the mid-1980s, a historiographical moment tinged by a feminist triumphalism born of Spain's then-recent legalization of divorce and abortion. Scholars like Monica Threlfall, writing in 1985, painted the inclusion of equal citizenship in the first post-Franco constitution as a distinctly feminist victory, and argued that the ruling socialist government's creation of a ministry to address women's issues represented a "conquest by the women's movement of a branch of state power."[28] This has proved an optimistic assessment, with subsequent historians—Pamela Radcliff in particular—questioning such triumphalist accounts, and instead advancing interpretations of the transition era as one in which negotiations between political actors were significantly more complex. Radcliff, for instance, has noted that the 1978 constitution's equal citizenship clause was politically expedient for male politicians hoping for acceptance from Western Europe, and that feminist demands thus did not factor into its passage.[29]

This book builds on Radcliff's work by similarly arguing that we need to understand ostensibly feminist victories as, instead, the result of negotiations amongst multiple actors, some with views counter to those of feminists, but who found that supporting feminist goals or adopting feminist rhetoric advanced their own political aims. It adds a nuanced understanding of Spanish feminism as polyvalent rather than monolithic, underscoring the conflict and divisions that have marked it since its modern inception. As such, my book argues against a triumphalist narrative that has portrayed feminist activism as beholden to a single set of beliefs and strategies, that has described this activism as uncomplicatedly successful, or that has understood seemingly feminist legislative progress as either unproblematically desirable or in fact as primarily a result of feminist efforts.

In addition, my book encourages a deeper look at the forms that feminist organizational efforts have historically taken, seeking to counter narratives that have argued for female inaction, weakness, and invisibility during much of the twentieth century and particularly under Francoism. In fact, Spain has a rich recent history of women's organizations, a history that includes a wealth of female-led agitation in the early twentieth century, as working-class women mobilized within their neighborhood networks to demand improvements in quality of life for themselves and their communities. Temma Kaplan's groundbreaking analysis of a series of strikes in Barcelona in the 1910s, for example, demonstrated that the authority women derived from responsibility to family and neighborhood enabled them to organize and wrest reform from reluctant government officials.[30] But women of the early twentieth century demanded more than neighborhood reform; as Mary Nash has shown, the feminist *Mujeres Libres* action groups helped organize women's contributions to the war effort during the Second Republic.[31] And women, at least in Catalonia, won access to abortion and the right to divorce before the Civil War. Here, Nash and Kaplan show two different types of female organization, but reading them together makes clear that networks of organized women—and, in Nash's argument, self-consciously feminist women—existed and flourished in early twentieth-century Spain, with women fighting for issues beyond suffrage.

These feminist antecedents are now well established; for years, however, the popular conception was that this early Spanish feminism had not survived the dawn of the Franco regime—Monica Threlfall even went so far as to describe the 1970s push for female autonomy as falling "on almost virgin soil."[32] Fortunately, in the last two decades historians like Kathleen Richmond, Aurora Morcillo and Inbal Ofer have used analyses of *Sección Femenina* (henceforth

SF), the Women's Section of the regime-sanctioned and ideologically fascist party *Falange Española*, to revise our understanding of how women's networks functioned under Francoist repression. Richmond showed that while *Sección Femenina* was a minority organization, counting a mere fraction of the total female population in its ranks, it was able to exert a great deal of influence. Indeed, as Ofer argues, SF "initiated" legislation "for the promotion of women's legal, political, and professional equality," including changes to the Spanish Civil Code in 1958 and the landmark Law of Political and Professional Rights for Women of 1961. In other words, SF successfully championed women's rights legislation *before* the booming Spanish economy of the late 1960s and early 1970s definitively convinced Francoist officials of the need for such reform.[33] Aurora Morcillo has similarly argued that though *Sección Femenina* rejected the label of "feminist," it also strategically paired an adherence to traditionalist gender roles with fervor for nationalist doctrines and activities to gain legitimacy to push for improvements in women's lives.[34] Richmond, Morcillo, and Ofer thus show that even women who believed in National-Catholicism, even at the height of Franco's power, worked together for access to the public sphere and for greater governance of their own lives at a time when women were legally under the power of their fathers or husbands.

Similarly, work by Temma Kaplan and Pamela Radcliff pushes us to think about other forms of acceptable female organization during the Franco era and how these groups evolved into the increasingly visible Spanish feminist movement of the 1970s. First, Kaplan and Radcliff argue that Franco-era female networks laid the groundwork for feminist consciousness to emerge in the late Franco period and during Spain's transition to democracy. Pamela Radcliff's monograph on female associational life in the 1960s and 1970s, for example, shows that government-sanctioned neighborhood networks amplified individual women's concerns by allowing them to find common cause with those experiencing similar problems.[35] In addition, Kaplan found that the *Movimiento Democrático de Mujeres* (MDM), which would come to play a significant role in Spain's feminist movement, began as a support group for women whose husbands had been imprisoned for their political activism and opposition to the Franco regime. Over time, this grew into involved women making demands for the right to vote, for access to birth control, and for legalization of divorce.[36] In this respect especially, the development of Spanish feminist awareness seems to have much in common with the consciousness-raising groups made popular by the 1970s American women's liberation movement.

Such parallels, this book shows, were not always coincidental. Beyond a few initial attempts at comparative analysis, the relationship between Spanish feminists and counterparts elsewhere in Europe as well as Latin America have yet to be widely studied; I argue that such transnational links in fact comprise a significant part of how feminists both within and outside Spain developed their ideas and managed their interactions with bodies like the European Economic Community, the European Union, and the United Nations, in addition to myriad NGOs. This research, then, aims to move scholarship on Spanish feminism beyond a purely domestic or otherwise strictly comparative analysis, placing these feminists in the international context in which they consciously chose to operate.

More broadly, this study seeks to revisit a longstanding periodization of Western feminist development. In the 1970s and 1980s, scholars of European feminism concerned with understanding the nature of these movements—work that was often as personal and political as it was scholarly, undertaken by scholars with ideological or organizational ties to second-wave feminist movements—sought not just to describe these feminisms, but to diagnose what conditions helped them function well and compile data to support the work of incorporating women into the public sphere.[37] These scholars traced where and when feminism emerged and catalogued which issues feminists concerned themselves with at which particular historical moments. To this end, historians offered summaries and case studies of the arguments that feminists in different nations had made; researchers like Gisela Kaplan and Joni Lovenduski understood Western European feminisms as developing in dialogue with different national paths toward industrialization and economic development, different types of government structure, and varying dominant cultural norms.[38] Such scholars also sought to understand the relationship between first-wave feminism and second-wave feminism by gauging the influence that different nations' first-wave movements had on the structure and ideology of their second-wave successors, and mostly shared the assumption that Northern European feminisms—in Britain and Scandinavia, especially—had developed earlier and with more clearly-defined demands. Some, such as Clyde Wilcox, further contended that these nations' successful first-wave movements had enabled "a continuous tradition of feminist activity," while other European nations instead saw an absence of feminism at mid-century or in the case of Catholic nations like Italy and Belgium, never experienced a first-wave feminist movement at all.[39]

Historians of Catholic and Southern Europe, as well as of US feminism, have countered this narrative, showing that first-wave feminism was not the exclusive domain of Protestant Northern Europe, and that nations beyond Britain did host nascent feminist organizations at mid-century. The feminist movement, this work has underlined, did not suddenly materialize in 1968: Nancy Cott, for instance, has argued that scholars have overlooked female activism after suffrage in the United States, misinterpreting the absence of a mass movement, which was due to ideological divisions among mid-century American feminists who continued to fight in more diffuse ways, as silence.[40] Claire Duchen has exposed similar misconceptions in the study of French feminism, noting that while she herself had formerly assumed that May 1968 had been the start of women's liberation in France, grassroots opposition to discriminatory laws was in fact already well established by then, and that if French women's activists at the time spoke of 1968 as a "year zero" for their cause, this merely spoke to either an ignorance or intentional misrepresentation of their own history.[41]

Meanwhile, historians of Spain have worked to reveal the extent of mid-century women's activism there by expanding our understanding of what such activism could look like. Temma Kaplan's work on women in the early twentieth century, for example, has provided a model for thinking about ways in which women banded together to push for change both in their lives and in the lives of their communities well before feminism emerged as a concept.[42] And indeed, histories of fascist and authoritarian women's organizations have underlined the difficulties in defining what is and is not truly feminist in such national contexts. Spanish historians have recently begun to wrestle with these issues by examining the role of *Sección Femenina* in the late Franco era's admittedly tepid social reforms, and by seeking to recover clandestine histories of organizations like the pathbreaking feminist organization MDM founded in the 1960s. Though consensus among historians of modern Spain is that *Sección Femenina* was decidedly not feminist, specialists studying both that organization and regime-sanctioned associations of housewives have added studies of Spain to the canon of scholarship demonstrating the agency of fascist women.[43]

From its foothold in Spanish history, my work advances this scholarly shift by complicating the picture of what feminist activism looked like under late Francoism and by exploring the consequences that this embryonic advocacy for expanded women's rights had for subsequent feminist organization during the transition era. It argues that, as with Duchen's discovery about French feminism, Spanish feminism did not have its own version of "year zero," even though contemporaries and Spanish historians have thought of 1975 in this way. While periodicals like the *New York Times* portrayed the nation's feminist movement at the time as backward, silenced by Francoist policies, and unable to participate in activism before his death, they also at times portrayed political activism in general as nonexistent in Spain prior to the regime's collapse, despite covering the actions of Basque terrorist group *Euskadi ta Askatasuna* (ETA), as well as student protests and labor strikes, all of which were, of course, forms of political activism taking place well before 1975.

Notably, this book also seeks to counter a too-common perception that a discrete set of vanguard women's movements were responsible for the subsequent birth of movements elsewhere, along with arguments like sociologist Valentine Moghadam's assertion that "prior to the mid-1980s the world's women had not yet developed collective identity, a collective sense of injustice, or common forms of organizing."[44] Such assertions overlook the sentiments, actions, and networks of grassroots feminists in European nations like (but not limited to) Spain, women who also worked in solidarity with North and Latin American counterparts. As noted earlier, this study uses the case of Spain to show that feminist internationalism, which well predated the turn of the century, existed before and only intensified during the latter half of the twentieth century as women's organizations exchanged information, participated in each other's initiatives, and pushed for standardized international protections for women.

Finally, and most broadly, work on women's organizations and activism offers an opportunity to intervene in larger debates about the extent to which Spain was indeed "backward" by comparison with its Western neighbors. Though the question of Spain's "backwardness" has mostly focused on Spanish political and economic development in the late nineteenth and early twentieth century, there has been a recent upsurge in scholarship posing this question for the Franco and transition eras. Historians are starting to examine Spaniards' insecurity about their status relative to the more economically developed, and more politically and socially liberal, Western European nations and the United States. As Julio Crespo MacLennan argues, beginning in the 1950s, Spanish officials who desired EEC membership saw Western-European style modernization as their path to inclusion. In practice, this process was equal parts economic development orchestrated by government officials and unplanned liberalization of cultural and social norms driven by exposure to Western European tourism and consumer culture during the 1960s and 1970s, as Sasha Pack and Alejandro Gómez del Moral have respectively shown.[45] A side effect of the economic miracle that tourism and consumer culture helped generate was the expansion of women's roles, particularly in terms of their ability to own property after marriage, to procure work without spousal permission, and to exercise individual legal rights without a male guardian—yet Franco's regime instituted these changes not out of any great desire to alter gender norms, but rather because the regime hoped to gain a more advantageous economic relationship with Western Europe without making substantive changes to Spanish society or to government structure.

The coupling of women's rights and a more general liberalization began under Franco, but it continued more aggressively after Franco's death in 1975. Post-Franco Spanish politics also revolved around an ongoing and extensive pro-Europe consensus and a wish to join the EEC, but unlike in prior years, it coexisted with citizens' awareness that the EEC was unlikely to accept a non-democratic Spain and with politicians' willingness to create actual change. Pamela Radcliff argues that politicians thought making women equal citizens would send a strong message about the efficacy of Spain's burgeoning democracy and its willingness to change. Yet throughout the transition to democracy, feminist dialogue about women's rights existed in parallel with the dominant political conversation. Spanish politicians took notice of feminist demands, but feminists lacked the ability to participate in political conversation in a meaningful way. Instead, journalists and politicians mocked and dismissed feminists—for example, openly feminist politician Carmen Diez de Rivera, Director of the Cabinet of the Presidency of Spain, was subject to crude sexual comments and insinuations she was King Juan Carlos' mistress, and was ultimately fired for her feminism—even as they sought to inscribe gender equality in the constitution.[46] For these men, women's equality was means to an end—recognition by Western Europe—and was not a serious attempt to incorporate women into Spanish society. Thus, the extent to which women gained entrée to public life was a byproduct and not a goal of constitutional creation.

This book examines the above patterns and the questions across five chapters. Chapter 1 argues that *Seccion Femenina*'s engagement with Cold War-era international women's rights debates, rather than just its National Catholic gender ideology, shaped its women's policy proposals. Similarly, Spain's desire for greater connection with Western Europe influenced the Franco administration's domestic social policy as well as its economic and foreign policy. Significantly, despite its reputation for fascist backwardness, passage of legislation like the *Sección Femenina*-backed and regime-sanctioned *Ley de Derechos*, which passed in 1961 and provided equal pay and an end to sex discrimination in hiring, positioned Spain as on the vanguard of nations crafting labor policy for women—enshrining in the nation's laws protections that member nations of the newly established EEC had not yet realized. Yet *Sección Femenina*'s place on the vanguard was short-lived. Shifting international norms coincided with Franco's death, ushered *Sección Femenina* into its dissolution during Spain's transition to democracy, and buoyed the rise of feminist agitation that would shape Spanish and European identities and women's policies for the remainder of the twentieth century.

Chapter 2 argues that, despite the Spanish government's abolition of repressive Franco-era legislation that, for instance, criminalized female (but not male) adultery, its passage of feminist-friendly legislation, international sympathy for the plight of Spanish women, and leftist politicians self-identifying as feminist allies, the feminist movement itself had no political leverage in transition-era Spain. Feminists lacked access to political debates, even when elected as members of the Spanish *Cortes*, and politicians with access to those debates introduced ostensibly "feminist" legislation that in fact excluded feminist demands and ignored feminist arguments. Consequently, what scholars have judged to be two major feminist political victories of the transition era—the inclusion of an equal citizenship clause in the 1978 Constitution and the partial legalization of abortion in 1985 (which allowed abortions in cases of rape or incest, "serious mental or physical defects" of the fetus, or poor mental or physical health of the mother)—were not feminist-driven.

Chapter 3 describes the shift from an international feminism driven by grassroots activists to an international feminism instead dominated by government-affiliated feminist organizations. Particularly in Spain, the creation of a federal women's bureau, the *Instituto de la Mujer*, disrupted long-established feminist methods of protest and caused tension between grassroots campaigners and women in the *Instituto*. Moreover, this chapter argues that a rhetorical shift also manifested at this time, reflecting the evolving goals of feminists. Whereas activists previously used the phrase "gender discrimination" to label women's lack of a discrete set of rights, in the 1980s addressing "gender discrimination" increasingly referred to a broader attempt to foster equality of the sexes by restructuring social and cultural relationships between men and women. For instance, Spanish opponents of gender discrimination in the 1980s and 1990s advocated coeducation as a method of normalizing the ideal of gender equality in young children, but funding for these programs came at the expense of funding enforcement of legislation aimed specifically at improving women's material and legal circumstances, like equal pay laws.

Chapter 4 analyzes the history of intimate partner violence legislation in late twentieth- and early twenty-first-century Spain.[47] Debates about this legislation shared a political moment with debates about the legalization of gay marriage and a revisitation of debates to expand abortion access. Feminists sought to leverage international human rights resolutions to reinforce their positions; conservative politicians also played to international organizations' expectations. That Spanish Foreign Minister Benigno Blanco (1996–2004) of the right-leaning *Partido Popular* (PP), for example, could equate abortion, which his party opposed, with "gender violence," and that PP supporters have labeled attempts to protect abortion access as "fascist," "totalitarian," and "Francoist" illustrates how conservative politicians have coopted internationally sanctioned feminist rhetoric in their attempt to deprive women of the very same rights such rhetoric was developed to protect. Moreover, this rhetoric demonstrates Spaniards' challenges in coming to terms with Franco's legacy: politicians and activists of all political stripes continue to apply the terms "fascist" and "Francoist" to policies they oppose, in an attempt to tar these with the brush of being backward and undemocratic.

Finally, Chapter 5 concludes this study by extending its analysis further into the twenty-first century. It examines the resurgence of the feminist movement in response to proposed restrictions on abortion in the 2010s, which was especially visible at International Women's Day celebrations. In similar vein, it follows the Spain's other recent political crises, which I argue are best understood as a constitutional crisis with roots stretching back to the transition period, and the outcome of which is likely to have significant implications not only for Spain, but for the European Union.

In the backdrop of all the chapters is the fact that Generalissimo Francisco Franco has been dead for only forty-one years, and his regime gone for fewer still. Indeed, critics of the integrity of Spain's current democratic process often make use of the concept of *franquismo sociológico*, "sociological Francoism," which denotes the collection of Franco-era social norms, beliefs, sites of entrenched political power, and practices that have survived to the present in Spanish society and politics, and continue to degrade the genuinely free quality of both. Spain has not yet celebrated its fortieth anniversary as a democratic nation, and the country is at the moment still struggling to define the terms of its democracy, a struggle that plays out most often in political, social, and cultural negotiations to delineate the rights of women.

1

Female Sentinels of Occident

The *Sección Femenina*, Women's Rights, and Francoist Spain's Search for International Acceptance in Postwar Western Europe

In 1961 the Spanish parliament, *Cortes*, passed a piece of sweeping legislation governing Spanish women's economic and labor rights at the behest of Pilar Primo de Rivera and the fascist women's organization *Sección Femenina* (SF). This legislation, popularly known as the *Ley sobre derechos políticos, profesionales y de trabajo de la mujer* ("Law on Women's Political, Professional, and Labor Rights," or LsD), guaranteed equal pay, made it illegal for companies to force women out of work because of their marital status, and expanded the range of professions open to Spanish women. For authoritarian Spain, which had existed under a dictatorship beholden to National Catholic gender ideology since 1939, the LdD was an unprecedented step toward broadening women's roles and liberalizing what Generalissimo Francisco Franco's regime deemed acceptable female contributions to Spain's labor market.[1] In its official magazine, *Teresa*, SF declared the new legislation a resounding victory over female inequality and gloried in the assertion that it placed "Spain on the vanguard of dignifying women's work." Among its pages was a laudatory description of the legislation by journalist—and *Bando Nacional* and *División Azul* veteran—Ángel Ruiz Ayúcar, who also compared Spain to other European nations that lacked such legislation and condemned "more progressive" countries who had, he argued, done less for women.[2]

As indicated by Ayúcar's and *Sección Femenina*'s assertions that Spain was "on the vanguard" relative to its European peers, *Cortes*'s passage of the *Ley sobre derechos* was about much more than its ostensible subject, and did not occur in a vacuum. It was influenced by the establishment of the European Economic Community (EEC) in 1957 and coincided with Spain's application for EEC membership, which the regime submitted in February 1962 following years of debate. Tellingly, when commenting on the *Ley sobre derechos* in the wake of its passage, *Sección Femenina* frequently made a point of favorably contrasting the rights that the *Ley sobre derechos* offered Spanish women with the rights that other nations, and especially EEC nations, guaranteed.

Placing *Sección Femenina* initiatives like the *Ley sobre derechos* in such an international context—a context that the organization itself sought to place its work within—provides a more nuanced understanding of *Sección Femenina*'s political agenda and struggles, including how these fit into the Franco regime's larger machinations, during the latter half of the dictatorship. First, even as the Franco regime strove to lessen foreign influence over its citizens, Spanish women's politics existed within and were influenced by international, and not purely domestic, concerns. The timing of the LsD's introduction and the way *Seccion Feminina* framed its impact both within Spain and beyond the nation's borders reveal that Pilar Primo de Rivera and her colleagues were aware of the regime's foreign as well as its domestic political goals, and that they made calculated political decisions to meet *Seccion Femeinina*'s goals even as they helped Franco meet his. The result of the calculation was that the *Ley sobre derechos* granted women rights that *Sección Femenina* had championed for a decade while also fitting neatly into the narrative the Franco regime was trying to create for mid-century Spain, that of a nation that could be as European—or more so—than the rest of its peers on the continent, without relinquishing its unique history, its Francoist ideology, or its non-democratic governance.[3]

This context also allows us to see that *Seccion Feminina* as an organization also looked beyond—and indeed sought to operate beyond—Spain's borders, and it existed at a complicated nexus: the organization was simultaneously radical within mainstream Spanish politics (which was, of course, governed by men who understood even an incremental expansion of women's rights to contravene National Catholicism), promoted policy in line with international organizations' stated values, and yet ideologically was far to the right of what international feminist organizations embraced.

Early Foundations for a Conservative, Transformative Activism

Sección Femenina originated in 1934 as the women's wing of Spanish fascist organization *Falange* and, over the following decade, evolved into an influential standalone organization with a voice in the political decision-making process of Franco's regime. SF leader Pilar Primo de Rivera so captured Franco's respect that he appointed her to the National Council of the Falange at the conclusion of the Spanish Civil War; upon *Cortes*'s formation in 1942, members of that council, including Primo de Rivera, also became representatives in Spain's new parliament.[4]

SF's position in the regime hierarchy allowed it to simultaneously contribute to the National Catholic ideological project and consolidate its grip on women's affairs over the 1940s as the nation dealt with postwar instability. Women's policy during the war and early years of the regime reinforced the new government's ideological principles, clearly defined gender roles, and made it difficult for Spanish citizens, but especially women, to transgress those roles' boundaries.[5] This took several forms. First, SF policies in the immediate post-Civil War period worked to mitigate the effects of the postwar economic crisis, known as the "hunger years," while also buttressing National Catholicism. For example, SF enforced the regime's pronatalism in part by creating subsidies to supplement families' meager incomes—desperately needed during Spain's depression, which squeezed working-class families in particular—but distributing them only to non-working mothers with more than two children.[6] In addition, SF wrested control of Spain's Social Service in the early 1940s and made participation in its programs mandatory for women hoping to work, hold a passport, or attend college.[7] These programs, though unpopular and sparsely attended, offered education in home economics and reinforced the Francoist ideal of women as responsible for their households' domestic affairs; the programs were designed to push generations of post-Civil War women into what Aurora Morcillo termed "true Catholic womanhood," making them paragons of Catholic virtue whose lives were dedicated to home and family.[8]

Postwar instability of the 1940s lent SF its initial opportunity for political leverage; dramatic economic and cultural change of the subsequent decade was the crucible in which the organization's political ascendancy and its approach to women's rights were forged. Spain maintained an isolationist stance immediately after its Civil War and throughout the Second World War, but by the early 1950s Franco reevaluated his position on international involvement. This was driven by Spain's dire economic circumstances: regime officials debated how to pull the nation out of its postwar depression, and increasing international trade relationships was the winning, if controversial, strategy. The decade thus saw the end of autarky in Spain, the appointment of technocrats to the National Council, and the implementation of an economic Stabilization Plan in 1959 that established a market economy and allowed an influx of international goods into Spain.[9] In addition, regime officials began courting foreign approval, which culminated in deals with the United States and the Vatican in 1953.[10] Yet despite Franco's intent for Spain to retain its unique character, the nation had been slowly liberalizing, in part as an involuntary reaction to European tourism but also in part to the demands of Spain's growing economy.[11] Early European integration and trade efforts in the early 1950s, leading to the establishment of the European Economic Community and signing of the Treaty of Rome in March 1957, further complicated Spain's economic policy options and made debates between regime officials about the desirability of Europeanization—that is, social, political, and economic convergence with Western Europe—increasingly contentious.[12]

During the 1950s, as Spanish and European leaders alike found themselves preoccupied with new economic pressures, SF shifted focus to begin advocating an expansion of women's civic and labor rights. Though SF leadership initially struggled to reconcile the tension between its National Catholic ideals and its position that women should have increased access to employment, by the end of the decade SF leaders no longer found the position contradictory and instead believed that increasing women's participation in the work force would enrich the nation as much as it enriched individual working women, thereby rendering its position ideologically sound.[13] *Teresa* tackled the controversial issue of women in the labor force in a recurring column titled "Women Want to Work," which featured individual women talking about their jobs and their worklife experiences. By 1960, with SF's blessing, the number of women in Spain's workforce had doubled.[14] In addition, in terms of civic rights, SF pressed the regime to remove statues in the Civil Code that discriminated against women, realizing sixty-six such revisions in 1958.[15]

The *Ley de Derechos*, the Issue of Equal Pay, and the EEC

From an economic, domestic political, and women's policy standpoint, the *Ley sobre derechos* of 1961 was in many ways a logical successor to SF's advocacy and achievements over the 1950s, such as its successful campaign for a reform of the Spanish Civil Code. To be sure, these changes had been real and were welcomed by many women. Yet, the group's ambitions when pushing for those reforms had remained limited by its commitment to preserving strict gender roles that required women to dedicate themselves above all to their families and to domestic life. And yet again, Pilar Primo de Rivera also felt that promoting women's participation in civic life would enrich their lives as well as the vitality of the *Patria*, the Spanish fatherland.[16] In this same vein, Primo de Rivera and

SF consistently stated that neither they nor the new *Ley sobre derechos* was in any way progressive, and in particular that the law was not feminist nor intended to foster equality of the sexes. Indeed, as SF National Delegate to the *Cortes*, Primo de Rivera herself declared during the parliament's debate on the proposed law,

> This is not a feminist law in the slightest. We would be faithless to José Antonio if it were ... In no way do we wish to make men and women two identical beings. Neither their natures nor their aspirations would allow it. But we do ask that if their tasks are equally important, their rights should be equal, too ... we ask that, by this law, when a woman is driven to work out of need, she is able to work in the best possible conditions. As such, rather than being feminist, this law is men supporting women—the weaker half—to make their lives easier. We would like nothing more than for men's wages to be enough so that women, especially married women, would not need to work ....But there are no shortage of families ... that cannot forego women's work so that they can properly provide for their children, which is matrimony's primordial aim ... an educated, refined, and sensible woman is a better mother and a better companion to her husband because she has those qualities.[17]

For *Sección Femenina*, then, the new *Ley sobre derechos* was the latest of a series of measures meant to address specific problem cases not accounted for in National Catholicism's sweeping gendered ordering of society, as well as to reconcile women's educational aspirations with the inviolable primacy of marriage and family as their ultimate destiny in life. It was, in other words, a direct heir to *Teresa*'s columns profiling working women.

However, other language that *Sección Femenina* and sympathizers used to talk about the law in the period surrounding its passage point to a shift in the group's discourse and agenda. In a novel turn, officially sanctioned SF commentary portrayed the LsD as not just policy that benefited Spanish women, or even Spanish national life as a whole—as Primo de Rivera's speech had—but as policy that benefited Spain specifically because of what its passage meant for the nation's position relative to its Western European neighbors. *Teresa*'s aforementioned declaration that the new law placed Spain on Europe's "vanguard" was one such instance of this. Even as he restated Primo de Rivera's claims that the law was not feminist and aimed to benefit society generally rather than women specifically, Ángel Ruiz Ayúcar's 1961 column also argued that women's inferior wages had historically been a product of "liberal capitalism's ... exploitation of the working classes, which gave rise to the proletariat, the cause of the era's gravest upheavals." He observed that "the principle of 'equal pay for equal work', while recommended by international organizations, ha[d] not [been] fully implemented by any nation." And the upshot of this was his article's titular claim: that Spain was now on Europe's vanguard on questions of women's rights.[18]

Similarly, in a March 1963 column featuring interviews with five Madrid university students on the topic of equal rights, *Teresa* printed twenty-two-year-old Political Science student Antonio Hernández's opinion that women were not naturally capable of running a factory floor or a country, but that otherwise they deserved equal labor rights. Thus, he argued, SF's new and "magnificent" law was right to still exclude women from such roles, and it also put Spain well ahead of many European nations on this issue. "Really," Hernández declared, "I think it is about time that we [passed this kind of law]"—a comment that seemingly acknowledged international critiques of Francoist Spain's perceived lack of freedoms, even as it also consigned these criticisms to the past and subtly echoed the regime's longstanding claim that Spain's rightful role in the world was to serve as a moral example for other nations amid parliamentary liberalism's decadence.[19]

This shift in focus toward Europe dovetailed with the Franco regime's own changing priorities. By the late 1950s, when *Sección Femenina* began to lobby regime policymakers to consider proposed measures would become the *Ley sobre derechos*, the regime had already moved toward opening Spain's economic and social borders to Western Europe, a process that would soon culminate with the Stabilization Plan of 1959 and continue thereafter. Economic exigency drove this policy shift in part, as the early Franco regime's failed strategy of autarky had contributed significantly to the widespread goods shortages and economic stagnation that marked Spain's "Hunger Years" in the mid- and late 1940s, and the regime's tepid and unsound efforts to open the economy in the 1950s helped trigger an inflation crisis in 1956-7. But the birth of the EEC in 1957-8 was equally fundamental: though Europeanization remained a controversial idea among Spain's political elite, Franco himself made clear that he wanted Spain to join the new economic bloc, and toward this end, the regime took steps during the late 1950s and early 1960s to align Spanish economic policy with EEC requirements, as well as to improve Spain's international reputation more generally.[20]

Teresa's portrayal of the *Ley sobre derechos* as a measure that now placed Spain on Europe's (and the world's) "vanguard" also aligned with repeated efforts by the Franco regime during the 1950s to improve Spain's image abroad. Ayúcar's article is again especially revealing. After observing that no country had fully implemented the principle of equal pay, Ayúcar went on to note that if women's wages were truly raised to parity, Western Europe's economies would suffer particularly severely due to a high reliance on female labor. This, he continued accusingly, was why "[though] the nations of the Common Market agreed in principle to equal pay for women's work, … this has not been put into effect … " France, the Falangist conceded, had made the most progress, but if anything this underscored his argument—for all of its talk of enlightened progress, the EEC had done little to better the lot of working women, while Franco's Spain had. And to drive home his claims of foreign hypocrisy and Spanish leadership, Ayúcar concluded by complaining that a certain "prejudice[d]" segment of the foreign press "will not forgive Spain for its successes over the past 25 years," and so refused to recognize this latest accomplishment.[21]

There was in fact considerable truth to Ángel Ruiz Ayúcar's damning analysis of the Western European record on the equal pay question, despite its self-congratulatory agenda. If *Sección Femenina* considered the newly minted *Ley sobre derechos* a watershed for women's rights and a significant moment too for Spain's place within a nascently integrating Europe, the foreign press did not seem to agree. No major European newspapers reported on its passage, and the EEC, moreover, made no institutional comment. As Ayúcar rightly observed, it was not that these nations were unaware of the equal pay issue, as the West German, Dutch, and French constitutions, all drafted or revised in the postwar era, each contained equal pay clauses, and it was France that pushed to include an equal pay clause in the EEC's founding document, the Treaty of Rome. But as Ruiz Ayúcar also suggested, this last initiative stemmed from economic concerns rather than any altruistic impulse. Though equal pay was ostensibly already guaranteed in all three nations as treaty negotiations unfolded in the mid-1950s, wages in France were far closer to parity than in West Germany or the Netherlands: in 1955, women's wages were 86 percent of men's in France, but only 63 percent in Germany, and 58 percent in the Netherlands.[22] Fearing that in the wake of the EEC's founding French businesses might move to other member states to access cheaper female labor, France fought for what became the Treaty of Rome's Article 119, which called on members to "ensure that the principle of equal pay for male and female workers for equal work or work of equal value is applied."[23] For the French, this was a question of protecting business competitiveness in the newly formed trade bloc, not of extending rights, in fact following a precedent set by member nations' existing equal pay laws, which were largely crafted to protect male labor, corporate profits and national economies, not women.[24]

Sección Femenina, then, aimed to depict Spain as Europe's true trailblazer in the field of women's rights, and so portray the nation as an especially attractive and appropriate candidate for the EEC membership the Franco regime sought—an agenda highlighted most especially by the curious timing of the law's introduction and its storied origins nearly a decade earlier. Though *Sección Femenina*'s campaign for a law expanding working women's rights seemingly unfolded entirely in 1960–1, SF founding member and jurist Mercedes Formica had developed its underlying principles in the early 1950s. In 1950, Pilar Primo de Rivera authorized Formica to form a research group to investigate and improve the state of women's employment and compensation in Spain. Over a period of twenty-two months, Formica and her team collected and analyzed data, developed what would become the *Ley sobre derechos* underlying principles, and drafted a presentation for a 1951 Hispano-American conference, which *Sección Femenina* was organizing to discuss women's issues, including women's labor rights. On the eve of the conference, however, Primo de Rivera cancelled Formica's talk, explaining that she had lost the presentation draft. Formica later recalled having felt distressed; she was even more so in 1960, when Primo de Rivera first unveiled a plan for the eventual *Ley sobre derechos* at *Sección Femenina*'s National Congress, a plan that contained Formica's research and recommendations but did not acknowledge her work. Primo de Rivera had not, in fact, lost Formica's research, but had instead buried it, only to pass it off as her own idea nearly a decade later.[25]

Primo de Rivera could have proposed a law based on this stolen research as early as 1952, but tellingly, she waited and chose a moment when the law's passage could benefit the Franco regime's foreign policy goals. *Sección Femenina* boasted that its new law placed Spain on Europe's vanguard just as the newly formed EEC had begun to reckon with what the European integration it spearheaded might mean, and as different ideological camps within the Franco dictatorship started to consider what their nation's place within this process might look like. Though it may not have been directly motivated by Francoism's hunt for acceptance in Europe—especially EEC membership—(re)introducing Formica's proposal furthered this project by fulfilling (and indeed, exceeding) the EEC requirement that member states implement equal pay provisions by December 1961. It likewise advanced the regime's then decade-old effort to rehabilitate its image abroad by portraying the nation as focused on social justice in ways that even other, self-professedly progressive European nations could not achieve.[26]

And Francoist authorities clearly approved of this rhetoric and of *Sección Femenina*'s agenda, as shown by the stature of the cultural figures and regime-affiliated professionals that Primo de Rivera's marshaled to voice and support these claims in *Teresa*'s pages—and indeed, by the fact that those opinions were even published. The choice of a contributor like Ángel Ruiz Ayúcar was not random. He was three times a Francoist military veteran, having served in Franco's forces during the Civil War and as a lieutenant in the volunteer Blue Division that Spain sent to fight alongside the Wehrmacht on the Eastern Front, before rising to the rank of Colonel and head of national traffic operations in the paramilitary *Guardia Civil*. He was also a professional journalist, meaning that he had weathered the regime's centralized and draconian credentialing process, which only approved candidates whose opinions and politics aligned with the regime's. In other words, Ayúcar was not only ideologically above reproach, he was in fact a notable figure in one of the most prestigious segments of Franco-era society—the military—and by both supporting the LsD's contents and echoing SF claims about Spain's moral leadership in Europe, he all but declared the Francoist mainstream's approval of such rhetoric. And in any case, like all periodicals at that time, *Teresa* was subject to a censorship process that rejected objectionable information about the regime and its policies *before* publication. If the regime had disapproved of the magazine's contents, it would not have circulated.[27]

The *Ley sobre derechos*, which arrived at a pivotal moment when the Franco regime weighed the benefits and risks that European integration presented, clearly dovetailed with the Franco regime's foreign policy even as it served *Sección Femenina*'s quest to influence Spanish society. And as such, the new law was arguably a product not just of *Sección Femenina*'s ambitions, but also arose from Francoist foreign policy deliberations and a shift in the regime's internal culture toward an embrace of an at least limited internationalism—both forces that helped to shape the legislation that Primo de Rivera's organization self-interestedly proposed. That is, even though the law originated within SF with the stated goal of expanding women's roles in Spanish society, its timing and content resulted not just from *Sección Femenina* ideology, but also from a strategic choice to introduce it when the law would coincide with Franco's own desire to draw Spain closer to the newly-formed European Economic Community.

The Context of a Europe before "Europe"

Again, this strategy of burnishing Spain's international reputation by casting it as a European leader on working women's rights and labor conditions could only hope to prosper because of the state of women's labor rights reform in the EEC, and still more significantly the ideological construct of an integrating, economically liberal and socially progressive "Europe," remained works in progress at the dawn of the 1960s. In other words, the Franco regime's claim to have succeeded in protecting working women's rights, while ostensibly "progressive" nations had not, required not only that the regime's own efforts at least appear substantial but also that Western European measures fall short by comparison. Fortunately for Franco, this was largely the case. Women's wages continued to trail men's in places like France, West Germany, and the Netherlands through the late 1950s, as noted previously; significantly however, they did so not just due to inaction from legislators fearful of compromising their nations' international trade competitiveness, but active choice driven by ideology. Though West Germany's constitution ostensibly guaranteed equal rights to women just as France did, the German judiciary held that this equality must still bow to natural differences between the sexes, which in practice meant that separate spheres ideologies governed labor policy such that virtually all women's work contracts stipulated wages 20–30 percent lower than men's. The West German Federal Labor Court only ended this practice in 1955. Dutch wage regulations were similarly rooted in a belief that men should be the family's sole breadwinners, and only required wage parity in trades practiced by both sexes so that those industries would not come to rely on female labor for its cheaper cost.[28]

This state of affairs, moreover, remained largely unchanged in Europe even after the Franco regime made its own bid to enshrine wage parity. Despite (or perhaps because of) the fear that had prompted France to champion Article 119—that any nation that independently guaranteed equal pay would undermine its industries' ability to compete abroad—the newly minted EEC's membership mostly ignored the clause. No member state implemented its provisions by the required December 1961 deadline, or even late into the decade. Similar efforts floundered outside the EEC as well: in 1946, the International Labor Organization (ILO), which had supported equal pay for women since its founding in 1919, became an agency within the United Nations, and soon after drafted the watershed Equal Remuneration Convention of 1951, which legally bound signatory nations to ensure equal pay for work of equal value. Yet, though the UN and its agencies could request that member nations ratify this and other such treaties and require compliance, it ultimately had no powers of enforcement, and indeed, Western European nations that ratified the convention took an average of fifteen years thereafter to pass domestic laws guaranteeing equal pay. Only France, Spain, the UK, and the Netherlands did so before signing; the latter two nations, moreover, waited almost two decades to ratify the document and did not guarantee equal pay until 1968 and 1970, respectively.[29] Inaction, noncompliance, and toothless policies were almost uniformly the response to the ILO, whose aim—equal economic rights for working women—was in fact one of the least progressive visions of female equality being contemplated at mid-century.[30]

The *Ley sobre derechos*, then, was in line with or even exceeded what the international community and intergovernmental organizations mandated, and its passage placed Spain in a vanguard of nations that had legally (even if disingenuously) enshrined a commitment to women's labor and economic rights. Eventually, even the previously silent foreign press took notice: in 1964, American women's magazine *Cosmopolitan* published an article lauding what it titled the "New Roles for Spanish Women," which noted of the new law's equal pay provisions, as well as of the rising number of women serving in the Spanish *Cortes* and studying at the University of Madrid, and favorably contrasted these changes with women's status in Spain before 1961.[31] Circumstances in the United States only underscored the column's argument—the US Congress had only passed its own Equal Pay Act a year before, in 1963, meaning that on this issue authoritarian Spain had beaten the United States to the punch.

In fact, while Franco's Spain was still no friend to women's rights or indeed civil rights in general, it similarly outpaced most of the Western political milieu simply by maintaining a dedicated women's ministry within the state apparatus. Only the United States had a similar organization, a Women's Bureau founded in 1920; French, German, and British equivalents did not follow until 1981, 1986, and 1997, respectively. Even the American agency only achieved signature victories like passage of the Equal Pay Act of 1963 after a second body, the President's Commission on the Status of Women (PCSW), launched that same year. And neither agency had the kind of access to the highest echelons of state that *Sección Femenina* commanded.[32]

As such, neither the Franco regime and *Sección Femenina* on the one hand, nor the EEC on the other, can be neatly understood as progressive or backward on the issue of women's labor rights. Despite publicly aspiring to "creat[e] a powerful, supranational human rights regime," and, more vaguely, to move toward a single European standard for social legislation or "social harmonization," the nascent EEC established itself as a primarily economic partnership.[33] West Germany and the Netherlands both adopted the view that social harmonization was inevitable yet would also be socio-economically harmful if artificially rushed forward. The Treaty of Rome's architects, moreover, feared that an overly politically ideological draft would meet the same fate as an earlier attempt to form a European Political Community, which France had rejected in 1953. As a result, the bloc initially set intentionally concise and vague political requirements for membership, especially when compared to expectations established in earlier integration measures such as the founding statute of the Council of Europe (1949) or the failed draft treaty for a European Political Community (1953), both of which expressed a commitment to protecting human rights and freedoms.

The EEC's latter-day, more sincere commitment to social progress instead developed out of a long-term process of negotiation and evolution that started with the Treaty of Rome and spanned several decades, a process that was catalyzed especially by Spain's application to join the Common Market.[34] In 1962, Spain applied for association with the EEC—a lesser status than full membership, it should be noted—fully expecting that its application could succeed, as both France and West Germany had previously backed Spanish accession to the Organization for European Economic Co-operation (OEEC) in 1958–9. However, even though Franco did not even seek full membership, the possibility that Spanish association might later lead to full EEC membership prompted both the EEC bureaucracy and outside agencies like the International Commission of Jurists to draft reports that restated the Franco regime's unacceptably repressive nature and formally outlined the need for any nation affiliated with the EEC to practice democratic governance and guarantee civil freedoms.[35] Despite its erstwhile ideological reticence, the bloc ultimately chose to reject Spain's application, deciding that Franco's policy successes were insufficiently compelling when his regime was still clearly repressive. In the end, though, the EEC's vacillation highlights how the compromises that this and other such intergovernmental organizations have accepted to enact expansive social and economic initiatives often excluded any real strides for women's equality.

This is not to suggest that the Franco regime or *Sección Femenina* were or even aspired to be socially progressive. As noted above, Pilar Primo de Rivera's consistent position was that the *Ley sobre derechos* was not feminist and was not intended to foster equality between the sexes. If anything, Primo de Rivera's group held that their law proved both that feminism had failed as a vehicle for the tangible improvement of women's lives, and that protecting women's interests and fascist convictions were entirely compatible—that a dictatorship could protect women better than democracies had, all while rejecting equality as a valid measure of women's dignity and the health of a society. Moreover, the law's purpose was clearly as much to advance the Franco's regime agenda in Europe as it was to better the lot of women. Subsequent public portrayals of the law's contents and significance built upon a regime-sponsored narrative that portrayed Spain as economically and politically similar to existing EEC member states, yet did so without challenging National Catholic ideology.

Put another way, the *Ley sobre derechos* allowed the regime to argue that it could fulfill so-called "European" values in a uniquely Spanish way. In fact, the law could even serve to support Francoism's founding doctrine of Spanish exceptionalism: from its inception, the Franco regime had sought to make Spain a part of Europe, yet also apart from and above it. Francoism considered Spain a spiritually superior nation with a destiny to serve as a moral leader within Europe; for the regime, the *Ley sobre derechos* could serve as evidence that in the field of women's rights and by Europe's own standards, Spain was already fulfilling this destiny.

The *Congreso Internacional de la Mujer* and *Sección Femenina*'s Failure to Adapt

Emboldened by their success in championing the *Ley sobre derechos*, as well as the belief that they had firmly established their global leadership on women's rights issues, *Sección Femenina* began by the late 1960s to express an ambition to guide women's rights policy internationally, not just within Spain, and toward that end they secured the Franco regime's permission to host an international conference, the *Congreso International de la Mujer* ("International Women's Congress"), in Madrid in 1968. Organizers stated their purpose as "try[ing] to achieve a more just world," especially for women. They observed that "being a woman still pose[d] many problems in all parts of the world," and they intended the *Congreso* as a venue where participants could, through "exchanging and contrasting opinions and exposing the realities of [life for women in] all countries," "provide solutions" to these "many problems."[36] Significantly, *Sección Femenina* leadership also billed the conference as "the first of its kind" because "it touche[d] absolutely all issues related to women."[37]

With their conceptualization of the *Congreso*, *Sección Femenina* billed itself as uniquely qualified for international leadership in women's rights and as in possession of a necessary and unique new vision for how to conceptualize those rights. In this way, they echoed Franco's own desires and motivations for international engagement. Franco wanted not just to be seen as *part* of Europe, but he wanted Spain to be a *model* for the rest of Europe, to have Europe as well as Spain itself recognize what he portrayed as his nation's exceptional character.[38] SF similarly conceived its role in global women's rights politics. The organization intended to serve as an example for other women's organizations, and sought to extend its vision of true Catholic womanhood and a platform of women's rights crafted with those gender roles in mind, worldwide. The *Congreso* was their vehicle.

Announcement of the *Congreso* in *Teresa*, SF's official magazine, described the conference and its organizers as heirs to the legacy of prominent early-twentieth-century women's rights activists: the *Congreso* was inspired by the "three Dutch commemorations of the International Congress of Women," likely a reference to the International Congress of Women held in The Hague in 1915, which prominent female activists from Europe and North America organized to demand an end to the First World War, as well as to demand that women gain the right to vote.[39] SF also framed the *Congreso* as a response to prior unnamed "feminist" international conferences that had failed because their alleged feminism prevented attendees from correctly identifying and resolving the challenges women faced.[40] In placing their own *Congreso* within this tradition of international women's rights activism, SF claimed the mantle of international, not just Spanish, leadership on women's rights policy while also signaling dedication to the Francoist regime through their stated political opposition to an undefined and bogeyman like "feminist" ideology.

For SF, international leadership was more than symbolic: it also involved building solidarity through interpersonal networking, though despite the organization's insistence that its *Congreso* was open to "all nations" and "all Spanish women who wished to take part in its tasks, without regard to political, religious, nor ... social affiliation" SF courted attendance primarily from right-wing women who ultimately made up the majority of the *Congreso*'s attendees.[41] Shortly after announcing the organization's intention to host an international *Congreso*, for example, Primo de Rivera and members of the SF leadership team toured Latin America in order to personally extend invitations to sympathetic women's organizations. They visited Peru, Honduras, Nicaragua, Costa Rica, and Colombia on their trip—all, with the exception of Costa Rica, fellow dictatorships—meeting with presidents and senior officials, holding events with these nations' first ladies, and meeting members of local women's groups.[42] The tour offered SF members an opportunity to burnish their foreign policy credentials as well as to build a network of similarly minded women's organizations with which SF could evangelize about their shared, fascism-tinged and Catholic infused, gender politics.

These meetings were successful, as were efforts to publicize the *Congreso*. Latin American delegates dominated the *Congreso*, but women from around the globe also attended, representing organizations from nations as far-flung as Iran, Cameroon, Taipei, India, and Vietnam.[43] SF leaders were thrilled about the turnout and envisioned the conference as the first of many. The LsD had put them on the map in Spanish political life and in the nation's women's rights policy development; they expected the 1970 *Congreso* to give them similar stature in international circles.

Despite welcoming conservative women to discuss a conservative agenda, the SF leaders also understood themselves as women's rights activists on a global scale, with the aim of serving as international ambassadors not only for Spain, but for their vision of women's rights. Yet SF's image of the *Congreso* and its significance stood at odds with reality. The LsD had dovetailed with Franco's attempts to court approval from Western Europe and had helped ease Spain's internal economic and societal pressures; it had also matched the predominant approach that Western Europe took to women's rights, which stressed legislative change to give women equal opportunities—especially equal economic opportunities—but which would otherwise render governments and bureaucracies unchanged.[44] In contrast, announcement of the *Congreso*, as well as the event itself, existed within a transitional moment for international women's rights activism as cultural unrest both in Spain and throughout the West in the late 1960s fueled the development of new feminist strategies and networking tactics.

Initial plans to announce the *Congreso* in 1967 coincided with a wave of labor unrest and student strikes in Spain that closed eight universities. In response, SF, in consultation with the Franco regime, chose to delay publicizing the *Congreso* until authorities quelled the protests.[45] But the protests and their impact were inescapable. More flourished in Madrid and Barcelona in 1968, and Europe and the United States also experienced a surge of cultural contestation when feminists, laborers, LGBT organizations, minority organizations, and students took to the streets to demand acknowledgment and reforms from their respective federal governments. These activists also increasingly held mass demonstrations calling for a rejection of fascism and colonialism.

The international movement for women's rights became swept up in momentum generated by the counterculture and split into two "branches"—an older branch that "usually work[ed] within the system to change laws and public policies unfavorable to women" and a "younger branch" that "typically focuse[d] on building alternatives outside the existing system, for instance, cooperatives run and controlled by women including economic enterprises, women's shelters, health clinic, and daycare centers."[46] The divergence in organizational strategy also pointed to an ideological divergence between the branches. Until the mid-twentieth century, women critical of government hierarchies languished on the ideological fringe and moderates with connections to establishment politics ran the show, but the 1960s countercultural fireworks brought the ideological fringe to the foreground. Female activists applied social and cultural critiques promulgated by countercultural organizations to the discrimination they encountered both in their daily lives and at the hands of their peers in radical organizations; as a result, feminists began to argue that women experienced a unique form of oppression that underlay every social and political structure, that the global community could take steps to alleviate it, and, moreover, that one of the unmet ideals of liberal Western democracy was its guarantee of female equality.

Sección Femenina, which had been more or less in line with international women's rights efforts in the 1950s and early 1960s, faltered in the mid-to-late 1960s and throughout the 1970s. Primo de Rivera's organization was of the "older" branch of women's rights organizations and emerging organizations of the more radical "younger" branch crowded out SF and other right-wing women as they found a voice in international women's politics during the 1960s.

This shakeup happened at the domestic level as well. While *Sección Femenina* delighted in its policy successes in the 1960s and planned the *Congreso*—its international coming-out party—the organization also experienced a membership crisis that it perceived to result from the changing political environment and the perception of young, educated women that *Sección Femenina* was "a devalued political organization" incapable of giving the professional opportunities they desired.[47] Also, for the first time under Franco, Spanish women who felt this way about *Sección Femenina* had other options, both legal and extralegal, for political involvement.

Beginning in 1964, Franco allowed the creation of a network of neighborhood and housewives' associations throughout the country. These associations were in principle apolitical and loyal to the regime—they would not have been legal otherwise—and though SF had no affiliation with such organizations, some individual members chose to participate in both the associations and in SF. However, the housewives' associations and SF attracted different kinds of women. Since SF only concerned itself with furthering its political capital as a "female political elite" and with recruiting "modern" women, the organization focused its activities on women engaged in professional activities and on university students who had begun eschewing membership in the organization.[48] Nevertheless, *Sección Femenina* was no longer the only option available to Spanish women who wished to become involved in politics—especially local politics—and who wished to improve their lives and those of the women in their communities.

Moreover, in Franco's Spain, feminist organizations formed and began to gain a following during the 1960s and 1970s, albeit clandestinely. *Sección Femenina* thus had to wrestle with both an emerging feminist-driven international consensus about how to work for women's rights, and with the emergence of feminist organizations within Spain that threatened the regime and the ideological foundations of *Sección Femenina*'s work. Over the course of the 1960s Spanish women increasingly turned to their nation's nascent clandestine feminism despite penalties for feminist activism that included hefty jail sentences and torture.[49] As early as 1965, the MDM, backed by Spain's clandestine Communist Party, recruited members for a women's rights movement. Most neighborhood associations were Francoist, but feminist organization *Movimento Democratico de Mujeres* (MDM) infiltrated some, resulting in five new MDM-affiliated homemakers' associations and thereby creating networks of feminist consciousness and solidarity in several working-class neighborhoods. Activists participating in this infiltration did so at great personal risk and when they were discovered, police raided their groups, disbanded them, and reiterated the illegality of feminism. Still, such attempts at infiltration continued and feminists also found other ways to organize. In 1967, the MDM gathered roughly 1,500 signatures on a petition demanding equal rights, including access to birth control and divorce.[50] Other women wrote anonymous letters critical of SF gender policy to sympathetic periodicals, which published the missives.[51] In all, despite the regime's harsh penalties for political dissidence, and despite their clandestine activities, feminist organizations nevertheless became so widespread that even SF had to acknowledge their existence.[52] Indeed, estimates suggest that shortly after Franco's death there were as many as ninety feminist organizations throughout Spain.[53]

These feminists engaged with, challenged, and condemned *Sección Femenina* and its *Congreso*. In addition to creating networks of solidarity by infiltrating housewives' associations, in 1970 the MDM also used such infiltration in a plot to sway SF's political platform and to exert influence over the conclusions of the *Congreso*.[54] Some high-profile Spanish women with links to feminist organizations participated in the *Congreso* and openly, if cautiously, disregarded SF's restrictions on what topics could and could not be discussed. Maria Campo de Alange and several members of her Women's Studies Sociology Seminar (SESM), for example, caused controversy when they insisted on promoting coeducation for children, one of the banned topics—though, as Mary Salas recalled, they had to speak of it in coded language as "the word coeducation could not be said then."[55]

Still others convened a clandestine, competing conference where they denounced SF's *Congreso*. In January 1970, representatives of feminist organizations from around Spain gathered in Madrid under the name *Mujeres Democraticas de España* (MDE). Their meeting's minutes included a rejection of the *Congreso*:

> We believe it important ... that this first general meeting took place months before the Women's Congress ... [This Congress is] sponsored by Pilar Primo de Rivera (observer of woman's awakening [in Spain]) ... [who] with typical Falangist demagoguery now intends to turn us into a means to integrate [women's activism] into the Regime, just as she formerly did all she could to marginalize us, "inspired" by the doctrine of José Antonio. We roundly denounce this Congress as foreign to the true interests of women.[56]

By sarcastically naming Primo de Rivera a mere "observer of woman's awakening" and referring to her legislative successes as "'inspired' by the doctrine of José Antonio," MDE positioned SF as regime henchwomen and not as the reformists that SF and its supporters believed themselves to be. Feminists at the time largely defined themselves in opposition to Francoism and their demands included the dissolution of the regime, amnesty for its political prisoners, and an end to the particular oppression women suffered under National-Catholicism; they also opposed SF's limited vision of women's rights, pushing for a more expansive vision of labor and economic rights, as well as for legalization of abortion, contraception, and divorce. In sum, despite *Sección Femenina*'s claims, MDE argued that the *Congreso* was simply an SF attempt to coopt and dilute feminist demands and not an honest attempt to represent Spanish or indeed any women.

Ultimately, both the sanctioned neighborhood associations and the feminist organizations challenged SF's control and illustrate the changing methods of working for women's rights. Of themselves, Spain's newly-legal, official neighborhood and housewives' associations did not challenge SF's claims to internationalism; their emergence did, however, represent an alternative to SF's erstwhile monopoly on women's activism while feminist infiltration of the associations blurred the boundaries between Francoist and radical. Over time even those associations supportive of the regime began to behave like the emerging "younger" branch of women's activism inasmuch as they used grassroots networks to advance the regime's ideology at the local level. Organizationally, if not yet ideologically, the nation's growing number of alternative women's groups conformed with rather than resisted shifts occurring in the international women's movement. Growing support for outright feminism, meanwhile, increasingly forced SF and the Franco regime to fight to retain Spanish women's loyalties as popular views on women's rights shifted to leave SF's by-then-antiquated reformism behind. Spanish feminists' approach to women's rights was not unique: it corresponded with the gains of international grassroots women's rights activists and centered on rectifying oppression as opposed to economic injustice. This ascendant movement increasingly outshone conservative activists and formal women's organizations, who now found themselves struggling for influence.

SF's sponsorship of and participation in the *Congreso*, and its representation of the *Congreso*'s aims and their hopes for action arising from the discussion topics, existed within a transitional moment for both domestic and international women's rights activism, which became increasingly clear as the 1970s wore on and came to a head with SF's participation in the 1975 WCOW in Mexico City. It is perhaps ironic that the very moment when SF's approach was becoming passé was the moment the organization chose to push beyond Spain's borders in search of solidarity.

The Transitional Moment and the International Women's Year (IWY)

Oblivious, perhaps, to the disconnect, SF members concluded the *Congreso* feeling optimistic about the state of women in Spain and around the globe, and about their role in championing women's rights. The organization's leadership excitedly jumped into preparations when the United Nations' General Assembly announced that 1975 would be the International Women's Year (IWY) and that its programming would include an international conference. Francisco Franco appointed Pilar Primo de Rivera head of the Spanish National Committee for the International Women's Year. News that the Committee had already held its first meeting on Spain's involvement in the World Conference on Women (WCOW) greeted *Teresa* readers in the magazine's August 1974 issue, along with the assurance that Primo de Rivera was preparing to host the second meeting "[a]t the time of drafting these lines."[57] Subsequent editions of *Teresa* provided in-depth detail about the National Committee's structure as well as about individual members of the committee, including Primo de Rivera, of course, but also Carmen Salinas and Carola Ribed de Valcárcel, each of whom were on the SF leadership team and were entrusted with important speaking or public relations roles during the WCOW.

SF approached the WCOW confident in Spain's exceptional record on women's rights. After all, they felt that though Spanish society still needed some work, Spain had already managed to achieve female equality. According to Pilar Primo de Rivera,

> Nowadays, one can almost say that woman is no longer subject to [male] tutelage, as she was before. Within the specific context in which she undeniably exists, she has beyond a doubt made enormous strides toward equality with man. Not acting against him nor placing herself ahead of him, but rather eliminating discrimination that kept her from developing her abilities, till now nearly always confined to the exercise of household duties or second-tier labors. Now woman studies, works, interests herself in politics, is in principle an equal member of society. This is more or less accepted today.[58]

In addition, *Teresa* reported on SF's continued international engagements in the lead-up to the first World Conference on Women, to be held in Mexico City in 1975, which they used to gauge reception of the Spanish delegation's ideas as well as to gauge what kinds of demands were in vogue in other nations. To this end, SF expressed surprise, wonderment, and amusement that the Swedish delegation wanted greater maternity and paternity leave while the Malian delegation desired access to technologies that could relieve housewives of their domestic labor.[59]

SF leadership felt secure that their calls for labor and financial rights for women were among the best proposals for international action. The Spanish delegation's fundamental goal for women's rights policy in the WCOW was twofold. First, Spanish delegates encouraged other nations to adopt "equality legislation and to negate all the rules that discriminate against women," which consisted first of "the establishment of equality in the field of political, professional and labor rights." In her speech to the WCOW Plenary Session, Vice-President of the Spanish Delegation Carmen Salinas allowed as how "most countries [had] resolved" this step, and posited that the next vital component of such equality was in ensuring "legal equality" and giving women "the same opportunities" as men. To this end, she exhorted women "that only with their effort and determination [would] they achieve their rightful place in the society of the future."[60] After securing legislative advances, then, Salinas and SF argued that the work of ensuring female equality fell entirely on the women who wanted equality. Women should be "integrated" or "incorporated" into society, but society should not be changed to accommodate them.[61] Instead, they argued, women should be given the legal equality and resources to work hard to exist in society in its present form.

Secondly, SF lobbied the WCOW to refrain from proposing a universal method of tackling women's inequality. SF once again asserted its exceptional character, arguing that because of Spain's special traditions and state of development, other nations' solutions or suggestions to improve the lot of women would not work there. SF delegates felt that the lesson Spain had to teach Europe and the world was about the need for nationally specific solutions, a lesson the government reinforced: Spanish Prime Minster Carlos Arias Navarro similarly argued that other nations also had their own individualized needs.[62] Spain's delegates were steadfast in their belief that the conference's participating nations would best be able to combat female oppression through individualized approaches tailored to their particular cultures and traditions, and remained convinced of this after witnessing the dramas of the WCOW.

Despite SF's confidence leading into the WCOW, the delegation failed to have its desired impact. Throughout the 1950s and 1960s SF was in step with the international consensus on women's rights politics, but by the 1970s tSF was increasingly out of touch, both organizationally and ideologically. Organizationally, a split emerged between older branches of women's rights activism and newer branches of second-wave feminist activism—the former intent on a bureaucratically administered top-down international solution to women's inequality, the latter influenced by the counterculture of the 1960s and reliant on the grassroots tactics of mass political movements pioneered in student uprisings, the Civil Rights Movement, and Vietnam War protests. Notably, WCOW organizers fell on the "older" side of this divide: American delegate and activist Arvonne Fraser described them as "CSW women ... bent on using the power of international institutions and governments as a vehicle for the transformation they desired," the antithesis of "newer" activists' goals.[63] The Spanish delegation fell into the "older" category as well, as much for their relationship with Spanish governmental institutions as for their disdain for the emerging feminism and its grassroots activism. Meanwhile, grassroots feminist activists involved in international women's rights politics attended the WCOW primarily through an associated NGO Tribune, which hosted organizations which were unaffiliated with the UN and were denied access to conference proceedings. The UN resented the new model of NGO involvement and attempted to soften their role in WCOW negotiations by cordoning off NGO staging areas, but NGO lobbyists found ways to connect with UN representatives and delegates, pushing grassroots-aligned NGOs' agendas into conference proceedings.

Ideologically speaking, the Spanish delegation also found itself isolated. First, the delegation's goals and beliefs were no longer mainstream, nor in line with what other international women's rights activists advocated. This was complicated by the particular political tensions that riddled the 1975 WCOW in Mexico City, as well as the two subsequent WCOW. Though the UN intended the IWY and its accompanying WCOW to find points of commonality and build networks for politically active women, the WCOW instead highlighted the differences between ideologically diverse groups of women and exacerbated relationships already fraying under Cold War tensions. Cold War political conflict between the Soviet delegations and the Americans fundamentally shaped the development and goals of international feminism, as well as the agendas of not just the first UN World Conference on Women held in Mexico City in 1975, but also the second and third, held in Copenhagen in 1980 and Nairobi in 1984. This clash marked the battle lines between women who, like the Soviets, felt that "gender equality could only be achieved within a more just economic system" and Americans who dismissed those arguments. That Soviets also wanted to expand the WCOW agenda to include conversation about international political issues beyond female equality frustrated American delegates. Moreover, Soviets, in a move antithetical to American and Western feminist beliefs, also put forth what scholar Kristen Ghodsee has called the "peace agenda" rooted in a cultural feminism celebrating differences between the sexes and offering solutions based on those differences.[64]

The more "radical" Soviet aims held sway at the Mexico City conference and through the following decade. Some of this was due to the American government's reluctance to invest in the WCOW proceedings, as officials generally believed that women's rights activism was a mere front for communist agitation. Arvonne Fraser's recollections of the US government's prohibition on female American delegates talking with Soviet women or advocating binding proposals are perhaps easier to comprehend within this context, as is the National Security Council's strenuous objections to US First Lady Betty Ford giving opening remarks on behalf of the American delegation at the conference. But the American government was not solely responsible for American activists' limited influence; their activist colleagues also marginalized and even mocked them. This conduct was so extreme that one conference attendee later recalled women pulling each other's hair in physical fights during mid-conference debates; in more prosaic opposition, the Mexico City WCOW's concluding documents contained multiple tenets with which American women were uncomfortable while both they and their foreign counterparts viewed resolutions about some issues, like Zionism, as referendums on American foreign policy.[65]

Neither of the two major branches of debate was compatible with SF ideals. SF defended capitalism and industrialization, unlike the Soviet bloc. The Western European side did desire increased labor and economic rights for women, but also advocated democracy and broader roles for women in civic life than SF supported. Moreover, in siding with the "Western European" nations, which Salinas did by identifying them as the only nations who had ideas worth entertaining, SF chose the "losing" side of the WCOW debate: as Ghodsee shows, the Western feminist perspective was roundly criticized during the first three WCOW and instead it was the Soviet ideologies which dominated for the next decade after the Mexico City WCOW. Spanish feminists, not SF, were in line with those ideologies and demands.

The Spanish delegation further distinguished itself by the lack of any objection among its membership to the inclusion of male delegates within their ranks. While feminist delegates from other nations resented the inclusion of men in their delegations, the Spanish contingent did not. Spain's explicit inclusion of men in its delegation and debates was a clear statement about the role they felt men ought to play in the process of determining women's rights, as opposed to the veiled role that men played in other delegations that declared their intentions to promote women's involvement while simultaneously pushing women and their opinions into the margins. Though women comprised 73 percent of the 2,000 WCOW delegates and headed 113 of 133 attending nations' delegations, many women nevertheless felt they struggled to make meaningful contributions to the conference agenda.[66] Arvonne Fraser recalled:

> Unnoticed by the media was the solidarity among women in recognizing discrimination even across lines of intense political disparities. Males headed virtually every government delegation, even in the preparatory conferences. Interested primarily in the political issues and protecting their country's point of view, they left their chairs to female delegation members unless a political issue was on the agenda; then the blue suits, white shirts, and ties would emerge en masse into the meeting hall. Women would turn around and look at each other knowingly as they relinquished their seats. Finally, in one preparatory meeting when the men emerged from the outer hall, a swell of spontaneous laughter greeted them. By 1985, many women led delegations and the political officers were more discreet.[67]

Though Fraser's numbers are inaccurate—women, in fact, headed the majority of government delegations—her anecdote nevertheless points to the feelings of irrelevancy some women felt even at a conference specifically for women, as well as to the significant role that men continued to play even in ostensibly women's politics. Fraser herself noted the phenomenon of "male delegates who thought the whole idea of a world women's conference was unnecessary."[68] Fraser was not the only delegate to feel this way. As Ghodsee notes, both the Soviet and the American delegations remained "under the firm control of male politicians back home," with American delegates forbidden to even informally engage Soviet women in conversation.[69]

More anomalous still was SF's repudiation of NGOs and radical feminist politics. Other delegations were willing to at least entertain radical feminist ideas, communicated most often to official WCOW delegates by unaffiliated activists in Mexico City for the NGO Tribune; SF eschewed them. In her post-WCOW remarks, Carmen Salinas in fact blamed NGOs for the radicalism of the WCOW and asserted that the conference's ineffectual conclusion was at least in part due to the presence of NGOs and their accompanying NGO Tribune:

> The problem stems from the clearly extremist position that some women's organizations have adopted. This is the case with the "free tribunal," an assembly formed in parallel to the Conference, and which more than 3000 delegates attended. At this free tribunal, highly daring topics were discussed, subjects that have nothing to do with the serious matters considered at the International Conference. I cannot speak to those topics [discussed at the Free Tribunal], as I did not attend any of the sessions and I am nearly certain that no members of the Spanish Delegation [to the International Conference] did either.[70]

This rejection of both NGOs and the new, feminist, wave of women's politics their representatives championed put SF firmly outside newly developing lobbying methods for international women's rights policy.

SF also represented a model of conservative female activism increasingly out of touch with even other Western groups that self-identified as conservative. SF was comfortable with UN involvement and with formal international women's networks, whereas conservative women elsewhere expressed concern about global politics crowding out individual choice and the sovereignty of national democratic governments. For example, the IWY and WCOW coincided with the controversial Equal Rights Amendment ratification process in the United States that propelled conservative women like Phyllis Schlafly, who spoke out against ratifying the amendment, to prominence. Schlafly and her supporters denounced the IWY and WCOW as UN attempts "to institute one-world government"; they also argued that President Jimmy Carter's establishment of a corresponding US-sponsored International Women's Year and subsequent American women's conference in 1977 was a "federally-funded effort to rally support for the ERA" and that it was "a front for radicals and lesbians."[71]

On the fringe and bereft of a bully pulpit from which to tout the strengths of Francoist gender ideology and the opportunities that Franco's Spain afforded women, *Sección Femenina* struggled to assert their ideas in the WCOW. The structure of the published conference summary is such that contributions of individual delegates and nations to phrasing of drafts are difficult to trace, but the record does reveal which delegations participated in which drafting processes and how delegations voted on proposed resolutions.[72] This record shows that the Spanish delegation contributed to just two resolutions. One stressing the importance of "education, vocational training, employment and housing" for women in "developing countries" and "in rural and low-income urban areas."[73] They also helped shape resolution 17, "The Family," which stated that "the family is the primary and fundamental nucleus of society" and recommended ways in which the state could protect the family unit.[74] Beyond this, the Spanish delegation abstained from every vote but one.[75]

Notwithstanding their experience at the WCOW, the *Sección Femenina*'s faith in Spain's exceptionalism remained unshaken: after the conference, SF leaders criticized other nations in attendance and reported back that they had been correct to feel so exceptional. Yet coupled with this sense of vindication was a deep dissatisfaction with the WCOW, its conclusions, and its organization. One key point of dissatisfaction was that the WCOW offered SF less opportunity for outreach and solidarity than its leaders had expected. In a January 1976 post-WCOW retrospective for *Teresa*, Carola Ribed, secretary of the Commission, contrasted the WCOW experience with SF's experience of prior conferences. Members of the SF leadership team had served on the Spanish National Commission of the IWY and attended multiple international conferences in the period between the *Congreso* and the WCOW, and Ribed recounted that she and other SF members had, for example, attended conferences in Ottawa, Paris, Brussels, and Bonn. She reported that each of them had "been very interesting seminars," and that at her favorite, Ottawa, "countries attended to engage in an exchange [?? likely 'of'] projects and come into contact [with one another] … it became clear that there was a need to create government organizations in the various nations specifically dedicated to dealing with women's issues."[76] Though Ribed seemed hesitant to provide explicit critique of the WCOW, the implication was that the WCOW had not represented a similar opportunity for the exchange of ideas.

SF leaders also felt that the WCOW failed to adequately address women's real problems. Salinas, for example, criticized the WCOW as a farce "politicized" by national delegations ultimately less interested in working together on women's rights issues than on forcing their agendas on the assembled multitudes. Kristin Ghodsee's work explains the dynamic between the United States and Soviet women that shadowed the conference; Arvonne Fraser noted those key conflicts in her recollections; Spanish delegates represented themselves as caught between warring factions. Salinas expressed particular frustration at the "interventions" of developing nations, which "used [the conference] to attack ... the issues of colonialism, neocolonialism, occupied territories, 'apartheid', etc." The nations included the "black countries [who] ... intervened extensively and ... lashed out against industrialized countries" as well as "Arab women [who] spoke in their own language, with no means of translating them and, even more, using a really unacceptable tone." The division was so all-encompassing, she noted, that "the mere mention of a Third World country, like Chile, started an endless amount of applause." Only "the interventions of the more developed countries—the United States, France, Holland, England—that is to say, almost all of Western Europe" passed Salinas's muster; other delegations' contributions crowded out opportunity to talk about women's "true social, cultural, and economic problems" to the point where the WCOW accomplished, in Salinas's eyes, little of consequence.[77]

Salinas hewed to Spain's exceptionalism while painting her nation as sharing Western Europe's cultural values, but in actuality Spain's emerging feminists more closely aligned with the new international paradigm on display during the IWY and at the WCOW than did SF or the Spanish WCOW delegation. And while these feminists did not participate directly in the UN's WCOW, they did engage with it. Spanish women of varying radical affiliations organized their own feminist conferences to coincide with the IWY and sent out press releases exploring the implications of the WCOW and responding to the UN's goals. The *Organizaciones de Mujeres de Madrid* (OMM), for example, laid out a specific program—with categories roughly corresponding both to the IWY development goals and to the *Congreso*'s categories of discussion—to improve Spanish women's lives. They deplored Spain's backwardness, stating that "Spain [was] one of the most backward nations in Europe," and proposed changes to bring Spain on par with Western Europe.[78]

On the other hand, the *Asamblea de Mujeres de Barcelona* (AMB) only halfheartedly welcomed UN support in publicizing women's problems and fighting their oppression. They interpreted the WCOW as "paternalistic" and denounced the Spanish delegation for buying into both the UN's paternalism and Spain's own: SF members were, the organization argued, "appointed by decree" and were not truly representative of Spain because they made up only a specific sector of the population. In addition to critiquing the Franco regime and the conservative *Sección Femenina*, AMB implied that the UN WCOW similarly allowed only a narrow group of women to share their experiences and participate in the negotiations. Yet, like the *Organizaciones de Mujeres de Madrid*, the women at the *Asamblea de Mujeres de Barcelona* used the WCOW as an opportunity to promote their own agenda and propose changes that they felt could address the real challenges women faced.[79]

Lastly, the *Movimento Democrático de Mujeres*, affiliated with the CCOO, agreed with OMM that

> the UN initiative to promote the International Women's Year is a positive measure, inasmuch as it has pushed women in all countries to take note of the discrimination to which they are subjected. We celebrate it as a measure that promotes women's movements that we believe have the duty to be the firmest and consequential defenders of the fight against discrimination.

But they also agreed with the Barcelona *Asamblea*'s prediction that the International Women's Year could have no effect on Spanish women's lives:

> [I]n our country the official celebration of the IWY is not having the least impact among the female masses, due to the fascist nature of the organizations to which the Government has entrusted the organization of the IWY in Spain, [organizations] that have done nothing more than try to keep women in the passive and isolated role assigned to them for all these years by the Dictatorship, and because of this the immense majority of women have confirmed that they can expect nothing from the current political regime—to the contrary, it is a reality that women themselves, despite the political and every other kind of repression [they face], are establishing their own popular and democratic organizations.

The simple fact, they argued, was that "the fascist dictatorship and liberation of women are incompatible and we reaffirm the conviction that the struggle against fascism, objectively, is a feminist struggle." In this regard, the MDM felt that the struggle against Spain's fascist dictator was a more important step than to work with the UN for increased protections for women's rights.[80]

SF remained on the margins and failed to meet its objectives during the WCOW, but the increased international attention to the issue of women's rights garnered during the IWY and the WCOW conversely gave Spanish feminists opportunities to create the kinds of solidarity that SF sought. If SF was out of touch with the dominant international consensus on how to work toward women's rights, and with growing conservative movements in other nations, Spanish feminists resembled their counterparts abroad who had mixed opinions about the conference but nevertheless tried to imagine ways it could improve women's lives. Yet for all that Spanish feminists were now in a position to speak, critiques of the IWY and international policy by emergent grassroots organizations heralded a new struggle on the horizon, one Spanish women had been fighting domestically and would now begin fighting abroad.

Conclusion

The *Sección Femenina*'s announcement of its *Congreso* and its international ambitions coincided with the shift in women's rights politics that left their policies and political approaches out of favor, though the shift did not become evident for another few years. Carmen Salinas's comments at the IWY show that SF leaders portrayed the *Congreso* as a great success for Spanish and international women's rights policy discussions even into the mid-1970s.[81] Still, *Sección Femenina* had struggled at the *Congreso*—it struggled to navigate participants' support for policies antithetical to fascism, it struggled with the emergence of feminist networks denouncing the conference specifically, and it struggled to recapture the attention of Spanish women who comprised its potential membership base.

These struggles came to a head at the WCOW. SF participants went to the UN conference hoping or expecting to be lauded for their work and, upon finding that they were not, realized that the changes that were taking place in global women's politics were beyond them. The growing women's movement had, by the time of the UN conference, left them behind. Grassroots and radical feminisms' influence on the conference agenda left *Sección Femenina* with nothing substantive to negotiate. The transition in international women's politics moved SF from mainstream to far right and thus made the organization irrelevant. That Franco died shortly thereafter completed the organization's fall from international and domestic power and paved the way for Spanish feminists to come out of hiding.

The divide between *Sección Femenina* and its domestic as well as foreign detractors, then, provides a lens through which to examine the culture of Spain in a moment of political-identitarian transition. By understanding how *Sección Femenina*'s policies reflected international trends in tackling women's rights, as well as how women like those in *Sección Femenina* interacted with their peers across the globe, we can better understand the ebbs and flows of international feminist activism throughout the mid-century. Moreover, the domestic narrative in which we can place *Sección Femenina* is significant on its own, but its intersection with broader international activist networks helps us explore how Spaniards debated and reconstructed their political and cultural environments as Francoism waned. Moreover, it allows us to better understand Spain's relation to and participation in the vibrant global politics of women's rights and the international negotiations to define modernity and progress.

Spanish feminism flourished in this international moment. Its emergence, and *Sección Femenina*'s dissolution in April 1977 as part of the transition government's dismantling of Franco's National Movement in advance of Constitutional negotiations, changed the landscape of Spain's female political activism. With that said, even as feminism overtook conservative women's activism, National-Catholicism's impact lingered and permeated political debates about the shape of the nation's post-Franco governance.

2

"What We Want is For Each Woman to Be Her Own Protagonist"*

Re-examining the Feminist "Triumphs" of Transition-Era Spain

From soon after Franco's death in November 1975 through the ratification of Spain's Constitution in December 1978, feminist magazine *Vindicación Feminista* ran a column called "Women in the World" that sought to inform readers about feminist movements in Spain and abroad. Authors Paloma Saavedra and Regina Bayo aimed to "report on existing [women's] groups, their lines of actions and programs," and envisioned the column as a "public forum for all groups who fight for the liberation of women."[1]

To this end, Saavedra and Bayo dedicated most of the column's inaugural installment in July 1976 to listing the organizations then advocating for women's rights in Spain, including a long list of political parties.[2] Many of these were radical leftist parties whose support for women's equality was likely unsurprising to readers, including the Spanish Communist Party (PCE), and the Patriotic Anti-Fascist Revolutionary Front's Popular Union of Women (FRAP-UPM). However, the list also had a glaringly anomalous inclusion: the politically and socially conservative Carlist Party, a longtime (albeit often uneasy) ally of the Franco regime since the Civil War and a consistent proponent of a strict and traditionalist gendered ordering of Spanish society with an ideology.[3] The Carlists, Saavedra and Bayo wrote,

> aim to end [women's] alienation through struggle ... a social and political struggle for progress [that] represents for [women] a recovery of two dimensions of their identities: their place in their communities as well as in worldly affairs. At this time, women's participation in the struggle is necessary for ending it, and

*James M. Markham, "Spain's Feminist Movement Concentrating on Rape Issue," *New York Times*, ProQuest Historical Newspapers, May 29, 1978.

women's response to the system['s dysfunctions] is already global/comprehensive in scope.[4]

Yet in the context of the democratic transition and Spanish feminism's changing fortunes, the Carlist party's seemingly incongruous ideological shift (or alternatively, Saavedra and Bayo's wildly inaccurate description of the party's position) made strategic sense. As *Sección Femenina* had discovered at the 1975 World Conference on Women, the mainstream international view on women's rights had moved past Francoism's once-successful marriage of substantive reforms and anti-feminist ideological immobilism, just as Spanish feminism emerged from its former clandestinity. Interest in feminist activism—including Spanish feminism—meanwhile grew abroad and domestically, spurred both by the growth of women's rights movements worldwide as well as Spain's sudden political mutability. For Spain's feminists, one result was that between Franco's death in late 1975 and the Spanish Constitution's ratification in 1978, they were able to engage heavily with international feminist networks that *Sección Femenina* had never successfully accessed. More generally, by the time that *Vindicación Feminista* published its first issue, appeals for female equality were fast becoming a powerful form of political currency—a currency that even the Carlists could desire to possess.

Moreover, there was seemingly also consensus among Spaniards and international observers that guaranteeing some measure of women's rights was a hallmark of democracies. As Juan Carlos's political machinations made democratization ever more likely even amidst criticism from public figures both on the left and right of the political spectrum, politicians of all political affiliations found themselves obliged to champion women's rights in order to demonstrate their commitment to the new Spain taking shape, and negotiating what these hitherto-undefined rights would comprise became key to negotiating the exact form of Spain's new democracy. Defining this democratic order included defining women's rights, and both were contested, all the more hotly because it happened under Francoism's lingering shadow. Some wondered what simply abolishing the remnants of National-Catholic policy would do for women's rights, whether this would so alienate Francoist stalwarts that they might attempt a coup to protect the Caudillo's legacy, or if such a reform was even possible. These debates also had significant potential international consequences. Negotiations over the shape of Spain's new government structure unfolded before a Spanish populace hoping to move on from Francoism, as well as European leaders demanding that Spain embrace liberal democracy, including a guarantee of women's equality, in exchange for membership in the European Economic Community (EEC).[5]

Yet, though feminism's visibility across Western Europe has seemingly contributed to this popular perception of a natural tie between democracy and guarantees of women's rights, in Spain negotiations about the precise scope of those rights took place both as the nation's politicians and the general public largely denounced feminism, and as feminists themselves struggled to access sites of political power. Spanish feminists' great domestic political challenge in the transition period was twofold: first, they sought to build consensus behind a shared feminist platform from groups of women who could not agree on whether to identify as feminist, what it meant to be feminist, or how far women's rights should extend. Second, feminists attempted to build relationships with the electorate and foster dialogue with politicians and major political parties about the extent to which Spain's as-yet-undefined democracy ought to include a coherent vision for achieving women's equality.

In the transition era, at least, feminists failed on both counts. As feminists' differing reactions to the WCOW in Chapter 1 foreshadowed, internal strife led to stark breaks within the feminist movement even at the outset of the post-Franco era as activists with conflicting strategies for expanding women's rights fought instead of finding common ground. Earlier shared enmity toward *Sección Femenina* and its vision for women's rights was no longer of primary relevance, as SF was unwilling to cooperate with any feminist groups and was in any case dissolved soon after in 1977 as part of the official dismantling of Franco's National Movement. Other conservative women unaffiliated with SF, however, did pose an organizational challenge for early feminist leaders when they expressed willingness to work alongside feminists, but only if these collaborations did not call themselves feminist.[6]

More consequential, this chapter argues, were disputes between double militant feminists—feminists who wanted to prioritize support for Juan Carlos's proposed democratic structure and work for increased women's rights from within the new government—and single militant feminists who rejected Spain's incipient democracy for retaining unacceptably close ties to Francoism and wanted the burgeoning feminist movement to focus on its own agenda, not matters of democratic statecraft. In general, double militants participated in the nation's governance as politicians, as administrators, and as staffers in bureaucratic divisions while single militants remained outside the government and instead worked through grassroots political channels. Both camps' demands were vague and lacked specifics, though single militants did generally propose policy and courses of action that Spaniards deemed "radical," most of which hinged on the core assertion that the structure of the new democratic state resembled Franco's own government too closely, and that its inability to break radically with Francoist politicians and National-Catholicism made it complicit in perpetuating the systemic discrimination carried out during the Franco years. Double militants voiced some similar concerns, but to a lesser degree; they clearly supported the Spanish democracy and perceived it to have fewer flaws than did single militants. These differences between double and single militants were present from the start, but, as this chapter shows, were initially only small stumbling blocks until the *Partido Socialista Obrera Español* (PSOE), which took power after winning the General Election of 1982, established a new state agency for women's affairs, the *Instituto de la Mujer*, in 1983.

Moreover despite feminists' desire to become more than "just a vote"[7] amid the Transition's political maneuvering, even double militants *were* just a vote, at least politically speaking, from the late 1970s through the mid-1980s. Women made up a paltry share of *Cortes* delegates during and following the transition period, and even left-leaning political parties like the PSOE rejected female members' requests to increase the number of female representatives on the party's slate of candidates for office.[8] Single and double militant feminists both lacked a say in the shape and content of major transition-era legislation. The Moncloa Pacts (an agreement between Spain's political parties regarding how the economy would be managed during the post-Franco transition), the 1978 Constitution itself, and the (partial) legalization of abortion all contained some policy for which feminists had fought—the Moncloa Pacts, for instance, included an agreement to decriminalize contraceptive use—but feminists were not included in developing these policies, nor did they have a voice in government discussions about how best to realize these women's demands.

In later years, a narrative would emerge that portrayed transition-era strides in women's rights as proof that feminist ideals had triumphed in post-Franco Spain; as the Transition still unfolded, feminists themselves similarly pointed to their swelling ranks, public influence, and ability to attract foreign and domestic media attention as evidence of their growing strength.[9] Yet this strength, I argue, was more apparent than real and did not translate into an ability to shape legislation or the new government's final form. Contemporary feminists' own views of what these changes truly meant for their movement and for Spanish women suggest as much: an ideologically diverse array of feminists decried the reforms, calling them mere salves for Spain's real sickness, which were the underlying patriarchal government and social structures that perpetuated female oppression.

Instead of treating transition-era women's rights reforms as genuine feminist victories, this chapter builds upon historian Pamela Radcliff's argument that male politicians of the time found it politically expedient to seemingly embrace feminist ideals—incorporating an equal citizenship clause into the 1978 Constitution, for instance, to gain acceptance from, and perhaps open a path to joining, the EEC.[10] Ironically, however, this chapter reveals that despite feminism's political usefulness, Spanish feminists themselves lacked any political leverage. Spanish feminists were already struggling to resolve their internal ideological schisms and to gain access to the political arena as politicians and parliamentary delegates; meanwhile, male politicians actively silenced and marginalized those double militant feminists who did become their colleagues, and also misrepresented feminist positions and demands, advocating instead for watered-down versions that little resembled what either single or double militant feminists wanted. Indeed, I show, two measures that are often cited as seminal transition-era feminist victories—the equal citizenship clause in the 1978 Constitution and the legalization of abortion in 1985—were neither feminist-driven nor significantly addressed actual feminist demands.

Post-Franco Feminism

For many Spanish women, advances secured by *Sección Femenina*, the Francoist women's organization, were neither advances nor secure. As Chapter 1 shows, late Franco-era feminist groups—at the time, still clandestine—already decried legislative changes put forward by Pilar Primo de Rivera's group, and rejected both the conservative vision of progress enshrined in the goals for the SF's International Women's Congress of 1968, as well as the group's claim that Spanish women's lives were improving, calling instead for what they considered real reform. Activism only intensified after Franco's death as feminists sought a public presence in Spanish political life. Women founded new feminist groups and joined women's wings of political parties, and the international and domestic press, eager to cover the upheaval in post-Franco Spain, catalogued events that activists organized to condemn Francoist policy and foster feminist solidarity.

Yet feminists, despite the appearance of strength, lacked centralized organizational structures and a coherent voice. They struggled to attract members and grow formal networks in comparison with other political organizations—including women's organizations with continued ties to the defunct regime, such as *Sección Femenina* (until 1977) and officially sanctioned Franco-era housewives' associations. Pamela Radcliff's study of Spanish housewives' associations, for example, estimates that many of these groups had thousands of members in the mid-1970s. The largest, in Barcelona, boasted 12,000 members; others had as many as 3,000 members or more, and membership in such associations was rising.[11] The *Sección Femenina* also had a hefty roster. Kathleen Richmond estimated the number of *mandos*—SF staff and organizational hierarchy—to have been 15,000 in 1968, a number that did not include the many more women who comprised the organization's membership.[12]

Feminism was less popular. "Dissident" housewives associations formed by radicals in the *Movimiento Democrático de Mujeres* (Women's Democratic Movement, or MDM) to further feminist aims had fewer members than their legal counterparts did. This divide persisted even after the transition, when such dissident groups became legal and more widespread—Barcelona's MDM branch peaked at just 2,000 members in 1979.[13] Attendance numbers for conferences and marches tell a similar story. SF held national congresses yearly until 1974, and though meeting minutes do not contain statistics on attendance, the organization nevertheless had a large enough attendance to sustain such meetings annually for several decades.[14] Looking at statistics for its Congreso Internacional de la Mujer also highlights the draw of SF-sponsored events. The conference report listed 885 presenters, a total that did not include SF leadership like Pilar Primo de Rivera, invited male "experts," or attendees not presenting. In addition to its international participants, it also drew Spanish women from over fifty organizations and from forty-two of the nation's fifty provinces.[15] In contrast, the First Conference for Women's Liberation, held in Madrid in December 1975, drew only 500 feminists from fifteen organizations, representing only a third of Spain's provinces.[16]

Moreover, membership in feminist groups was divided across dozens of small organizations with no shared centralized leadership. The diversity of feminist organizations and perspectives was apparent to outsiders as well as to feminists themselves. According to Pamela Radcliff, for instance, a Catalan journalist observed at the time that "atomisation was the first impression one got [of the feminist movement]," and that feminists published "periodic 'dictionaries' … to distinguish between a variety of groups" with confusing acronyms and unclear alliances.[17] Particularly after the legalization of political parties in July 1976, feminists also faced competition from other political organizations, including some founded by long-exiled communists, socialists, labor activists, and other left-wing groups that hoped to capitalize on Franco's death by pushing for radical social reforms. Anny Brooksbank Jones, for example, has estimated that over 300 political parties formed for the 1977 elections.[18] Housewives' associations and *Sección Femenina* had faced no such political or ideological competition when recruiting.

Feminists' immediate impact on Spanish culture likewise fell short of what the *Sección Femenina* and housewives' associations had achieved. The *Sección Femenina*, as Richmond shows, measured its impact less by membership numbers and more by "the fact that SF's moral and cultural standards were embedded in colleges, institutes and university residences throughout Spain."[19] In practice, this included scenarios such as "a government-run nursing school that hired SF teachers on staff to teach political, domestic and physical education classes."[20] Even once SF disbanded, the gender and moral order it had fostered retained its impact on Spanish cultural consciousness and imbricated social structures.

Feminists relied on demonstrations and feminist-produced print media to attract members and sway public opinion. SF did publish a succession of magazines, including *Y* (circulated 1938–46), *Medina* (1941–5), and *Teresa* (1954–77), but these catered to existing members and reinforced messages that readers implicitly understood and ostensibly bought into. SF had other ways to attract members, not least of which was withholding social and cultural benefits from those who refused to participate in its programs. Feminists, who could not similarly rely on the complicity of the Spanish state, turned to one of the few tools available to them—magazines—to articulate and disseminate their message. They had markedly less success than SF. Major feminist periodicals like *Vindicación Feminista* and *dones en lluita* had comparatively long runs of three to four years, but more typical were smaller magazines like *Opción* that lingered for a handful of issues before folding due to financial pressure. Indeed, feminist magazines sold so poorly on public newsstands that even sympathetic vendors refused to stock them.[21]

In some cases, feminist magazines' sales woes were likely due in part to expensive pricing. Other women's periodicals like *Telva* cost 35 pesetas,[22] and general interest titles like *Interviú* or *¡Hola!* cost 45 or 25 pesetas.[23] Their direct competition, the *Sección Femenina*'s *Teresa*, cost 25 pesetas through 1975.[24] *Vindicación Feminista* and *Opción*, by contrast, cost 80 pesetas, almost three times as much.[25] A vicious cycle developed: beleaguered feminist editorial boards often could not sell enough copies to stay solvent, and once insolvent, struggled to fund new issues whose sale might have saved their enterprises. In desperation, these editors tried other tactics. They asked women to use personal connections to sell copies, sold through feminist organizations that bought and distributed copies for members, set up kiosks on street corners, and canvassed for subscribers—any way to sell copies when newsstands would not stock them. Self-financing was not an option, either. Middle and upper class feminists predominated on these editorial boards, but few women had the financial resources to keep a fledgling magazine afloat. *Vindicación Feminista* was a telling exception: its longevity was in large part due to prominent feminist Lidia Falcón's ability to bankroll the publication with her personal savings.[26]

Less expensive feminist publications experienced financial strain, too. *Dones en lluita*, which first circulated in January 1978 at a mere 20 pesetas per issue, raised its price to 50 pesetas by the printing of its combined March/April 1979 issue. The editorial board addressed rising prices in the January 1979 issue, reminding readers about the magazine's subscription plans before laying bare its dire financial situation and imploring readers for support. This was not a gentle plea. The editors berated their readership for not buying or selling enough copies to sustain the magazine:

> This is the tenth issue of the Bulletin ... During this time we have experimented. We are in search of a magazine that is a strong, true spokeswoman of the feminist movement and which would interest women in general at the same time.

What means have we all during all this time? And what is the support we have received? Little, very little. In the majority of cases we had to chase people to deliver items on time. The majority of vocalías and groups are limited to receiving five or ten bulletins, many are slow to pay or don't pay. They seem to forget that the idea of creating a newsletter was not ours, but the Assembly's, and we do not do anything other than execute an agreement of the Assembly every time a new bulletin comes out. Why then is there no way to find women to assume its distribution? We do not understand why Dones en Lluita was created, if we do not fight to be read by as many women as possible.

> The situation in these moments is practically unsustainable. Almost half of the costs of an edition of "Dones en Lluita" are fixed. This means we have to pay as much to make one copy as we do to print 20,000 copies. Right now we print 2,000 copies, of which 25% remain unsold each month. How can we propose, in these conditions, to increase the number of pages or increase the quality? This would mean an overwhelming increase of fixed costs, and naturally implies a significant increase in the sales price.

> There is only one alternative. We sell "Dones en Lluita" everywhere and immediately begin an aggressive subscription campaign so we can increase sales, or it dies in our hands and we are left without an important tool. DO WE, OR DON'T WE, ASSUME THE BURDEN OF DISTRIBUTING THE BULLETIN? DISTRIBUTING THE BULLETIN IS A TASK OF MILITANT FEMINISTS![27]

This tactic seems to have failed. In 1981 *dones en lluita*'s editors called a hiatus to evaluate the magazine's revenues, which totaled over 12,000 pesetas in losses as of December 1980. A few months later *dones en lluita* returned as a quarterly priced at 150 pesetas per copy, but published only eight more issues before folding in March of 1983.[28] Like other such periodicals, *dones en lluita* had a limited readership that seemed to mainly consist of women already involved with, or sympathetic to, the feminist cause. It failed to connect with a broad audience that could engage with feminism through journalism.

International and domestic newspapers unintentionally filled the gap left by magazines like *dones en lluita* through their reporting on feminist activities, which made these more visible and amplified feminist voices, but feminists had little control over this exposure. Foreign journalists offered the most sympathetic coverage. They portrayed Spain's emerging feminist movement as part of a righteous global feminist wave pushing democratic nations to better themselves. In these stories, journalists depicted nations that adopted women's rights legislation as beacons of progressivism. Articles often compared Spanish feminists to counterparts abroad, implying that Spain still lagged behind other, more advanced Western nations, but was starting to follow in their footsteps. Italy was a frequent point of reference, where feminists overcame the Catholic Church's influence to secure abortion rights in 1978. Onlookers wondered what this victory might portend for women's rights in Spain. Comparisons to the United States also abounded, especially as Betty Friedan's National Organization of Women gained prominence and the feminist movement radicalized.

Spanish media portrayed feminists in a more negative light. Even leftists—"authors of defamatory libels"—participated in what Lidia Falcón in a January 1977 *Vindicación Feminista* column called "the offensive against feminism." According to Falcón, feminists had suffered, and continued to suffer, "an exhaustive series of insults, disparaging descriptions, and aggressions [that had been] published in print," which were all the more wearying because the attacks came not just from conservative foes, but from groups that feminists would have otherwise considered allies.[29] Indeed, to the limited extent that Spanish journalists portrayed feminism positively, they merely echoed the international media's view that Spain's embrace of feminism would push it onto a progressive path and reinforce its democratic trajectory. As Pamela Radcliff has put it, this coverage was "not about women's agency, but about specific injustices that had to be corrected for Spain to join the world of modern democracies … feminism was discussed in the context of Spain's identity, not female empowerment."[30]

Finally, as they already struggled for members and the means to assert demands on their own terms, Spanish feminists also struggled because their movement's ideological diversity hindered organizations' ability to build consensus. This picture of fractious feminists runs counter to the prevailing historical portrayal of the movement in the transition era. Radcliff, for example, argues that feminists reported experiencing their gatherings as productive, empowering, and more-or-less unified, but an admittedly unfriendly Spanish media was able to make much of the discord between ideologically opposed feminist groups. Celia Valiente has asserted that political change was the priority for the "majority of women's rights groups."[31] Yet transition-era feminist media of all kinds, ranging from published conference proceedings to magazines to pamphlets to the internal communications of political parties' women's sections, show that feminists felt themselves to be irreconcilably divided over how, and even whether, to support Spain's transition to democracy.

Divisions between activists were so profound that initially they struggled even to agree on embracing the feminist label. In the late Franco years MDM had worked to devise a women's rights platform acceptable to both clandestine Communist Party members and devout Catholics, who together made up much of the group's ranks, and as a result, had already resolved in 1971 that it could "not propose a separate women's movement, but ... [rather] activities tied to other democratic sectors of the country that are fighting against the dictatorship."[32] In 1975, participants in the First Conference for the Liberation of Women, held in Barcelona, faced a similar dilemma. Though attendees negotiated a platform and a set of demands, the conference's published findings noted that there had been contentious debate on a number of points and included an addendum to the platform that housewives' associations and religious women's organizations had insisted on: a signed statement declaring that these groups disagreed with the platform delineated in the conference conclusions and specifically objected to calling the women's rights movement "feminist." Echoing the MDM's decision four years prior, these activists "support[ed] the conclusions but not the distinction of 'feminist'. [They] [a]dvocate[d] not creating a pro-feminist movement but women's awareness through extensive mass movements."[33] In both instances, religious and conservative women interested in women's rights activism withheld their full support for an emerging feminist movement that they believed did not encompass their perspective or meet their needs.

Other problems meanwhile developed among self-identified feminists. As with feminisms in other nations, a chasm opened between those feminists who identified as "single militant" and those who identified as "double militant."[34]

Generally speaking, single militants argued that the only answer to female oppression lay in a large-scale reconception of political, social, and gender relationships. According to Basque feminist Begoña Ibarrola, who penned several first-hand accounts of the Spanish feminist movement, single militants supported "militancy only for the women's movement." This was in large part because single militants felt that discrimination existed in all societies and forms of government, and so securing women's rights necessitated ensuring that cultures and social structures were built from their inception in ways that placed women on an equal footing with men. This could happen within a democracy or some other form of government, excepting dictatorship or a monarchy—single militants only cared that this government, whatever it may be, guarantee equality to all, and especially to women. Double militants, on the other hand, committed to "militancy in a leftist political party while in the feminist movement." They were, in other words, willing to work within an imperfect system for changes both to that system and to policies buttressing women's oppression.[35]

Ideological discord was not exclusive to Spanish feminism, but it did impact Spain's feminists in unique ways. In Spain, single militants fought against the very fact of the Constitution and the transition process. They believed that the new democracy was built atop the foundations of Franco's order, that it reproduced class divisions and patriarchal oppression, and that therefore it could not yield advances in women's rights. Spain's double militants, meanwhile, accepted and even cheered the transition, planning to work within the nascent democratic system to secure policy and legislative changes that would protect and enforce women's rights. They prioritized refining the nation's new democracy: for them, according to Ibarrola, "the problem of women [was] secondary."[36] Resolving the nation's struggle to evolve into a healthy democracy had to happen before women could be assured of their rights.

The approach that the Federation of Feminist Organizations of the Spanish State took toward constitutional deliberations in 1977 is indicative of how double militants worked. The federation's constituent organizations rejected what they knew of the draft constitution, but did so because they felt it failed to guarantee their rights, not because they believed democratic systems were inherently tainted. The group's response to the draft, headlined with the slogan "We do not want to be just a vote," stressed that the right for women to participate in the elections was not enough to meet their demands of equality.[37] In addition, conference attendees devised a "feminist minimum" for upcoming electoral campaigns. Their platform put reform of Spain's laws on adultery and related issues like custody, divorce, and division of marital property at the top of their list of demands. It also demanded contraception, abortion, and educational programs designed to eliminate gender discrimination. Rather than rejecting the constitutional project entirely, these double militant activists were willing to work for a version of it and of the new government that they felt could meet their needs.

The fundamental incompatibility of single and double militant ideologies, even leaving aside the other ideological camps that also worked under the feminist umbrella, was enough to cause friction during events and in organizations designed to present a unified feminist front. In May 1976, for example, conservative women's rights organizations attending the First Catalan Women's Conference withdrew because they objected to the conference's goal of restructuring gender relationships in Spain. In an opinion diametrically opposed to that of most of the conference's other attendees, these conservatives described the fight for women's rights as the pursuit of discrete legislative solutions for the problems women faced.[38] In other cases, feminist organizations with diverse membership bases struggled to accommodate all of their members. ANCHE, a women's activist group, reported having just this problem in 1977 as a dispute over the organization's goals resulted in dissatisfied women leaving to form their own group.[39]

Still, single and double militants did find a sliver of common ground: though they disagreed about whether having a democracy was desirable, they did agree that the version of democracy promoted by Spanish officials in the late 1970s failed women. Their objections to the October 1977 Moncloa Pacts and, increasingly, to the 1978 Constitution as it took shape centered on a shared conviction that the constitutional order's architects sought only to pacify them, not to actually satisfy their demands. And indeed, the Moncloa Pacts were a product of private negotiations between male members of the nation's liberal and conservative political parties, who aimed to boost Spain's struggling economy as well as to mollify activists agitating for social and cultural change. Domestically, these men hoped the Pacts' provisions would stabilize Spain politically in advance of Constitutional ratification. Internationally, they hoped to signal their liberalizing intentions to European onlookers. It is no surprise, then, that the Moncloa Pacts incongruously included seemingly feminist legislation—both the legalization of contraception and heightened penalties for rapists—alongside economic reforms.[40]

Feminists chafed at Moncloa Pact reforms to varying degrees and their objections temporarily, and tenuously, united single and double militants under one feminist umbrella. Both single and double militants resented that politicians continued to ignore or deny their requests for involvement and transparency, as well as for more structured efforts to combat discrimination against women on a social and cultural level. Mainstream male politicians' failure to consult feminists on the Moncloa Pacts or on how best to meet their demands alienated even those feminist groups inclined to sympathize with the transition government. Feminist Paloma Cruz Pepa-García addressed this in an article for the left-leaning periodical *Triunfo*. Pepa-García acknowledged that "[w]ithin the framework of the Moncloa Accords there are a series of positive aspects" which included, in her opinion, "the disappearance of Article 416, which penalized the use, sale, and advertising of birth control methods; creation of family planning centers within Seguridad Social (Spain's national healthcare service); disappearance of the crimes of adultery and unmarried cohabitation; creation during 1978 of 200k free preschool spaces [presumably freeing mothers of young children to return to their careers]." Yet she also assserted that the Moncloa Pacts were not feminist. "It is evident," she wrote, "that this is no feminist milestone; among other reasons, because the influence of different women's groups and movements have been pretty minimal within the Spanish state; rather [the motivating factor has been] converging with European ways in these areas." For Pepa-García, the Moncloa Pacts could not be feminist because feminists had no voice in their creation and because politicians crafting the Pacts' "positive aspects" did so more for political purposes—"converging with" Europe—rather than because they felt motivated to address women's concerns.[41]

Feminists also objected to the Moncloa Pacts because they feared that inclusion of women's rights legislation in that forum was politicians' way of sidestepping the issue of whether to include such provisions in the Constitution. Pepa-García's article in fact hinted at this concern, noting that the next "task" for feminists after the Moncloa Pacts was for "feminist groups [to] take on" reforms "that remain purely on paper"—most likely the Moncloa reforms themselves, the implication being that they remained cemented either in transition era legislation or in social consciousness.[42] Indeed, feminists like Pepa-García argued that unless enshrined in the Constitution, the Moncloa Pact reforms would soon become a dead letter as political tides changed. As one *dones en lluita* columnist, a double-militant who theoretically supported the transition to democracy and the Constitution, explained:

> With the Moncloa Pact agreements on adultery and contraception, the UCD government has tried to give us something of what we requested, to make us believe that we can collect our demands, and thus to more easily silence us; but

we women are not fooled, even as we admit that this is a positive step in achieving our demands. The decriminalization of adultery and contraception is progress achieved through the struggles of thousands of women across the country. But this conquest … is a measure that has no value when not contained in the new democratic constitution … "[43]

Once it became clear that politicians would not introduce comprehensive women's rights reforms into the Constitution, feminists and like-minded leftists led the charge against it. As one OCE Bandera pamphlet titled "Women, The Constitution is not for us, No to the Constitution" declared, "the Constitution institutionalize[d] woman's oppression."[44]

"The Constitution is Made By Men and For Men"[45]

Despite these objections, Spaniards overwhelmingly approved the Constitution, with 91.81 percent of voters favoring ratification.[46] Domestic and international observers lauded the result as a great progressive victory, and in some ways it was. The Constitution of 1978 was Spain's first since the Second Republic's Constitution, which had lasted from 1931 to 1939, and it soon presided over a peaceful transfer of power from Adolfo Suárez's UCD to the PSOE after the general elections of 1982. Observers also found its equal citizenship clause worthy of acclaim. International leaders lauded Spain's new democratic structure, contemporary feminists like PSOE delegate Carlota Bustelo pronounced it a triumph of feminist activism and influence.[47] However, further scrutiny suggests that constitutional ratification in December 1978 was not evidence of feminist strength and that politicians' embrace of feminist talking points was motivated primarily by a desire to win approval from Western Europe.

To begin with, Spanish feminism lacked domestic social capital: despite its visibility in the mid-to-late 1970s, public perception of the movement was mixed, at best. Even as the feminist movement garnered media attention and publicity for activists' demands, the Spanish public mocked both feminism and feminists. Some of this came from women unsympathetic to feminist demands, like lawyer Montserrat Amat Roca who in a 1976 letter to *La Vanguardia* argued that "the laws in [Spain were not] discriminatory and slanted against women, but rather [recognized] that man and woman [were] simply different and the law treats us correspondingly differently." According to Amat Roca, feminists were, moreover, not representative of all Spanish women:

As a result of all of these opinions voiced in favor of adultery and the public protests that a series of women have made in the city streets, we might be left with the impression that all women in Spain want the divorce law approved. If we stop to count the number of households in which peace, love, and tranquility reign, however, we realize that reality is very different, and that the majority of Spanish mothers don't dedicate their time to screaming in the streets but to caring for their families ...[48]

Amat Roca dismissed feminists as shrieking harpies who neglected their domestic responsibilities and were ungrateful for what she believed were the sufficient protections Spanish law already afforded them.

Citizens opposed to feminism expressed this type of disdain for the movement and its participants throughout the transition period. Even in May 1978, as female equality seemed widely accepted and the Constitution was actively being debated, *ABC* ran an article by prominent fascist journalist José Luis Calleja. Like Amat Roca two years prior, Calleja unflatteringly caricatured a feminist demonstration against adultery laws to portray feminists' demands for legal divorce as absurd: "'I am an adultress!', one [picket sign] screamed. 'I am an adultress!', the next one seconded. 'I am an adultress!' the last one confirmed ... My God: they are adultresses and proud of it. Well then, what do they want divorce for?"[49]

Male politicians likewise rejected feminists and their demands, silencing and marginalizing their feminist colleagues. Openly feminist politicians in particular suffered discrimination and saw their political reputations and careers lag behind their male colleagues'. The professional fate of one of the transition's most prominent female political figures, Carmen Diez de Rivera, is illustrative. Diez de Rivera seemed heir to the kind of political influence that Pilar Primo de Rivera had wielded at the height of her power.[50] She became personal friends with Prince Juan Carlos and his wife Sofia in the early 1970s and worked alongside Adolfo Suárez at the national broadcasting service, Radiotelevisión Española. When Juan Carlos appointed Suárez Minister-Secretary General of the National Movement, Suárez named Diez de Rivera head of his cabinet and then promoted her to Director of the Spanish President's Cabinet upon his confirmation to the Presidency. In this role, she helped negotiate the legalization of Spain's Communist Party in early 1977 and handled delicate diplomatic talks between warring political parties in the early months of Suárez's tenure.[51] For her efforts, and inspired by her aristocratic background, notable *El Pais* columnist Francisco Umbral dubbed her the "Muse of the Transition."[52]

But Diez de Rivera never acquired leverage to rival Primo de Rivera's. She initially faced opposition due to her gender. Shortly after Diez de Rivera joined Suárez's cabinet, a columnist for the well-established news magazine *Blanco y Negro* described the public's negative reaction to her political ascent: "The first woman came to a position of responsibility in the new government. And the commotion arose. And all for that, for being a woman."[53] In addition, Diez de Rivera's gender-bending traits as a jeans-wearing, beer-sipping policy wonk with expansive knowledge and a forceful personality made men in Spanish government uncomfortable. As a Spanish editor later explained to an American journalist from *Newsweek* in 1977, "[Diez de Rivera's] style rubbed people around Suárez the wrong way. Imagine: a woman with power; a beautiful woman who knows as much or more than they do, a woman who can influence the Premier and perhaps the King, a woman who speaks her mind."[54] The SF's formidable leader had coupled her women's rights policies with condemnation of feminism and a professed desire to lead women out from under its thrall. Diez de Rivera's championing of feminism from a similar position of influence was unacceptable, and doubly so because unlike under Franco, feminism stood a chance of instigating change as the transition unfolded. Being a woman was forgivable. Being a feminist was not.

As *Newsweek* noted, Diez de Rivera ultimately lost both her position and (temporarily) her professional reputation in May 1977 when she "irked the men in government" by publicly identifying as a feminist and calling for the legalization of divorce, abortion, and free contraception, the latter of which violated a ban on public expression of opinion about these issues.[55] And this was not just an American interpretation of what transpired: Diez de Rivera did remain a prominent political figure, but she never again wielded comparable political power and after her death in 1999 Spanish media looked back at what they considered her unfair treatment, describing it much as the 1977 *Newsweek* article had. One journalist's retrospective in *El Mundo*, for example, lauded both her beauty and accomplishments, reminding readers that no woman had since held a government post as lofty as Chief of Staff, and detailing some of the discrimination Diez de Rivera had experienced, including lewd sexual insults during diplomatic missions and intimations that she got her position because she was the king's lover.[56]

Women in the transition, especially in the wake of Diez de Rivera's fall from grace, lacked the benefit of a model and advocate like Pilar Primo de Rivera—her deeply conservative ideology notwithstanding—who had enmeshed herself in the regime and had thus been able to champion reform. *Sección Femenina*'s dissolution in 1977 further complicated women's access to political negotiations. On the one hand, SF had represented only a subset of women's interests. The lack of a women's bureau during the transition meant that women with diverse perspectives—and feminists certainly held a diversity of perspectives—could in theory make them known in the *Cortes*. On the other hand, *Sección Femenina*'s political access and the respect that Pilar Primo de Rivera herself commanded had given women a voice in even Franco's political decision-making. And though women sat in the *Cortes* from 1977 onward, in the transition period there was no centralized, government-affiliated women's group that could match SF's political stature. In *Sección Femenina*'s absence, then, Spanish women participated in government solely as elected delegates *Cortes* or as appointed members and staff in government ministries, roles in which their ability to articulate feminists views was limited.

There was no significant increase in the number of female delegates in the *Cortes* that might have compensated for the loss of the defunct SF's political clout, either, and even those parties officially championing women's rights had few female delegates—a situation that would not improve until the PSOE instituted a gender quota system for its delegation in the 1990s.[57] Meanwhile, the 598-member Constituent *Cortes* that met between July 13, 1977, and January 2, 1979, included only twenty-seven female representatives, a mere 4.5 percent of total seats, or 6 percent of the Congress of Deputies and just 2.4 percent of the Senate. Tellingly, the majority party, the centrist *Grupo Parlamentario de Unión de Centro Democrático* (GUCD), had the lowest ratio of women, at 4.1 percent. The Communist and socialist parties had the highest, yet even this only ever rose as high as 13.6 percent.[58] Women's—and feminists'—lack of representation in *Cortes* translated directly into a lack of input in the Constitutional drafting process. On July 26, 1977, a thirty-six-member, all-male, Commission of Constitutional Affairs picked seven male representatives from Spain's major political parties to be the "fathers of the Constitution."[59] They met over a series of months to draft the Constitution without oversight from the press, the public, or their colleagues in *Cortes*; once the appointed "fathers" completed the draft in April 1978, the Commission of Constitutional Affairs debated and refined it. Only then did the document come to *Cortes* for a vote.

The electorate bore limited responsibility for low numbers of female *Cortes* delegates. The leaders of Transition-era Spain's major political parties, all of them male, tightly controlled their parties' political activities and worked to ensure that there were few female politicians available for election. In this environment feminist politicians' demands took a back seat to larger party goals.

Women who could and did speak during *Cortes* debates were beholden first to their parties—which chose who spoke during debate, and whose platforms did not always prioritize women's rights—and only then to their personal principles. Moreover, male party heads and delegates, even ostensibly progressive ones, rejected female colleagues' requests for greater representation. One member of *Mujer y Socialismo*, a feminist caucus within PSOE, recounted to historian Monica Threlfall that she and her peers pushed the party to place more women in political positions, urged the adoption of a quota system as early as 1979, and drafted a list of potential female candidates for the PSOE to run in the 1979 election. PSOE leadership rejected these proposals.[60]

Feminists consequently found themselves in a strange position. Even as female *Cortes* delegates grasped for leverage and feminist organizations decried the Constitution's shortcomings, feminist rhetoric when wielded by male politicians seemed powerful. Feminists bemoaned the powerlessness of women in politics and the fact that, for Spanish politicians, voicing solidarity with the feminist movement's goals seemed in many cases to have become a useful political tactic, not a genuine ideological position. As one columnist in the October 1978 issue of *dones en lluita* complained: "Feminism is an exceedingly serious thing to [have] become this year's laughingstock … and it's sad that some parties, moved by what I assume is a momentary political tactic, and not by women party members' wishes, have agreed to participate in the charade."[61]

Feminist causes and activism found a positive reception in domestic media only when male politicians spoke of their work to improve the new Spain and provide women with a new slate of rights. Or as Pamela Radcliff has observed, "[f]eminism received positive press when it was something done *for* women, not something done *by* them."[62] And indeed, male politicians' support of the Constitution's equality clause made it appear as if they embraced feminism. Yet they did so not to improve women's representation in politics or to satisfy feminist demands—the left-leaning PSOE's silencing of its women's wing, and feminists' steadfast contention that the Constitution and other supposedly "feminist" legislation ignored their desires, among other things, show otherwise—but rather, as noted previously, in the hope of proving Spain's liberalizing bona fides to international observers and gaining Spain admission into the European Economic Community (EEC).[63] In this way, the very male politicians who had silenced and marginalized their female colleagues, especially those pushing for feminist legislation and for greater representation in party politics as did Carmen Diez de Rivera and the women of the PSOE's *Mujer y Socialismo* caucus, wielded and gave legitimacy to "feminist" rhetoric in the transition era while also reducing feminists themselves and feminist causes to a joke or an afterthought.

For these reasons, though Carlota Bustelo called the Constitution a feminist triumph, many feminists did not agree.[64] The overwhelming feminist reaction from both single and double militant feminists was to decry women's lack of input in the Constitution. For *Vindicación Feminista* columnist Lidia Falcón, one of the nation's most prominent feminists, women's exclusion from the drafting process meant that "the Constitution [was] made by men and for men."[65] But lack of input was not the only flaw feminists identified. As Paloma Pepa-García's article hinted and a *dones en lluita* contributor explicitly stated, feminists also felt that the Constitution failed to enshrine rights they had explicitly demanded. Feminists had, for instance, wanted the Constitution to incorporate the Moncloa Pact's provisions in order to provide constitutionally and not just legally guaranteed access to divorce, contraception, and childcare support, along with decriminalization of adultery. Lacking such clarity, the equality clause's declaration that "Spaniards ... [are] equal before the law and [that they] may not in any way be discriminated against on account of birth, race, sex, religion, opinion or any other personal or social condition or circumstance" seemed troublingly sparse. It provided no additional guidance for defining or enforcing the equality it proclaimed.[66] As expressed in OCE Bandera's pamphlet, many feminists consequently felt that without more comprehensive protection for women's rights, the Constitution perpetuated discrimination against women.[67] Summing up the general feminist sentiment about the Constitution's value, the Women's Assembly of Vizcaya, for example, declared that "for women, the Constitution is not worth the paper it's written on."[68]

Post-Ratification Feminist Strategy

Feminists' inability to substantially influence the political conversation in transition-era Spain was not limited to their meager impact on Constitutional debates. Women continued to make up a small percentage of *Cortes* delegations until the Spanish government adopted a quota system in 2007 requiring that party delegations consist of no more than 60 percent men; neither did their roles as politicians or members of government bodies—the latter greatly increased with the creation of the *Instituto de la Mujer* (*Instituto*), or Women's Bureau, in 1983—offer them platforms from which to advocate reform.[69] Moreover, the coopting of feminist rhetoric by politicians styling themselves as, but not acting as, feminist allies carried over into subsequent women's rights debates, further limiting the impact that women themselves had on legislation seemingly designed to meet their demands.

Feminists' fight to legalize abortion offers an especially clear lens for understanding these continued patterns and the development of post-transition feminist organizing. After the Moncloa Pacts, Constitutional ratification, and the general liberalizing legislative impulse during the transition, legal abortion was feminists' most sought-after individual reform. Additionally, feminists' linkage of individual demands under the umbrella of dismantling repressive social and cultural forces is especially visible in the debate over legal abortion, not least of which because that debate intrinsically involved larger questions like the extent to which women should have bodily autonomy. Yet examining the shifting public opinion on abortion's legality demonstrates that feminists' broad ideological arguments did not resonate with the Spanish public. Instead, even as feminists continued to argue that the problem facing Spanish women was a flaw in Spanish culture that perpetuated women's oppression, a narrower argument won the day. Activism portraying abortion as a public health crisis disproportionately affecting poor women was what ultimately shifted public opinion and put abortion reform on the table. This strategic change was key to feminists winning abortion reform but was also a factor in feminists' inability to influence the final legislation. Moreover, political change in the early 1980s that placed the socialists in power also created formal divisions between feminists, who had been nominally united during the 1970s despite intense ideological division.

Feminists' understandings of their demands as interlinked predated Constitutional ratification. For example, a February 1978 article in feminist magazine *dones en lluita* about the prevalence of sexual violence explained feminists' perspective: "to understand rape as an individual phenomenon is a distracting maneuver that cannot deceive us … rape has social and political content, it is a weapon employed by men to defend their patriarchal society …."[70] In other words, the article asserted that the problem with rape was not just the harm it caused to the woman raped, but rather that its prevalence indicated men's attempts to control and subdue women in general. As such, their calls for increased criminalization of rape were a stopgap measure on the way to ending patriarchy and granting women autonomy. Discrete demands such as calls for legal abortion, contraception, divorce, and stricter penalties for rapists were simply incremental requests, ways to address individual symptoms of the larger problem as feminists perceived it.

This pattern of incrementalism likewise manifested in late 1970s and early 1980s feminist platforms that presented abortion not solely as a goal in and of itself, but as the linchpin of interlocking oppressions that women continued to experience. *Vindicación Feminista, dones en lluita,* and *Opción,* along with *Tribuna Feminista,* a Madrid-based feminist magazine launched in 1983, published numerous articles detailing the ways in which feminists felt abortion's illegality repressed women. As a 1983 *Tribuna Feminista* editorial explained, "[w]omen are ... interested in winning the battle of the right to abortion, because we are the ones who directly suffer the impositions of society, about our sexuality, our motherhood, work, education."[71] Feminists argued that lack of access to abortion was yet another indication of women's subordinate position in society, and that their calls for access to abortion were not about abortion *per se* but about gaining bodily autonomy and women's liberation. A Catalan feminist pamphlet from the period similarly asserted that in demanding abortion, Spanish women "[were] demanding the right to our own body, to do with it whatever we like and nobody but us deciding about it."[72] Emphasizing that feminists understood their demands for abortion as about bodily autonomy as much as about abortion, a 1984 *Tribuna Feminista* issue proclaimed the slogan, "We want the right to abort. We do not want to abort!"[73] And minutes from a December 1981 feminist gathering, representing activist groups from across the nation, resolved that

> the fight for the right to abortion represents something greater than fighting to improve our lot as regards abortion alone ... Rather, it is also a major step forward in the fight for women's liberation, for putting an end to the roles imposed on us and institutions that do nothing but keep us oppressed and discriminated against ... the struggle for abortion rights has a fundamental role in our struggle to change society.[74]

Feminists also understood abortion's criminalization as an insidious side-effect of the entanglement between church and state, and they denounced how the church-state relationship affected public policy and hindered reception of their demands. Radical organization L'eix Violeta, for example, appropriated a government-sponsored public health campaign encouraging condom use for its own, more expansive messaging.[75] The organization's poster, released in the early 1980s, depicted a graffiti statement on a brick wall that began with the initiative's slogan "Put it on you, put it on him," and then continued on to say "Why aren't there: Family planning centers? Sexual education in schools? Free and legal abortion? Sex education and information for gays and lesbians?" Around the poster's edge ran the statement "Birth control is a right, and abortion is too. If

Bishops could become pregnant, condoms would be given out for free." This campaign tied multiple issues together by fusing an appropriated but also shared call to use protection during sex, with the message that access to contraception was good, but not enough. Feminists also chafed at restrictions imposed either formally, through political and legal channels, or informally, through Church influence and social pressure from conservatives. L'eix Violeta's poster text hinted at the depth of frustration; its graphic content, of a priest trapped inside a life-sized condom and struggling to get it off while the graffiti artist (and presumably his entrapper) ran away giggling, further illustrated how deep the resentment ran.[76]

Such depictions of Catholic figures, particularly images of priests, commonly appeared in feminist media as targets of mockery or, less humorously, as targets for elimination. The cover of a pamphlet titled "Abortion Without Restrictions! Women Decide!" featured the latter.

In it, two men cower, one wearing a suit and using the other, dressed in a clerical cassock, as a shield. They face a woman twice their size, holding a knitting needle like a spear, staring intently at them, and taking aim in their direction. This ad, on its face about abortion, was also anti-capitalist, anti-patriarchy, anti-militarist, and anti-religion; in sum, it opposed everything that feminists perceived the government to be protecting and that they hoped to reform and repeal through attention to and action about issues like abortion. In particular, the imagery—of a government figure using a bishop as a shield—points to feminist resentment that the government continued to protect church interests and use appeasing the church as a reason to continue restrictions on reproductive freedoms that feminists found onerous and discriminatory. Tellingly, the weapon that threatened the literal embodiments of religion and the government was a knitting needle—an abortifacient, an instrument of one of the rights that women demanded and claimed for themselves.[77]

These campaigns appear compelling, but there is no evidence that they significantly impacted public opinion in Spain. More demonstrably effective were campaigns that fostered empathy for female victims of injustice. Grassroots feminists had worked within their communities to assist women seeking abortions and to promote better sexual health practices even during the late Franco years. They initially canvassed working-class neighborhoods, going door to door with liberal priests who helped deliver pamphlets and lectures about contraception and family planning. In the years after Franco's death, feminist organizations in other nations helped Spanish organizations by supplying these materials, though supplying such information about birth control remained illegal until 1978.⁷⁸ During and after the transition to democracy, feminist abortion-rights activists engaged with the public, gauging demand for legalized abortion among women from all walks of life, and raising awareness about the economic and physical hardships faced by poor women seeking the procedure. The feminist underground also secretly chartered planes and arranged international flights to London and Amsterdam for Spanish women seeking abortions.⁷⁹ In an *El País* retrospective about abortion laws, published in 2013 when abortion rights in Spain were once again up for debate, a woman identified as Cinta described her trip to Amsterdam in 1980.⁸⁰ The procedure alone cost 30,000 pesetas, nearly one-and-a-half times an average monthly income, which she had to borrow from friends.⁸¹ Despite the expense, over 30,000 women per year made such trips.⁸² So many Spanish women visited foreign clinics, with or without feminist help, that clinic administrators hired Spanish-speaking staff. And meanwhile, in 1978 the estimated number of abortions performed yearly in Spain still totaled 300,000.⁸³

The percentage of women who could afford to avail themselves of these feminist networks was limited, as Cinta herself noted and, additionally, women like Cinta faced a number of hardships in procuring abortions, not all of them economic. Women getting clandestine abortions, whether in Spain or internationally, could be imprisoned or face social ostracism even in more progressive regions. Carles Gómez del Moral, a middle-aged Catalan man, recounted a memory from his high-school days: one of his friends had traveled to London from Barcelona for an abortion, and when school officials discovered it she was called out of class and expelled.⁸⁴ Women also risked illness or death. At least one major feminist demonstration in 1977 was prompted by a woman's death after having an abortion.⁸⁵ Protestors sought to foster empathy for such women and to illuminate the health risks that lack of abortion access precipitated.

Still, activists did not gain traction on abortion reform until they found a focal point for their campaigns in 1979, when officials charged eleven working-class Basque women with participating in an abortion ring: a mother-daughter pair with having performed abortions, and nine for having received abortions. The uproar surrounding this case had a newfound intensity, an activist later recalling that the Bilbao case had "mobilized activists and women's organizations in an unprecedented way throughout the country."⁸⁶ Feminist media continued to draw connections between abortion legislation and women's oppression by patriarchal structures, while feminist organizations mobilized specifically around the issue of abortion and planned demonstrations to highlight its effects both on women in general and on a specific population of women—the poor.

Even then, feminists faced opposition to and retribution for their activism. At one feminist demonstration in Madrid, "police drove buses at a column of marching women to disperse them."[87] At another demonstration in Bilbao, feminists holding a sit-in were clubbed by police.[88] The Church also used its significant influence to condemn abortion and speak out against its legalization. The Spanish Episcopal Council issued multiple bulletins pleading with members not to vote for political parties that supported abortion rights, bemoaning the state of Spanish society, and threatening Catholics' eternal souls if abortion became legalized;[89] it also had enough political and social cachet to pressure regional governments to alter their messages of support for abortion and contraception. In the early 1980s, the Generalitat de Catalunya, Catalonia's regional government, undertook a public health campaign titled "No Undesired Pregnancy" that promoted the safe use of contraceptives but also tacitly alluded to the benefits of access to abortion. The Catholic Church fought the campaign, objecting to its apparent support for abortion access. One proposed ad depicted a bib embroidered with a personal ad stating "seeking mother who wants me, between 20–35 years of age, in good health (... and two siblings would be enough)." Underneath ran the campaign's slogan—"not a single undesired pregnancy." The Church and conservative groups successfully barred its use because it too explicitly addressed abortion and so, to feminists' consternation, another ad ran in its place.[90] This one was more ambiguous, featuring a blindfolded woman with the caption "Love is blind, but you must see clearly. Do not renounce your freedom as a woman. No unwanted pregnancy."[91]

Yet, as the 1980s dawned, the Spanish public showed signs of growing increasingly sympathetic toward abortion activists, as illegal abortions caused a public health problem in need of a solution.[92] Women from around Spain participated in demonstrations and direct actions to humanize women who sought abortions. Some turned to time-honored methods, like activists who "held sit-ins for two years" to support the women on trial in Bilbao and denounce abortion's illegality, not just in the Basque regions or in the capital, but in cities as far-flung as Sevilla.[93] Feminists repeatedly stormed the courtroom as well as the courthouse steps and atriums, chanting and picketing with demands that the defendants be released. Since the key stages of the trial happened in the summer and the room was not air-conditioned, the court had to keep the windows open; protesters' cries were so disruptive that proceedings were repeatedly suspended.

Other forms of protest aired feminists' demands in more creative ways. Women with widely varied backgrounds came forward to publicly discuss their abortions, including female politicians participating in *Cortes* debates about legalizing abortion. In one demonstration that made national news, 1,300 women lined up in a public square to announce that they had had abortions, signed a registry to that effect, and had their pronouncement notarized. Organizers ultimately gathered around 25,000 signatures.[94] In addition, 1,200 men, including prominent politicians, also signed and sent a letter to *El Pais* saying they had helped women get abortions.[95]

These and other such acts attracted media attention so intense that the trial was postponed twice in a bid to calm the furor and so ensure a fair trial. International as well as domestic newspapers drew attention to the plight of Spanish women seeking abortions, amplified and provided legitimacy to arguments painting women as victims, and reinforced the view that Spain was behind the curve on abortion rights in Western Europe. It was one of only four countries with abortion bans, which international newspapers noted when covering feminist protests.[96] In response, politicians also began to back abortion reform in ways more substantive than signing a petition. Some municipal governments bowed to public pressure, with Oviedo and Valencia both "pass[ing] motions in favor of abortion decriminalization and of acquitting the Bilbao women."[97] The Communist Party, the most radical party with representation in government, and which had a strong women's organization, had long advocated women's right to abortion even before the Bilbao case hit the headlines. With support from feminists, the party had introduced three bills to legalize abortion on demand between 1978 and 1981, which got a great deal of press and generated heated parliamentary debate. By the end of the Bilbao case in March 1982, in which ten of the eleven were acquitted and the eleventh recommended for immediate pardon,[98] the Spanish public was willing to accept legislation loosening restrictions on access to abortion.

Spaniards' new openness to legalizing abortion also coincided with a dramatic shift in the political environment that made such reform possible. Disagreements about the role of the Church in public life, as well as the appropriate Catholic reaction to divorce legislation, broke apart Adolfo Suárez's governing coalition and paved the way for a PSOE takeover in 1982.[99] Once the PSOE gained a majority in *Cortes* and formed its own strong coalition, socialist leadership took steps to reinforce the party's image as friendly to women's rights. After all, feminist activists identifying as double militants had worked with and within PSOE since its legalization, including feminist PSOE delegates advocating for abortion in *Cortes* debates in 1978, and PSOE political materials already incorporated some feminist goals and the goal of female equality.[100] And so, on February 25, 1983, three months into its tenure, the PSOE introduced a bill to legalize abortion. This was not a political party's first attempt during the transition to reform the nation's approach to abortion. It was not even a party's first effort since the Bilbao trial's conclusion. PSOE delegates, along with other left-leaning and feminist delegates, supported each of those failed attempts. This was, however, the first moment at which the public's desire for legal abortion coincided with a favorable political atmosphere.

"A Form of the Most Brutal Misogyny":[101] Abortion's Legalization on Male Terms

Feminist activism had changed public opinion on abortion, and passage of the PSOE's bill to decriminalize abortion (albeit only on restricted grounds) seemed proof of feminist influence in government and of the movement's success. The PSOE's creation of a new government ministry dedicated to researching, communicating, and crafting policy to address women's concerns, the *Instituto de la Mujer*, added to this perception. Unsurprisingly, perhaps, scholars and contemporaries concluded that feminists gained power with the PSOE's rise—that feminists helped craft party policy, particularly the abortion bill, and that the *Instituto* played a powerful role in shaping the Spanish legislative agenda.

Yet, to the contrary, feminists' role in the PSOE's drive for abortion legislation began and ended with their grassroots organization over the late 1970s and early 1980s. Grassroots activists were outsiders to the legislative arena, and feminists in government, even PSOE delegates and, later, *Instituto de la Mujer* members, had no say in shaping in abortion legislation's final form.[102] Moreover, the formation of the *Instituto* also broke apart the already-fragile single-double militant feminist coalition, such as it was, and created a clear division between the ideological camps as the *Instituto* offered double militants a formal avenue for incorporation into the government. Single militants chose to remain separate from the government and in independent feminist organizations. Ultimately and ironically, though grassroots activism fostered by single and double militant feminists instigated change, these changes were not necessarily what feminists themselves envisioned or even desired. Instead, the abortion law heralded the ascendancy of male politicians' political goals, primarily maintaining the stability of the still-fragile new democracy by placating both leftists and rightists within Spain.

The PSOE's abortion bill of 1983 reflected the party's internal changes since assuming majority power in 1982 and its attempt to strike a careful balance between conservative and liberal sentiments in *Cortes*. The PSOE that had advocated women's right to abortion in the transition era was a different PSOE with different constituent parts and a different relationship to Catholicism than the PSOE which governed in early 1980s and introduced legislation decriminalizing abortion in 1983. The PSOE of the transition did not need to cater to conservative political rivals—they filled the role of opposition party to Prime Minister (and transition architect) Adolfo Suárez's governing Christian-democratic and center-right political coalition, the *Unión de Centro Democrático* ("Union of the Democratic Center," or UCD). At that time, the PSOE had accepted a "split" within its membership between those advocating radical legalization of abortion and those supporting more limited reform, as its primary political goal was to combat the majority party—the UCD—and secure its own rise.[103] Socialists in favor of small-scale reform won out after the PSOE's ascent to power because party leaders, in an effort to appeal to a broader electorate, made a calculated decision to move away from radical politics and toward moderate positions. The party needed to clarify its position, which it did in 1982 when it publically supported limited decriminalization.

The PSOE's approach to abortion regulations also reflected that the path to smooth governance rested on finding common ground with the Church and with conservatives like *Alianza Popular* ("Popular Alliance," or AP), then the leading right-wing political party, which retained ties to the Church.[104] Contrary to some scholars' view that the Spanish Catholic Church had grown politically weak because it was unable to block abortion's legalization, or had otherwise taken a step back from a role in influencing Spanish society,[105] the Church could and did influence governmental policy and political negotiations both directly and indirectly. Though the 1978 Constitution had failed to meet the Catholic Church's moral requirements it did nevertheless acknowledge and protect Catholicism's ties to government, declaring, that the state would "maintain relations of cooperation with the Catholic Church," much to the dismay of liberal politicians and progressive activists who had hoped that the break with National-Catholicism would lead to a separation of church and state in the new democracy.[106] Subsequently individual *Cortes* delegates' personal relationships to the Church remained strong enough to precipitate the UCD's political crisis and fall from power in 1981.

Even after this political shakeup handed the PSOE a parliamentary majority, Catholic conservatives still made up a large portion of the *Cortes* and political parties loyal to Francoism's ideals remained present and wielded substantial political leverage.[107] The relationship between church and state had changed since the collapse of Francoism, but the state still allowed the church a role in shaping policy and influencing cultural and social expectations of Spaniards. The abortion law's final, relatively restrictive, form thus also reflected *Cortes* delegates' personal ties to Catholicism. Large numbers of Catholic conservatives from Alianza Popular voted for the 1985 abortion law, despite the Church's pleas to the contrary, but PSOE party leadership did not want to push its luck and its mandate by attempting further liberalization. Rather, PSOE leaders perceived that their ability to govern rested on finding common ground with conservatives like Alianza and feared that formulating a more liberal abortion law would alienate those colleagues as well as the more conservative wing of the PSOE's own base of support.[108]

The *Instituto de la Mujer*, meanwhile, lacked enough political clout to counteract this conservative influence over the abortion bill. Indeed, the relationship between the *Instituto* and the Spanish government highlights how even ostensible feminist allies reproduced patterns of discrimination against women, often by excluding women from debates concerning the exact issues the *Instituto* was founded to research and advise the government on. For several reasons, the *Instituto* was unable to participate in the debates over abortion legislation. First, it was only founded seven months after PSOE introduced this legislation, and so did not contribute to its drafting. This foreshadowed the *Instituto*'s subsequent politically weak position: its newness translated into a lack of impact. The organization had a small budget that increased only incrementally over the late 1980s, so it had few resources to fund policy research and proposals. It also took two years for the *Instituto* to be fully staffed and for its leaders to establish a functional organizational structure. Once it was staffed and running, the *Instituto* did participate in abortion debates, but its real influence lay in helping with the law's implementation, not its creation.[109] Moreover, the *Instituto* was a subdivision of a Ministry and not a Cabinet position, which put distance between it and the locus of government power.[110] All of these factors minimized the *Instituto*'s influence over abortion rights and in Spanish politics more generally. Meanwhile, independent feminists had helped organize the grassroots demonstrations drawing attention to the problems that the criminalization of abortion caused and shifting public opinion on abortion's legality, but this was the extent of their influence on the proposed legislation.

If anything, the PSOE's creation of the *Instituto* weakened feminist activism and presented new challenges for feminists calling for abortion reform as well as for feminists in general. While women working within the *Instituto*—institutional feminists—were double-militants comfortable with the political structures created in Spain's transition to democracy, activists outside the *Instituto*—independent feminists—were single-militants who rejected Spain's new form of government and so also opposed many of the agency's campaigns, strategies, and reform suggestions on principle even when their own organizations' strategies dovetailed with the *Instituto*'s efforts.[111] If the *Sección Femenina* had been the voice for a certain brand of conservative women's rights activist, the *Instituto de la Mujer* was its liberal counterpart. The *Instituto* advocated for women's rights from a perspective that independent feminists did not consider liberal or progressive, and so the ideological divide and the dynamic between the *Instituto de la Mujer* and independent feminism was similar in some ways to that of *Sección Femenina* and the emergent feminisms of the late Franco period.

The PSOE's own female delegates also figured little in the debates surrounding the socialists' abortion bill. While the 1983–5 *Cortes* debates about abortion legislation seemed a reaction to feminist outcry and appeared to be an opportunity for feminist representation in devising government policy, only three women spoke in support of abortion during the *Cortes*'s debates. Women's silence was such that in the 1983 debate Juan María Bandrés of the Mixed Parliamentary Group decried the lack of female representation in debate about an issue that he felt "affects women fundamentally, if not almost exclusively." Moreover, Bandrés was the only delegate, male or female, to discuss the gendered nature or gendered consequences of abortion policy.[112]

With women taking a backseat in the debate, the PSOE championed the bill without using feminists' arguments about bodily autonomy or female oppression. In this respect, feminists' success in getting public support for abortion based on its effect on public health worked against their larger ideological goals. PSOE's representatives in *Cortes* argued for expansion of abortion access, by reasoning that abortions would happen regardless, and so should be legal and safe, that abortion reform would make Spain more like other European nations, most of which allowed abortion, and that the abortion bill was actually moderate rather than liberal, since the majority of Spaniards favored it. When those favoring liberalization did refer to the impact of abortion on women, they framed their arguments in terms of the socioeconomic injustice done to women and not the gender injustice: rich women could afford safe abortions (usually by going overseas), but poor women could not.[113] The PSOE-sponsored legislation also legalized abortion in only three narrow cases: during the first trimester in the case of rape or incest; during the first twenty-two weeks, if two physicians confirmed that "the fetus would be born with serious mental or physical defects"; or at any time during the pregnancy if two medical professionals unaffiliated with the abortion clinic affirmed that the pregnancy posed "a serious danger" to the woman's mental or physical health.[114] The *Cortes* overwhelmingly voted in favor of the bill in July 1985, but feminists were not satisfied because the new law failed to address their concerns about abortion access as well as the larger issue of women's oppression. Even after the law's passage, its restrictions kept abortion out of reach for many women. In witness, there was a dramatic decrease in the number of women who left Spain for abortions after 1985, but women still sought abortions abroad because of the obstacles the law put in place domestically.[115] Spain's legislation on abortion remained among the most restrictive in Europe, even compared to policies in conservative Catholic nations like Italy, which as of 1978 allowed women to abort their pregnancies within the first ninety days for any reason, and where voters in 1981 rejected an initiative to repeal abortion rights.[116]

For these reasons both independent and institutional feminists, rather than cheering abortion's legalization, criticized the law for failing to deliver what they understood as real change for Spanish women. This was hardly a new complaint. Feminists, as we have seen, had objected to the Constitution on similar grounds. They felt similarly about the legalization of divorce, as a 1983 *Tribuna Feminista* article recapping major feminist issues and demonstrations illustrated—it asserted that the divorce law "did not reflect the aspirations the feminist movement had had for some years."[117] The article's coverage of the PSOE's abortion legislation repeated the dismissive claim, almost verbatim: "the introduction of the PSOE Act in Parliament ... does not capture feminist aspirations."[118]

Contributors to *Tribuna Feminista* were not alone in their ire, either. Independent feminist organizations around Spain held demonstrations to condemn the new abortion law. In a move that decried the law while also restating the feminist view that all oppression women experienced was interlinked, the organizers of International Women's Day 1986 in Barcelona chose the law as one of the event's focal points, sandwiching the call for "Abortion on Demand and Free" between demands for "No NATO" and "Jobs for All Women" on the event's promotional poster.[119] In addition, that December, independent feminists from across Spain participated in a Madrid-based tribunal that heard and recorded testimonies from women affected by Spain's abortion law. Conclusions published and distributed by the tribunal's organizers condemned the law, in part for the burdens it placed on women seeking abortions, but also because they perceived the law to be more evidence of the government's continued support for "maintaining the subordination and dependence of women in relation to men." These findings furthermore singled out specific members of government, in particular PSOE leader and Spanish president Felipe González, his minister of justice, other socialist government ministries and administrators, judges who were "applying laws contrary to the rights of women and which [were] a form of the most brutal misogyny" and both municipal police as well as the paramilitary Guardia Civil, whom the tribunal deemed responsible for "defending the patriarchal order."[120] Institutional feminists were less overt in their criticism, but nevertheless added to these critiques by trying, albeit unsuccessfully, to push for further reform despite being tasked simply with managing the law's implementation.[121]

Conclusion

The visibility of grassroots feminist activism in the late Franco years and during the transition, coupled with Spain's seeming rejection of the Franco-era gender order, led feminists and scholars alike to hail the Constitution's ratification in 1978 and the legalization of abortion in 1983 as feminist triumphs and proof of Spain's willingness to embrace women's rights. Yet despite appearances, transition-era feminists in fact struggled for political leverage and had little influence on either the contents of the Constitution or the form of abortion's legalization.

This lack of influence was in part due to feminists' struggles both for unity and for an audience receptive to their demands. Internal debates about feminism's future and its desired outcomes proved too delicate for the movement to maintain internal cohesion. Factions within Spanish feminism disagreed about how to structure the government, what aspects of Spanish society needed reform, and whether "feminism" was even an appropriate label. Though Spanish feminist organizations cultivated extensive international connections and involvement, at home they struggled to stay financially solvent and to disseminate their views as feminist print media lingered on the fringes of journalistic culture. They likewise had difficulty bringing new women into the fold, attracting fewer members than other women's organizations. The challenges were still more imposing given feminism's difficult cultural position, as journalists, politicians, and public figures mocked prominent feminist activists, pushed feminist politicians out of power, and derided feminist demands. Paradoxically, the dissolution of *Sección Femenina* only exacerbated women's lack of access to politics. Since the transition government did not establish a new women's ministry in its place, women lost an avenue for influencing government decisions and promoting women's concerns.

Even as feminists struggled for a foothold in Spain's political arena, feminist rhetoric found a receptive audience in Spanish politicians and citizens eager to rehabilitate Spain's international reputation. Feminism was popular, but only when espoused by *men*. The elision of women's rights with democracy meant that voicing support for female equality was a politically expedient tactic and arguably a necessary one for Spanish politicians hoping to marshal political power or gain international cachet in Spain's new age. The contents of Spain's 1978 Constitution must be seen through this lens—not as evidence of feminist demands influencing Spain's new democratic shape, but rather as indicative of male politicians' self-conscious political maneuvering in front of a European audience weighing whether Spain was liberalizing enough to gain both international approval and EEC membership. From feminists' perspective, the new Constitution was insufficiently democratic and did not address women's concerns. Equal citizenship seemed a salve, not a solution. Indeed, women had little to no say in the Constitution's contents: no women sat on the drafting committee, female *Cortes* delegates (of which there were few) could voice dissent but were overpowered by their colleagues, and last-ditch feminist efforts to persuade voters to reject Constitutional ratification failed.

Ratification of the Constitution was a turning point in Spanish feminist activism. Grassroots activists in the late Franco era and during Constitutional debate framed diverse forms of women's oppression as interlocking pieces of one large puzzle and urged Spaniards to craft and support comprehensive legislation protecting women's rights instead of addressing single problems ad hoc and piecemeal. Following the Constitution's ratification, these feminists continued promoting their view of women's oppression within feminist circles but focused their broader activism around discrete issues with simpler messaging. This is evident in how feminists framed their demands for legalized abortion—the first major women's rights legislation since the establishment of the Constitution. In feminist media, women presented abortion as a manifestation of lingering patriarchal oppression, normalized during the Franco dictatorship. To the public, activists framed lack of access to abortion as both a public health problem and as socioeconomic injustice, since poor women disproportionately struggled to afford safe abortions.

Feminist arguments about public health and socioeconomic injustice resonated with the Spanish public, and legislation to legalize abortion found traction in the *Cortes* when a political shakeup lifted the PSOE to a parliamentary majority. But interpreting the legalization of abortion as a feminist success obscures what feminists most wanted and how Spanish citizens and politicians perceived feminists. As the debate over legalized abortion shows, both independent and institutional feminists lacked a voice in parliamentary proceedings, despite the socialist party's ostensible support for women's rights as expressed through their creation of the *Instituto de la Mujer*. Politicians, even those identifying as allies of women's rights, spoke for women instead of allowing women to speak for themselves and made arguments that either ran counter to feminists' own claims or addressed concerns that women had not voiced. For politicians like those of the PSOE, legalized abortion was politically expedient and helped expand their party's base. For feminists, the legislation was a disgrace that denied women agency and perpetuated both the broader oppression they experienced as well as the public health problem and socioeconomic injustice that limited access to abortion caused.

However, as the next chapter shows, Spanish feminists' fight for legalized abortion resonated beyond Spain's borders. As the relationship between the Spanish government and Spanish feminists evolved, culminating with the creation of the *Instituto* and the final division of feminists into institutional and independent organizations, so too did the relationship between these groups of feminists and their counterparts in other nations. During the 1960s and 1970s, international feminist networks drew Spanish activists into a common feminist culture that transcended the use of shared visual elements and chants, extending also to exchanges of tactical advice and argumentation. In the 1980s and beyond, the *Instituto de la Mujer*, though largely ineffective in Spanish politics in its early years, added another layer to this network by providing both institutional and independent Spanish women access to international political debates even as feminists in both camps struggled to contribute meaningfully to political debates on domestic policy issues.

3

Transnationalizing the Transition and Beyond

How Domestic Feminist Conflict and Global Feminist Networks Affected Late Twentieth-Century Spanish Politics

By the 1990s, grassroots feminist activism in Spain, now dominated by the nation's independent feminist organizations, lacked the momentum, visibility, and political leverage that had marked its activism in the 1970s and early 1980s. The PSOE's founding of the *Instituto de la Mujer* in October 1983 had created a new body where women's concerns could be addressed and equality policies debated; as a result, independent feminists using grassroots organizational strategies no longer drove the political or cultural debates about women's rights. Instead, both independent feminism and its grassroots organization, eclipsed by the *Instituto*'s efforts, faded into the background. Independent feminists recognized this decline, discussing it at conferences and in pamphlets, and blamed it on the rise of the *Instituto*.[1] Yet, though diminished in number and influence, they continued their work, in part by pressing the *Instituto* as well as various regional Cortes to back their domestic policy proposals.

This shift in visibility and political leverage from independent activists using grassroots methods to institutional feminists operating within a state framework reflected a larger change unfolding contemporaneously in international feminist activism. This shift saw newly formed national women's bureaus lobby organizations like the UN and EEC for female-friendly policy changes.[2] Independent feminists recognized the impact that institutional feminists' international connections could have on their own activism, and, for example, in October of 1996, an independent feminist contingent from Valencia touched on just this subject in a presentation at a major feminist conference. Their "Manifesto for Equality" declared:

We who are committed to a society where equality and solidarity are principles and values that characterize it, we who, like so many, have struggled to achieve equality between men and women, we are not willing to retreat back a step in our achievements. What's more, we will not stop, we will continue forward in our purposes to achieve a real Equality.

It is for this reason that we turn to the members of the progressive forces in the Valencian Parliament to ask them to share our purpose and … concentrate their energy and commitment in the Struggle for Equality … in the Valencian Cortes, the Government of the Generalitat and the Central Government, [and] the application of Equality Policies in compliance with the Constitution, the European Union Regulations and the commitments of Beijing.[3]

In addition to pushing their local government to cede their demands—here, a vaguely conceived "real equality"—these independent feminists also implored both regional (the Valencian Cortes and Generalitat) and national (central government) arms of the Spanish government to abide by international edicts on equality policy, including those of the EU and those resulting from the World Conference on Women (WCOW) held in Beijing in 1995.

This invocation of international agreements followed a larger pattern evident during the transition and in post-transition Spanish politics. In some ways, the story of the Spanish transition is the story of how Spaniards of different political affiliations and identities envisioned, depicted, and fought over their interpretations of a post-Franco national identity for the embattled nation. Politicians worked toward crafting a post-Franco national identity that observers in liberal democracies, like those in North America and Western Europe, could find palatable. As Chapter 2 discusses, feminists and politicians battled over what democracy could and should mean for women's rights—what did those rights encompass? How far did they extend? And how much representation ought women have in forums intended to settle the matter? As a rule, even ostensibly sympathetic leftist politicians had their own agendas, which differed from feminists'.

This chapter explores how and why feminist organizations, both independent and institutional, reached for international connections that could help them provide solutions to the inequality they felt women still suffered. First, instead of marveling at the smoothness of the transition, feminists used global networks to examine and denounce the oppression women still experienced. Single and double militant feminists initially undertook this work together in the 1970s, as this chapter discusses, but even after feminists' split into independent and institutional organizations, each group continued to foster its own unique international networks for this purpose. Their efforts lasted through the end of the twentieth century and remain ongoing in the twenty-first. Indeed, though it came twenty years after Spanish feminists' initial experiments with internationalism, the Valencian activists' reference to EU and UN policy in 1996 was itself a denunciation of Spanish democracy, if a veiled one in the form of the implication that Spain (and Valencia) fell short of meeting the internationally mandated equality policies mentioned.

Feminists of the transition era used connections with feminists in other nations to work toward solutions not only in Spain, but in other nations, and with an eye to improving conditions for women worldwide. Their connections flourished throughout the mid-century via pamphlets and magazines, relationships between feminist organizations that transcended national boundaries, and a common culture that spanned not only nations, but continents. The PSOE's creation of the *Instituto de la Mujer* in 1983, which provides a bookend to thinking about the role of general grassroots feminist activism in Spain's political transition, meanwhile created another opportunity for feminists to build international networks—this time for institutional feminists working through official government channels that plugged them into the inner workings of the European Economic Community (henceforth EEC, which Spain finally joined in 1986) and the UN's equality bodies.

Instead of alleviating the challenges feminists in general faced, however, the creation of the *Instituto*, the organization's flaws, and its reach for international networks of its own merely added layers of complication for both independent and institutional feminists seeking political solutions to their problems. Even as international organizations passed resolutions that should have allowed feminists of both camps the political leverage to bring greater awareness to women's problems and to create domestic policy, the state of feminism within Spain hampered feminists' efforts.

These problems manifested in two significant ways. First, the *Instituto*'s decentralized bureaucratic structure hamstrung the organization's ability to craft centralized policy proposals and coordinate across Spain's regions. In addition, the longstanding animosity between independent and institutional feminists meant that they also bickered about the desirability of this new internationalization of feminist activism, and that independent feminists increasingly understood institutional feminists' entrenchment in officially created networks to be evidence that institutional feminists were feminists in name only. Independent feminists developed a deep ambivalence toward institutional feminists and their policies: on the one hand denying their counterparts' identities as feminists, while on the other hand recognizing that they sometimes needed the political leverage that institutional feminists and their networks could apply even though they disliked, disagreed with, or disavowed institutional feminism itself. The pleas of Valencian independent feminists for the creation of regional state-affiliated equality bodies, which opened this chapter, help highlight these complexities. Valencia had no regional *Instituto* as of 1996 and in its absence had no official avenue for local feminists, either independent or institutional, to push for advancement and alleviation of problems facing the region's women. The most powerful international networks that Valencia's independent feminist activists could draw upon were those in which the national *Instituto* participated, even as they disagreed with its ideology as well as with most of its stated policies and goals.

This chapter argues that the relationships between competing groups of self-identified feminists, in addition to the political leverage that feminists derived from internationally accepted and in some cases internationally mandated policies, shaped the rights and the political representation that ordinary women could access in Spain. The shift from grassroots activists' internationalism to the decreasing possibilities for international engagement that independent feminists still using grassroots organizational techniques faced once the *Instituto*'s own internationalism predominated, the limited role of the national *Instituto* in deciding women's rights policies for the whole of Spain, and the conflict between ideologically opposed groups of self-identified feminists over what equality meant and who got to be feminist all illuminate the ways in which Spanish feminists of different ideological camps mobilized for and effected domestic political change in the late twentieth century.

Transition-Era Grassroots Feminist Internationalism

In 1975, British feminists organized a demonstration against the Franco regime and the repressive gender norms that they felt underlay it as well as all fascism. An article written by the group for an issue of *Red Magazine* recounted:

> Our group came together when some fifty women gathered at a picket outside the Spanish Embassy on 5th October, coinciding with a demonstration at Hendaye on the Spanish border, organised by the French women's movement. We did not know each other but we did not stand in silence. We began to talk. The discussion became a meeting and from the meeting came a resolution to

meet again—and to organise. It was not enough to simply stand in silence for a few hours and then return home. So we have formed the Women's Campaign Against Fascist Spain. We believe that fascism is based on sexism and as women we must fight both. We must fight to ensure that the liberation of the Spanish people means the liberation of women too. We will fight as women—nonsectarian collectively; and our first aim is to tell women in the movement here about the situation of their sisters in Spain and enlist their active support.[4]

As the Women's Campaign Against Fascist Spain's words underscore, national borders did not constrain European feminism of the late twentieth century. Instead, feminist politics of the era confronted problems that activists believed affected all women, regardless of nationality. Activists sought political and cultural solutions tailored to their nation's unique political culture and set of problems but worked for change in other national contexts as well, assisting feminists from those countries in their fights. In this sense, feminist activists functioned within an international network of solidarity whose mission was not to pass specific laws or policies—though that, too, as the case of abortion rights activism in the mid-1970s showed—but rather to lessen women's overall experience of oppression worldwide.

Spain's delicate coalition of single and double militant feminists, both under Franco and after his regime's fall, existed within this network and shared its feminist culture. They perceived themselves to be part of an oppressed class that stretched beyond Spain's borders and linked them with women throughout Western Europe, the United States, and Latin America. Activists in the network shared a symbology and vocabulary, exchanged ideas and messages of solidarity, helped women in other countries distribute educational and ideological material, and participated both in international conferences as well as directly in demonstrations to overturn or protest domestic laws. Spanish feminists, like those with whom they built relationships, felt they were part of a system whereby gains for women's rights in another country would necessarily lead to improvements in women's lives everywhere, either because women in nations with lesser developed rights systems relied on travel to access more liberal women's rights laws (abortion) or because change in one nation set off a pattern or increased momentum for change everywhere.

The international feminist culture necessarily shaped Spanish feminists' domestic activism and local feminist networks. Spanish feminist magazines of the period reflected this internationalism and its refraction into Spain's unique political environment. Articles placed Spanish feminism in historical context globally as well as domestically; urged readers to contact feminist organizations in other countries, forging transnational ties of solidarity and action; and analyzed the major problems that women faced not just in twentieth-century Spain, but across the globe.

To begin with, feminist magazines placed Spain's feminist history within the historical narrative of the international feminist movement. *Opción*, for example, ran a recurring column called "The Other History" about the precursors of and foundations for twentieth-century feminism. Its first iteration explored "the birth of feminism" with the creation of French Revolutionary women's organizations and activists participating in the Seneca Falls Conference in the United States in 1848.[5] Subsequent columns delved into the historical roots of Spanish feminism as well, describing the achievements of Spanish women in the late nineteenth and early twentieth centuries and the prejudices they overcame.[6] Throughout, these columns positioned Spain's experience as part of a larger pattern. For example, writers discussing the relationship between social class and access to equality in the Industrial Revolution stated that women's rights in Spain, as elsewhere, were initially "for the bourgeois" and that working-class feminism only came of age with the Industrial Revolution.[7] They also discussed the evolution of specific rights, like women's suffrage, and contrasted Spain's experience with that of other European nations.[8] *Vindicación Feminista* and *dones en lluita* contained similar columns.

These magazines also studied the major problems that women faced not just in twentieth-century Spain, but across the globe. *Vindicación Feminista* dedicated a significant amount of space to long-form journalism about women in other countries. Its first issue, for example, included articles about lesbian activists in Brussels, abortion rights protests in Italy, and a liberation movement in the Western Sahara which, significantly, Spain had decolonized only a year before at the behest of the UN and which was then fighting for self-determination against Moroccan and Mauritanian control. Subsequent issues ran articles about topics as diverse as women in communist China, domestic violence in Italy, life for women in Eritrea, and Chilean women opposing fascism.[9] Throughout its tenure, *Vindicación Feminista* covers frequently either featured women from other countries or explicitly promoted articles on global topics: a photograph of a Western Saharan woman comprised the cover of the magazine's first issue, for example. And, befitting a magazine aspiring to global scope, it solicited subscriptions from readers in Europe, Morocco, the Americas, and the United States as well as from Iberia.[10]

Dones en lluita and *Opción* similarly covered international events. Though *dones en lluita* focused primarily on domestic affairs during the first half of its twenty-three-issue run, later issues of the magazine regularly ran stories about feminism and politics in other nations. Indeed, one of its most striking covers, from an October 1981 issue devoted to opposing NATO and militarism, featured an altered version of Botticelli's "The Birth of Venus." A well-muscled Ronald Reagan cloaked in an American flag and hugging a skeleton stood in for the angel, and swooped menacingly over the figure of Venus.[11] By the publication of its last issue in June 1983, *dones en lluita's* feature articles often focused on international events and global feminism, running the gamut from Palestinian women fighting for independence,[12] to prostitution in Nicaragua,[13] to "feminism in England: past, present, and future."[14] Meanwhile, feature stories in *Opción's* first issue—which are indicative of the magazine's focus for the rest of its run—included a piece about women in India and the Middle East being sold as brides, as well as a piece on sex education in Paris. Other stories included coverage of the female governor of Washington state, Dixie Lee Ray, and short articles on a radical Italian feminist group and female political figures in the IRA.[15]

This internationalist bent was not just voyeuristic. The goal of these articles was in fact to foster international activism, not just to inform. In addition to reporting on feminism in other nations, Spain's feminist magazines also drew parallels between contemporary feminist fights in Spain and elsewhere and drew inspiration from other feminists' experiences. Most common were articles using women's experiences getting an abortion as a point of comparison, with journalists looking to Italy, France, Portugal, the United States, and England to provide both anecdotes and information about the intricacies of these nations' abortion laws.[16]

In addition, writers urged their readers to reach out to feminist organizations in other countries, creating transnational networks of solidarity and action. Paloma Saavedra and Regina Bayo's "Women in the World" column in *Vindicación Feminista* attempted to provide a space where, as neutral moderators, they could tease out the nuances of different domestic and international feminist groups' ideological positions, describe how women across the world tackled problems that all feminists faced, and give Spanish feminists the foundation to understand and contact feminist organizations in other countries. Though their first column mostly focused on Spain's own feminist organizations, it also included two pages of material about French feminist groups, complete with contact information for interested readers.[17]

Another magazine, *Tribuna Feminista*, specialized in encouraging these kinds of connections, by reporting on both national and international feminist activities. In its inaugural issue alone, the magazine promoted Italian feminist publications, describing Italy as "one of the European centers of international feminist activity." It provided a blurb and contact information for the *Centre de Recherches de reflexion et d'information féministe* (CRIF), a Parisian feminist study group, alongside an informational paragraph about a feminist gathering in Brussels. And it included information about a gathering of 600 Latin American women in Lima, Peru that was also attended by women from France, Britain, Germany, and—very specifically—"the Spanish state."[18] Subsequent issues included an article about Dominican feminists accompanied by a list of thirty-one Latin American feminist organizations, periodicals, and their contact information,[19] as well as a short article discussing the influence of French feminism and containing the translation of a French feminist poem.[20]

Such magazine copy reflected a common desire for connection; the symbology and visual culture that Spanish feminists shared with women across Western Europe and North America highlight the depth of those connections. The woman symbol, often encircling a fist, predominated. It served as the initial "O" in the title of the feminist journal *Opción*, for instance, and appeared alongside *Tribuna Feminista*'s title on that magazine's page headers. Feminists also made widespread use of a hand gesture where the maker created a diamond shape representing the vagina by facing her palms outward and pressing together the tips of her index fingers and thumbs. These signs, along with slogans like "Basta!," meaning "Enough!" in the languages of Italian, Spanish, and Catalan, permeated feminist media, adorning magazines, posters, photographs, and cartoons.[21]

A 1978 pamphlet titled "Abortion Internationally" offers as an especially clear example of this visual lexicon and the extent to which feminists from across Europe used, understood, and related to them. This pamphlet's cover photograph depicted two demonstrators making the diamond symbol together and holding signs, one featuring the "Basta!" slogan. Inside the pamphlet, a woman symbol encircling a fist accompanied a pro-abortion quote. As its title indicated, the pamphlet discussed international abortion laws, and to that end included articles on China, Chile, Italy, Spain, the United States, and Bangladesh. The publication was British, as were most of its contributors, and it was written in English—but Italian protestors served as its cover models, one of its contributing writers was Chilean, and Spanish feminist archivists at *Ca La Dona* consciously preserved the copy consulted for this study, despite its language and place of origin, because Spanish feminists shared it amongst themselves and then donated it for preservation alongside locally produced materials.[22]

This flow of information ran both ways: just as Spanish women consumed feminist media from Belgium, England, Italy, France, and the Netherlands as well as more local sources, their own feminist magazines and pamphlets promoting diverse causes and public acts like local International Women's Day events found their way into foreign feminists' hands. Often the authors actively hoped for this, as when Spanish feminists organizing their first (ultimately cancelled) conference in 1974 "produced and circulated [the program] to other countries so that the different movements would discuss it and thereby enrich [their] own practice and analysis."[23] In other instances, Spanish and foreign feminists alike went a step further, sharing printed material directly with one another. In particular, the flow of pamphlets educating women about their reproductive systems and reproductive healthcare options illustrates feminists' close international ties. Pamphlets like "How to avoid a pregnancy," a comic book about women's reproductive care and birth control options from approximately 1974 to 1975, came to Spain from Italy courtesy of Italian feminist group *El Colective "Consulterios" del Movimente Italiano de Liberación de la Mujer* (MLD).[24] MLD shared the pamphlet with a neighborhood Spanish feminist association in Barcelona, which translated it to Spanish from the original Italian. Two other pamphlets from the same time, one about how to identify and cure vaginal infections and the other explaining how gynecological exams worked, were first published by the Italian *Gruppo Femminista per la Salute della Donna* and then, as the front covers proclaimed, "translated and edited for [the] *Vocalía de Mujeres del Carmelo*" by Italian group *Spina Piazaa Monte di Pieta*.[25] Though originally produced specifically for the *Vocalia de Mujeres del Carmelo* in the 1970s, the pamphlet on vaginal infections also had an afterlife and a larger circulation: it appeared, excerpted, in *dones en lluita's* last issue, published in 1983.[26] Of course not every Spanish feminist could read other languages, and so in some cases Spanish magazines relied on multi-lingual friends or readers to translate interviews or articles from other publications and report on those for their readership. Mirea Bofill, for example, was fluent in English as well as Spanish and so served as translator for several feminist organizations and periodicals.[27]

Spanish feminists also benefitted from international exchanges of information about how to travel to various countries in order to receive care that their nations prohibited—specifically, abortion and contraceptive services. The last few pages of "How to avoid a pregnancy" dealt with just this issue, offering annotated listings for abortion and family planning clinics open to Spanish women in places like England, Switzerland, the Netherlands, and Italy. England and the Netherlands, for instance, were listed as being "cheap," readers were warned that the Swiss clinic would help them "only before the third month," and a note at the bottom of the pamphlet cautioned: "In November 1974 abortion was approved in France. We do not yet have data on Family Planning and Abortion Centers in this country, but in any case, it is necessary to take into account the fact of the geographical proximity. Ask."[28] Similar pamphlets continued flowing into Spain from European nations throughout the 1970s and into the early 1980s, including the aforementioned titles from Britain and the Netherlands as well as additional translated pamphlets from MLD.[29]

Spain's grassroots feminists were not alone in accessing these resources. It was so common for European women to seek abortions abroad that nations with more permissive abortion laws reached out to women in nations with more restrictive laws—Spain, but other nations as well—to offer options for circumventing those restrictions. Once the Netherlands legalized abortion in 1981, for example, the Dutch organization *Stimezo*, which worked to help women get abortions in safe and hygienic conditions, distributed a Spanish-language pamphlet that detailed how to come to the Netherlands for an abortion and noted how *Stimezo* had helped women from all over Europe access abortions. The pamphlet included prices, locations, procedures, lists of paperwork women needed to enter the country, a map with cities and clinics marked, and, lastly, a catalogue of which clinics did and did not speak Spanish.[30] And, as discussed in Chapter 2, such contact extended beyond instructions printed in pamphlets. Feminists in nations like the Netherlands and Britain worked directly with Spanish feminist groups to organize travel and accommodation for Spanish women seeking abortions, and even hired additional Spanish-speaking staff in local abortion clinics to accommodate the influx of new, foreign customers.

Finally, Spanish feminists and their foreign counterparts also directly joined one another's battles for feminist-friendly legislation both to show solidarity and because they believed all feminists' fates to be linked. For example, when the British National Abortion Campaign convened a "Tribunal" in 1977 to protest a proposed bill that would restrict women's access to abortion in the UK, British feminists asked colleagues from seven other countries to come testify about how their own nations' abortion restrictions had impacted women.[31] Dolores Thomas of the Barcelona Women's Liberation Movement was among the invitees, and when sending her regrets after visa trouble ultimately prevented her from attending the Tribunal, she tellingly declared, " … I and the women of Spain depend on your solidarity and wish you the best. If the Benyon Bill is implemented, many of us will be the first to suffer. We want to hear the results of your Tribunal and hope that we can attend your demonstration in May." Testifying to the depth of the connections that linked Spanish and British feminists, and more generally to how feminists were willing to involve themselves in fights beyond their own national borders, the organizers included Thomas's letter in the tribunal's official materials. And, underscoring the breadth of Spanish women's participation in these networks, while Thomas missed one specific event, Spanish feminists from four different organizations did attend an International Campaign for Abortion Rights meeting in Paris in 1978.[32]

And, as Thomas's story suggests, feminists also frequently traveled to participate in one another's protests. Because of the networks these women constructed, changes in laws—particularly laws regarding abortion practices—affected women in more than one country. In this case specifically, the restriction of abortion in Britain would have impacted Spanish women's access, as Dolores Thomas noted. Though a national law, it had international repercussions, which feminists understood, and which bound them together in networks of solidarity and action. Notably, these kinds of demonstrations also provided a pattern for how to do feminist activism. Nearly ten years later in 1986, Spanish feminists held their own tribunal to judge Spain's new abortion law and its implementation—a tribunal patterned on the earlier British example in which Dolores Thomas had sought to participate.[33]

Through the 1970s, then, feminist activism was the domain of grassroots feminists who spurred their communities to action and took inspiration from their connections with feminists doing the same work in other nations. An international network of feminists transcended national boundaries and shared vocabulary, ideology, and imagery as well as tactical plans and overarching strategies designed to cement rights for women in a multitude of nations and not just in a sole national context. However, this was not to last. As the decade waned, a series of domestic and international institutional changes, whose start coincided with the launch of the World Conference on Women series in 1975, heralded a slow shift in international feminist engagement. Increasingly, the feminism of spectacle that had flourished in grassroots transnational networks gave way to formal, coordinated international diplomacy and negotiation for women's rights undertaken by or on behalf of individual nations.

Shifting Feminist Internationalism—From Insurgent Spectacle to Formal Diplomacy

The PSOE's creation of the *Instituto* in 1983 opened new channels for feminist international outreach that only grew after Spain joined the EEC in 1986. It also coincided with a larger transformation, a shift over the course of the 1980s and 1990s in how feminists built international ties and pushed international organizations to recognize sites of injustice. In the 1980s, women's rights and human rights advocacy intersected on the global stage, as feminists worldwide increasingly prioritized convincing international organizations to publicly subscribe to the position that women's rights were human rights.[34] In addition, the 1980s also saw a dramatic shift in how activists built solidarity networks, moving from grassroots methods to formal diplomatic negotiations that national women's ministries undertook on behalf of their governments.[35] In Spain, the result was that institutional feminists were thrust into newly formalized international feminist networks—networks from which independent feminists, as this chapter will later show, meanwhile found themselves increasingly isolated. Then, in the 1990s, international women's rights activism also began to move away from advocacy for isolated women's rights causes like guarantees of equal pay and legalization of abortion and toward a more holistic concept of equality. In this vein, feminist activists working with and/or within the UN pivoted to what gender and sexuality politics scholar Elizabeth Friedman has called "gendering the UN agenda,"—that is, a fight both to keep women's issues from being relegated to the WCOW series instead of being addressed in more broadly influential international bodies, and for these groups to "recogni[ze] that the structure of society and all relations between women and men ... [needed to] be revaluated."[36]

The UN and EEC—after 1992, the EU—acceded to feminist demands and reimagined their missions in the late twentieth century to include ensuring gender equality and eliminating gender discrimination. Human rights and international women's rights scholars, as well as participants and subsequent UN documents, have interpreted the 1995 Beijing WCOW as the turning point when these international organs bowed to feminists' gendering of the UN agenda and in response began to implement a policy of "gender mainstreaming." This policy required that government and administrative bodies consider the gender impact of all proposals, at all levels, to ensure that they would not create or reinforce structural discrimination or inequalities; meeting gender mainstreaming standards meant only implementing proposals that ensured women, as well as men, had equal access and equal opportunity.[37] By the late 1990s gender mainstreaming was firmly entrenched in UN talking points, policy, and administrative culture. Contemporaneously it also became influential in the EU, which had observer status at the UN. Though the European Court of Justice does not rely on international precedent to adjudicate cases (and so does not look to UN policy when making decisions), the Beijing WCOW nevertheless brought gender mainstreaming into the EU lexicon and into EU policy making.

Gender mainstreaming also made inroads in national politics. Women in national government felt that international organizations set precedents on which they could draw to persuade their nations to adopt new policies: when the international community used rhetoric that gave credence to feminist views, activists could then argue that local governments should heed these declarations when setting policy. Gender mainstreaming additionally provided a new common vocabulary and universal rhetoric that women agitating in different national contexts could use to frame their concerns. Moreover, international acceptance of the language of gender and women's equality—whether international laws and resolutions proved binding or not—gave women leverage to argue that in order to meet international standards and be respected on the international stage, their nation needed to implement changes and create new laws to protect women.[38]

Yet gender mainstreaming had its limitations. First, it was not a defined, prescribed plan but rather a vague blueprint for achieving a similarly vaguely defined equality. Implementation of this principle suffered as a result. Torild Skard, a Norwegian sociologist, activist, and politician who has worked extensively with women's rights organizations on an international level, criticized UN implementation of gender mainstreaming for being "slow, cumbersome, and incomplete."[39] More specifically, one serious problem, according to Skard, was that men dominated leadership and management roles in UN bodies, which meant they had to not only approve the implementation of new policies like gender mainstreaming but also ensure that their bodies adhered to its guidelines.[40] Adherence remained a challenge in part because of "a lack of training and subsequent confusion about concepts, goals, and means," but also because "there was a tendency to dilute the radical feminist texts of the world conference recommendations." This meant that, when applied on an administrative level, "power aspects [of terms like gender, empowerment, and self-determination] ... [were] denied and the need for a basic restructuring of society concealed." As a result, Skard reported, "implementation measures ... [did not address] the specific gender dimensions and political aspects that were at the core of the original recommendations," a problem Skard termed "gender malestreaming."[41]

In addition, gender mainstreaming resolutions that feminists used to promote women's rights suggested, but did not require, that nations meet gender equality benchmarks or institute legislation protecting women's rights. In an EU context, as Mariagrazia Rossilli shows, this meant that resolutions represented an open conversation, and not a foregone conclusion, about the desirability of legislation protecting women's rights. Most often feminists took responsibility for convincing their governments to conform to EU resolutions, but the public nature of their lobbying left room for non-governmental organizations of all persuasions to participate in and co-opt individual nations' political conversations.[42] Indeed, conservatives also had networks with global scope—including the Catholic Church and right-leaning family values groups with influence across Europe and in the United States. As a result, feminist arguments were not always effective. Feminists' ability to leverage connections for legislative reform varied despite the enduring popularity and prevalence of rhetoric supporting human rights.

Moreover, complications in finding the balance between men and women's interests, needs, and priorities included the erosion of programs that had been designed to bring women to parity with men. As Jane Jenson argues, one unintended consequence of the new focus on gender discrimination was that organizations discontinued practical initiatives to protect specific women's rights and so eroded feminist gains. For example, the EU defunded results-oriented women's rights programs such as those mandating equal pay and monitoring compliance in favor of instituting new pedagogical techniques in early childhood education in an effort to prevent gender discrimination in future generations.[43]

These problems presented unique challenges for feminists, both independent and institutional, within Spain. Institutional feminists working within the *Instituto*, like their foreign counterparts, brought home policy proposals discussed or ratified in international conferences or by intragovernmental organizations and attempted to leverage international agreements into domestic policy change in Spain. There as in other countries, this tactic faced roadblocks from politicians and legislators unwilling to pass such policy in Spain as well as from international organizations unwilling to enforce their own mandates.

The primary challenge institutional feminists faced was the *Instituto*'s lack of effective centralized authority over the whole country. When the PSOE established the *Instituto*, it only provided for the creation of a Madrid-based national agency, not for additional branches around the country or for a central means to coordinate with policymaking bodies in Spain's emergent autonomous communities. This was in no small part a consequence of democratic Spain's complex and decentralized system of governance, which developed during the transition through an uneven process of case-by-case regional devolution. Under this system, the national government shared power with the governments of the nation's seventeen autonomous regions, affording each a host of powers while also reserving some—foreign relations, for instance—for the central state.[44] However, this autonomy was not the same everywhere: as part of the change, individual regions were invited to apply for devolution, which included drafting formal statutes of autonomy. And while regions with strong identities, like the Basque Country and Catalunya, secured extensive autonomy by the early 1980s, others only finished the process a decade later, and claimed far fewer powers.⁴⁵ This motley and unfinished structure affected the implementation of equality policy inasmuch as it also impacted how regional governments organized the bodies that could create the policy in the first place. Autonomous communities decided for themselves whether to have regional equality bodies, what relationship to regional government those bodies would have, and what those bodies' priorities would be, all of which consequently varied widely between different regions.

Institutional feminists bemoaned the structural challenges posed by Spain's decentralized *Instituto*. In an editorial in a 1996 issue of the Andalusian *Instituto*'s magazine *Meridiana*, for instance, regional director Carmen Olmeda Checa noted just how widely regional *Institutos*' political circumstances could vary: while six autonomous communities had powerful *Institutos*—Catalunya, the Basque Country, Aragon, the Canary Islands, and Andalucia—others had newly created agencies, like Navarra, where after winning control of the parliament in 1995's regional elections, the PSOE created a local *Instituto* separate from the Institute of Social Welfare, where women's equality issues had previously been handled. Still others, like Asturias and Murcia, had equality bodies whose staffing, budget, and even position in the regional hierarchy shifted with every election and change of reigning political party.⁴⁶ This variety, coupled with a lack of coordinated central leadership, meant that regional equality agencies' priorities were set by autonomous communities and not by, or even in consultation with, the national *Instituto*. And in some cases, these priorities did not align with what the national *Instituto* had negotiated with the EU. In Valencia, the regional government "slowly abandoned" EU-financed and approved plans to support women's associations and advance coeducation. The Asturian and Murcian regional governments similarly stopped implementing EU equality initiatives whenever these ceased receiving European funding.⁴⁷

Shifting political tides could also alter these groups' priorities—sometimes even longstanding policies changed or fell by the wayside when a new party came to power. In these situations, local *Institutos* struggled to maintain coherent policies and provide women with a consistent slate of services, diminishing their practical impact on women's lives. The phasing out of EU programs in Valencia, for instance, coincided in 1996 with ascent of the right-wing Popular Party (PP), which soon closed the region's *Instituto* and gave jurisdiction over women's equality matters to the Ministry of Labor, where the approach to these issues shifted to "empowering housewives" and "strengthening the family bond." Practically speaking, this meant that the government replaced regional coeducation initiatives, originally instituted to comply with EU gender mainstreaming objectives, with a system of subsidies for families providing at-home care for elderly relatives. Similarly, the closure of the General Directorate for Women in Murcia precipitated reorganization of a program to stop abuse against women; the program was placed under the Social Assistance branch of the national social security system, which helped all citizens, meaning that a domestic violence program created to help abused women would now service men as well. This, the *Instituto*'s branch in neighboring Andalucia judged, sent the message—inappropriate, they implied—that such violence was "not an exclusively female problem." Following that pattern, Madrid incorporated the formerly independent Directorate for Women into the Ministry of Health and Social Services which *Meridiana* likewise lamented was "diluting" efforts to help women in large part because of an ensuing "reduction of workshops, publications, subsidies, and aid" meant specifically for women.[48]

And meanwhile, the scattered nature of feminist organization in Spain also foreclosed institutional feminists' ability to fully cultivate their international connections and parlay them into domestic policy advances. The case of gender mainstreaming is revealing: independent feminists shared the aims and backed implementation of gender mainstreaming in Spain, at least in theory, and they were to an extent willing to work with institutional feminists to achieve it. Yet, the *Instituto* remained hampered by a decentralized structure that limited its influence over regional policymaking and its ability to build the kind of national cohesion such a policy required. As a result, independent feminists who had initially supported gender mainstreaming came to distrust institutional feminists' intentions when advocating for it, and likewise questioned whether these *Instituto* activists were acting in good faith when promoting policies derived from negotiations with international entities like the UN and EU.

The differing equality policies between regions and the lack of centralized coordination hindered Spanish institutional feminists' international outreach efforts. Domestically, the *Instituto*'s agents struggled on the local and regional level to create and access their own versions of the networks that grassroots feminists had cultivated for decades. As a result, institutional feminists across the country sometimes lacked clarity about their comrades' aims and resources—and even about how many other women shared their goals. And crucially, when institutional feminists from different regions tried to collaborate in building international ties, their differing views on equality policy affected their ability to work together effectively. As late as the 1995 WCOW in Beijing, one Andalusian institutional feminist described, she and her colleagues struggled to take advantage of the networking opportunities such meetings offered due to the radically varied organization of their regional *Institutos*:

> despite [the federal Instituto] having sent almost six hundred women, our presence [in Beijing] was almost completely invisible. However, for many of us, the forum was the place where we first came into contact with other Spanish women from different places, and only those who had come from well-coordinated organizations ... could take advantage of these meetings.[49]

In response, Andalusia's institutional feminists sought to build greater links between Andalusia's women's associations, as well as between Andalusia and the national *Instituto*. One potential vehicle they identified was the European Women's Lobby (EWL), formed five years earlier, in 1990, to represent women's interests in the EU; women's organizations in nations across Europe joined and/or created new organizations to affiliate with the EWL. Seeking to expand both their domestic and international networks, feminists from the Andalusian *Instituto* advocated for "integrati[ng] into the ... Association of Support to the European Lobby of Women [henceforth ASEWL],"[50] a Spanish affiliate founded in 1993 and linked politically with the PSOE.[51] ASEWL membership, these women hoped, would give them a role in "organization and coordination of the NGO State Platform for Beijing" as well as provide them with a "link to several European [feminist] Networks."[52] Ultimately, though, Spanish institutional feminists still found themselves both frustrated in their efforts to access negotiations abroad on women's rights policy, and bereft of the political leverage needed to push for reforms at home. This only increased the animosity that independent feminists felt toward institutional feminists and diminished their already-low goodwill. Perhaps, independents reasoned, institutional feminists' entrenchment in government networks, combined with their ineffective activism, was a sign that they were not actually feminist at all.

In sum, feminist successes at intervening in the international political agenda and making women's rights part of broader conversations did not always or easily translate into domestic feminist successes. Within Spain specifically, the *Instituto de la Mujer* participated in international events and cultivated its own formal international networks with bodies like the EU and UN, but it lacked domestic organization and cohesion. Ultimately, the fractures caused by the *Instituto*'s decentralized structure prevented it from generating political leverage it might otherwise have amassed in a moment of intense international attention to precisely the issues it was founded to address. This breakdown also affected institutional feminists' ability to create potentially useful domestic channels of solidarity and communication. Perhaps most ominously, though, the leadership vacuum created by domestically weak national and regional *Institutos* allowed debates over Spanish feminism's aims and methods to reopen, at least on the regional and local levels where independent feminists' grassroots networks, though losing influence abroad, still held sway. By the 1990s, this shift meant that competing groups of self-professed feminists once again battled over the aims of feminist policy, with consequences for how Spain's regions implemented gender mainstreaming recommendations promulgated by the UN and the EU.

Independent Versus Institutional Feminists in Spain

As *Instituto* agents worked to parlay their newfound international access into real foreign ties with tangible benefits, Spain's independent feminists by contrast remained dependent on their established grassroots networks. Consequently, once they encountered new economic and ideological obstacles to cultivating new links abroad, they quickly fell behind their institutional rivals. Indeed, they were in at least one instance literally left behind: in 1985, independent feminists hoping to attend an NGO Tribunal taking place alongside that year's WCOW in Nairobi petitioned the *Instituto* to defray their travel expenses so that representatives of Spain's poorly financed independent feminist movement could make the trip. No agreement was reached and independent feminists, outraged at what they considered a silencing of their perspective and an *Instituto*-led monopolization of the Spanish feminist mantle, bitterly denounced the agency in a column printed in *Tribuna Feminista*'s July 1985 issue. Appealing to Spanish activists' desire for international connection, the indignant authors opened by accusing the *Instituto* of having violated the recently ratified CEDAW tenet that "induce[d] governments" to "facilitate the presence of autonomous organizations in international forums" by failing to subsidize their travel.[53] Echoing the terms of feminists' criticisms of the *Sección Femenina*'s participation at the 1975 WCOW in Mexico City, they asserted that without grassroots activists present as a counterbalance, the *Instituto*'s participation made it appear that Spanish feminism had attended when in truth it had no representation at the conference. And this, the independent feminist authors concluded, "demonstrate[d] [the *Instituto*'s] desire to control the Spanish presence in the Non-Governmental Forum" that accompanied the official WCOW.[54] In other words, independent feminists strongly implied that they did not in fact consider institutional feminists to be feminists at all.

This was more than a rehashing of well-worn slurs and longstanding ideological divisions. The *Instituto*'s creation and subsequent efforts to assert itself both abroad and domestically changed and significantly escalated the conflict that had split Spanish feminism. To be sure, debates about women's rights—what these rights were, which women ought to have them, and how governments could best ensure them—occupied Spain's public, politicians, and feminist activists, as well as international observers, from the late Franco years through Spain's democratic transition. And the feminists who had helped make these debates central to transition-era politics disagreed especially frequently on this issue, with tensions between the period's single and double militants dating to this rift's earliest days. Yet despite this, both camps had ultimately found unity enough to advocate for change even (or perhaps especially) when shut out of political decision-making as a post-Franco democracy took shape. At that time, feminists' primary conflict was over the practical issue of whether to cooperate with the democratizing process then unfolding; notwithstanding, feminists of all kinds worked to define and seek protections for women's rights. The creation of the *Instituto* in 1983 changed the terms of Spanish feminism's fundamental schism by creating a fixed, tangible barrier between the two sides, as double militant/institutional feminists now had a place within the state edifice they hoped to shape, affording them (at least in theory) increased influence over women's rights policy and its implementation. And as the international paradigm for women's rights activism shifted toward state-affiliated, bureaucratized feminist groups working through official political channels like UN conferences, they were similarly well-positioned to participate in international negotiations on women's policy.

This represented a major shift in how Spanish feminists could access and engage with the political sphere. Again, during the late Franco years and early transition period feminists had all encountered similar limits to participating in high-level political debate, and had fought the Spanish government for recognition that women faced oppression and that oppression should be rectified. From the 1980s on, by contrast, institutional and independent feminists had radically different levels of access to political decision-making and championed different ideas of what it meant to be feminist, how to define "equality," and how best to create and implement policies to guarantee that equality for Spanish women. In this sense, late twentieth-century Spanish feminists' greatest struggle was arguably not for recognition that women should have rights, but over which group of self-identified feminists, independent or institutional, had the right to claim the mantle of feminism and set the agenda for protecting women's rights.

Above all, independent feminists condemned their institutional rivals for what they described as a willingness to play politics with equality, like male politicians had, instead of being genuinely interested in making concrete change. Institutional feminists' "integration" into the Spanish government, their critics argued, had made them complicit in the government's continued oppression of women. The proceedings of the IV State-level Independent Feminists' Conference, held less than a month after the *Instituto*'s founding, underscore these concerns. The conference had been organized to explore the state of Spanish feminism, and participants indeed expressed concern over its future and its goals. One presentation, titled "Feminism and Power," stressed the "need to review the politics of the feminist movement to explain its current stagnation … and therefore, the loss of its character as a social movement." Authors Lola G. Luna and Maria Luisa Marino i Serra, who hailed from Oviedo and Barcelona, respectively, went on to warn that the feminist movement as they had known it was "scattered and isolated" and that "for a few years now, it [had] been difficult to find many independent feminists."[55]

Both women, along with other presenters, ultimately laid blame for feminism's "stagnation" on double militants—institutional feminists—whose "integration" into the government meant an end to the potential to restructure the social relationship between men and women through activism. To open the conference, Luna and Marino i Serra's intervention argued that activists incorporated into the state "[did] not hesitate to apply all the techniques and strategies learned as political party militants, in order to retain their hegemony."[56] The next presenter, Karmele Marchante Barrobes, extended this critique by rejecting institutional feminists' claim to the feminist label, arguing that such women "have their exact role to play within their organization and they have stopped asking questions. Of course, they would not have an answer, either, because they are in a different orbit from the feminist galaxy."[57]

Ten years later, the Basque independent feminist magazine *Lanbroa* took this critique further still, suggesting that institutional feminists' integration into the fabric of the Spanish state had not come from a genuine desire to create change—rather, these women were willing, and perhaps even actively sought to buttress patriarchal power: "Society is interested in a certain kind of feminism," they wrote, "from which it can … extract something for its benefit and to control its interests."[58] In an interview with the magazine, prominent Spanish feminist Lidia Falcón similarly opined that Spain's institutional feminism was ineffective because, unlike in the United States, feminists in Spain had not "become independent from the intellectual colonization that the men of the parties have had over women."[59] And mere months later, journalist and scholar Concha Fagoaga also accused institutional feminists of being knowingly complicit in women's oppression. When asked the admittedly leading question, "how important do you think it is that the feminist movement be autonomous," she responded that this was of utmost importance because "today Party feminists also know how easy it is within those organizations to postpone feminist goals again and again, waiting for the timing that is never timely."[60]

These tensions permeated Spanish feminists' engagement with the international community as well. In the 1980s, independent feminists coupled their critiques with pleas for the same level of international exposure that *Instituto* feminists received, and for enough financial support to be able to attend international conferences that set the global agenda for feminist activism. But by the 1990s, Spain's independent feminists no longer clamored for a seat at the table. Embittered, they now rejected the international networks in which institutional feminists across Europe participated, and condemned institutional feminists, both Spanish and foreign, for being brainwashed at best and at worst power-hungry.

The early and mid-1990s also saw independent feminists expand their critique of institutional feminism's "integration" into the state's power structure to also include critique of the "integrationist" policies that such state institutions promoted—in Spain's case, the *Instituto*'s adoption of the UN and EU's gender mainstreaming policies and equality frameworks. To this end, contributors to *Lanbroa* argued that "Equality Feminism's integration into modern democratic society," common across Europe, was in actuality an integration of only "the least revolutionary discourses of alternative movements," advancing true radicals' marginalization and with it "the silencing of the [critical] analysis of the power relations between men and women."[61] Independent feminists argued that the kind of equality that gender mainstreaming ultimately offered was tantamount to forcing female integration into the male world instead of making a world designed for both men and women:

> People no longer openly defend misogynistic behaviour or laws that explicitly discriminate against women; to the contrary, they are careful to make statements, especially written statements, affirming that women are 'equal to men'. They begin by using the term 'equality' as a shorthand for equal opportunities or equal rights, but end up not meaning the sameness of rights ... but rather a goal for which women must now strive: conformity with the male world.[62]

In this sense, Spain's independent feminists' critique of gender mainstreaming echoed Torild Skard's: both asserted that gender mainstreaming became stripped of its radicalism in institutional contexts and that, as a result, the policy designed to provide equality for women instead primarily helped men. Skard, of course, still believed in gender mainstreaming; Spain's independent feminists found it to be a deliberate rerouting of women's rights efforts away from the possibility of real change.

Yet for all of their venom, independent feminists' denunciations lacked specificity and moreover reached only a small, specialized audience that remained limited largely to independent feminist circles and did not include the broader public. And so, the conversations that feminists had with and about each other often did not resemble or reflect what Spaniards uninvolved in feminist groups had to say about feminists and their goals. In addition, independent feminists' failure to communicate or even formulate a platform of concretely defined problems and potential solutions perhaps accounted for some of the misunderstandings and misgivings that ordinary Spaniards had about their brand of feminism and their intentions.

And the Spanish public was far from silent about feminism or oblivious to feminist demands. Though press coverage of feminism routinely failed to draw distinctions between feminist groups in the ways that feminists themselves did, coverage of feminism throughout the 1980s and 1990s was nevertheless extensive, and it focused heavily on discrete issues like divorce, legalization of abortion, and calls for domestic violence reform.[63] It also included reviews of works by prominent international feminists, occasional opinion pieces by journalists and intellectuals about the state of feminism in Spain, and ordinary readers' letters to the editor. Again, though, the flood of reporting on feminist issues neither explained the nuances of different ideologies within the feminist movement nor even hinted there *were* such nuances beyond a general mainstream feminist versus radical feminist divide, which mapped only inexactly onto the institutional versus independent divide. And with few exceptions, those espousing feminist viewpoints in major periodicals were the same kind of feminist—mainstream and institutional—and even those who otherwise felt comfortable aligning themselves with feminism rejected so-called "radical," or independent, feminists.

Spaniards may have seemed to agree that "feminism" was a good idea, then, but in fact feminism appears to have been broadly acceptable in the 1980s and 1990s only when defined as a vague recognition that men and women should have equal rights. This held true even for progressives who ostensibly held fast to feminist ideals. At the height of the progressive PSOE's political reign in 1986, for example, and as the party was working to secure what it defined as feminist goals, an ABC article described Prime Minister Felipe Gonzalez's wife Carmen Romero as having "[become] the star of [a] massive gathering of socialist women organized by the PSOE in Torremolinos." The article then quoted Romero as saying that she rejected what most Spaniards would have defined as "radical" feminist views: "I do not understand feminism more than as a collaboration of men and women to social progress, I do not understand a movement that marginalizes men ... "[64]

The construction of a dichotomy between radical feminists who seemed to hate men and femininity and more mainstream feminism that embraced the opposite sex extended to descriptions of feminist politicians as well. In 1990, in an article lauding Isabel Donaire, the newly elected female mayor of Jerez in 1990, ABC for example described her as "feminist, but very feminine."[65] Meanwhile, the portrayal of radical feminism as divisive and undesirable was not limited to politicians and their families. Spanish model Raquel Revuelta shared a similar sentiment in a 1989 interview: "I am against radical feminism. I do not share their theories ... Feminism had its *raison d'être* in its time, when women achieved, fighting, achievements as transcendent as the feminine vote. But now, those arguments have become obsolete, because nowadays men and women have the same opportunities as long as they show their personal worth."[66] Revuelta's perception—that feminism's moment had come and gone now that women could vote and feminist demands had been answered with legislative concessions—was widespread: many women voiced that Spanish women still needed to fight for equality, but no longer needed radicals' feminism to do it.[67]

Institutional feminists helped reinforce the conceptions of mainstream and radical feminism in the national press. In 1990, *Blanco y Negro* ran an article on Naomi Wolf's pathbreaking book, *The Beauty Myth*, and used it to discuss the trajectory of feminism. The article, titled "Twenty Years Later: The Resuscitation of Feminism," posited that feminism within Spain had died over the prior decade of the 1980s, but that Wolf's book resonated with a new generation of feminists starting to become active in the last decade of the twentieth century. Much of the five-page article summarized Wolf's conclusions, but its last pages also offered a mini-feature titled "Spain, Past and Future" that discussed the nation's history of feminist activism and asked women to weigh in about the state of feminism in Spain. Meanwhile, the *Instituto*'s director, Carmen Martínez Ten, rejected claims that feminism had died, arguing instead that it had simply "changed much over the decade of the 1980s" and that it had "become more diffuse ... less radicalized, but more widespread" with the result that most Spanish women "favored equality between both sexes." She also noted that "[h]er preferred definition of feminism [was] 'a heartfelt appeal to the common sense of society so that men and women develop as people on equal terms, regardless of their sex.'"[68]

In each of these instances, Spaniards identified only with a mainstream conception of feminism; independent feminists, deemed "radical," faced simplified mischaracterizations of their ideas (as in Romero's concerns about the marginalization of men), derision, or, as with Martínez Ten, a sentiment that radicalism's time had passed. Moreover, editorials and letters to the editor penned by Spaniards far less famous than Romero or Revuelta echoed these figures' rejections of radical feminism. Most newspaper letters to the editors focused on what they felt was feminism's attempts to eradicate differences between the sexes. Some writers felt that these differences were "natural" and that trying to make men and women equal was upsetting the balance.[69] Others felt that equality seemed like a good idea, but that, as one letter-writer suggested, radical feminist over-reaching made life worse for all women:

> The worst thing of all in this disaster is that almost always we come across as horribly ridiculous because people are able to see through us, because even when the most ardent feminist digs her fingernails into her palms to keep from telling her fiancé that she wants to marry a lo Pantoja [this references the desire to have an extravagant wedding] and the housewife hits the bottle to not tell off her husband who has her completely out of sorts with his unwillingness to take on any responsibility, men immediately perceive our schizophrenia and end up handling us as they like—without the advantages, of course, that came with being so managed back in our grandmothers' time, because then men could do as they liked, but some little courtesy or gift always came your way, and now you're the one who has to invite them to the movies.[70]

Once again, aside from writers who rejected feminist calls for equality outright, most rejections of feminism were in actuality rejections of what Spaniards considered "radical" feminism and not rejections of mainstream, institutional feminist calls for equality of the sexes and legislative changes designed to help the process along. All of this is to say that Spain's independent feminists had a circumscribed audience: unlike in the 1970s, major periodicals now largely ignored independent feminists' viewpoints, though when independents did receive newspaper coverage they were dismissed in similar, if perhaps less biting, terms than single militant feminists had been in prior years.

However, despite independent feminists' failure to impact public debates, they nevertheless were able to make strategic choices that provided them with a foothold for influence on political negotiations for equality policy in Spain. Independent feminists understood the power of gender mainstreaming rhetoric and positioned themselves as the real arbiters of gender mainstreaming, as opposed to the *Instituto* who they felt implemented it poorly. This choice, combined with the *Instituto*'s organizational challenges, put independent feminists in a strong, if unremarked upon, political position. Ultimately, independent feminists claiming to uphold the values of gender mainstreaming enmeshed themselves in regional political structures dominated by the *Instituto*, as a way of using political leverage to force the "integrationist" institutional feminists to take independent feminist views on feminism and equality seriously. Thus, despite their stated animosity toward both institutional feminists and institutional networks, independent feminists' political strategies betray what seems to have in fact been a deep ambivalence.

The ensuing dynamics were on display as a battle unfolded in the Basque country over how to improve coeducation in the early 1990s. Independent feminists already at odds with the *Instituto* over their ideological differences accused its proposed coeducational programs of being poorly thought out, insufficient, and staffed and managed by individuals so unqualified as to prevent the schools' success. They followed this by immersing themselves in regional politics, the structure and content of which had been dominated until then by local politicians and institutional feminists. When the Basque regional *Instituto*, *Emakunde*, published an Action Plan in 1991 for reshaping the region's coeducation system, radical feminists sought appointments to government-established Coeducation Advisory Boards (CAB) tasked with surveying the education system and instituting change.[71] And when these feminists failed to win enough seats to give them influence, they sought it in other ways, like controlling the staffing of teacher training programs so they could influence their curricula.

Independent feminists' involvement in regional politics also helped shape the priorities of the national *Instituto*.[72] In at least one instance independent feminists sought to shape not just the priorities of their regional equality body, but the existence and structure of the body itself: as noted at the start of this chapter, on International Women's Day in 1996 independent feminists in Valencia—at the time still lacking a regional *Instituto*—begged their regional parliament to create what they termed a Woman's Council (*Consejo de la Mujer*) with which local women's associations could affiliate, calls they repeated at a feminist conference the following year.[73] Despite their ideological differences with their institutional counterparts, these independent feminists also recognized the utility of state-affiliated agencies that, when free of cynical politicking, could leverage their local power to catalyze national change, something scholars Alba Alonso and Tánia Verge have called "level shopping," meaning that independent feminists generally reliant on grassroots organizational methods worked their way through different "levels" of government administration seeking a level through which they could effect change.[74] In these exchanges, independent feminists often exerted political leverage in Spain from the bottom up, aided by rhetoric and policy formulated and implemented through international bodies like the EU and UN even as they rejected institutional feminism and institutional feminist networks.

Conclusion

The later decades of the twentieth century saw the development of sophisticated, transnational grassroots feminist networks through which women produced an international feminist culture. Women in these networks not only shared solidarity, but also strategic and tactical information as well as practical advice about such matters as how to obtain abortions or help women learn about their reproductive systems. Significantly, women within these networks understood themselves as working for a common goal that transcended their ambition for individual pieces of legislation in their national contexts; they believed that women in all nations were affected by similar political milieus that routinely denied women rights and thus that the plight of women in other nations was their plight also.

During the 1980s and 1990s, however, international feminist networks underwent a dramatic shift, moving from a system in which grassroots feminist activists organized protests and direct actions that transcended national boundaries to a system in which government-affiliated women's ministries sent delegations to international conferences organized by intergovernmental bodies and negotiated for women's rights policy through diplomatic channels. This shift transformed feminist activism into a career for a subset of feminists. Those feminists working within government ministries could aspire to titles, offices, and salaries; the professionalization of feminism gave women's rights activists legitimacy, some measure of access to the legislative process, and the possibility of increased leverage to request policy change and influence their national governments.

Meanwhile, as international feminist networks changed, so too did the goals of such activism. In the 1990s, feminists had successfully lobbied intergovernmental organizations for a new way of conceiving, measuring, and implementing equality measures. EU gender mainstreaming policy, for instance, required that member states take the potential impact on women into consideration when weighing any organizational decision.

In Spain especially, these shifts upended the already uneasy balance between double- and single-militant feminists. The creation of the *Instituto de la Mujer* in 1983 gave double militants, now institutional feminists, a home within the government they had defended; single militants, now independent feminists, lacked such official recognition. Independent feminists developed a deep ambivalence for institutional feminists as dominant methods of feminist politicking changed. On the one hand, independent and institutional feminists shared some goals. Notwithstanding independent feminists' reservations about its implementation, gender mainstreaming was one such goal: it satisfied both groups' desires to pinpoint and resolve at least some of the causes of discrimination that women suffered in Spanish society. And as their request for financial assistance to attend the 1985 WCOW NGO Tribunal shows, independent feminists also clearly hoped to benefit from the same institutional feminist "integration" that they criticized.

However, institutional feminists' political failures, as well as what independent feminists perceived as their ideological shortcomings, served as the foundation for a dispute about who should have the right to define feminism as well as for a political battle over the right to define equality. A struggle ensued over which feminists should design and implement legislation and policies to protect this still-undefined equality, primarily at the local and regional levels as the *Instituto*'s decentralized character left an institutional feminist political power vacuum in those places. In this way, both institutional and independent feminists' desire to influence domestic politics, and to reach toward Europe for solidarity, reproduced and ossified decades-old arguments about how best to define and protect women's rights after Francoism and trumpet Spain's post-Franco national identity. In other words, international representation and connection simply became new sites for feminists intent on waging their identitarian battles as each ideological camp persisted in its belief that the other did violence to the larger feminist cause. Soon, however, as activists of the late twentieth and early twenty-first centuries gained ground on an increasingly publicly debated issue—the problem of domestic abuse—feminists of all varieties would concentrate on combating a more spectacular and far more material brand of violence.

4

Violent Inequalities

Debates on Intimate Partner Violence, Gender Equality, and the Ongoing Struggle to Define Post-Francoist Democratic Spain

On December 4, 1997, Ana Orantes, a middle-aged Spanish housewife, mustered the courage to appear on a popular daytime talk show broadcast on Spain's *TeleCinco* television channel, where she testified to the abuse she had endured during her forty-year marriage to José Parejo Avivar. Over the course of the interview, Orantes described daily beatings and screamed epithets, revealed how her husband had raped her while she was postpartum, talked about her greatest fear, that her spouse would similarly abuse their children (including a daughter whom she suspected he had already sexually molested), and questioned her God for seemingly sanctioning such a match for her: "Now Christmas is coming and I have no joy in life," she sobbed. "I'm as if buried alive, and I just want to cry. I ask the Lord why I had to come across this man."[1]

Orantes never fully explained her willingness to share such a personal story with *TeleCinco* and its viewers, but there are some clues about why she may have wished to. A recent fight, in which her husband had choked her, had given Orantes courage to ask for a divorce. But escaping the legal bonds of marriage did not mean escaping her ex-husband: the court refused to grant Orantes alimony, sole custody of their eleven children, or possession of the house. Lacking financial independence, and with her life inextricably intertwined with his, Orantes's only option was to continue living with her abuser. She created a makeshift apartment on the top floor of the house the couple had previously shared. This proximity enabled Parejo's bullying to continue. He no longer beat her, but even after he moved out to pursue a new relationship, he often returned to threaten Orantes. "I start to tremble when our dog starts barking," Orantes told TeleCinco, "because we know [that means] that he's coming."[2]

Thirteen days after the interview aired, Orantes's ex-husband stomped up the stairs to threaten her for the last time. But this time he did not stop at the threshold and wound her with words alone. This time he burst through the door and bludgeoned Orantes until she crumpled to the floor. He threw her from the second-floor balcony and into the courtyard below, where he then doused her with gasoline and lit her broken body on fire. The couple's fourteen-year-old daughter discovered the horrific scene—Orantes's body still smoldering—upon her return from school. Parejo claimed temporary insanity as his motive for the crime. Orantes had insulted him, he said, and provoked him. An enraptured nation watched the murder trial, and when it was over, with Parejo sentenced to seventeen years in prison, a public outpouring of support for Orantes turned into a national call for stricter intimate partner violence laws.

This public attention seemed a windfall for feminist activists who had sought intimate partner violence reform since the late Franco years and had campaigned on behalf of victims of sexual and intimate partner violence since Franco's death. Moreover, as discussed in Chapter 2, feminists had long framed their advocacy for women's rights, including their calls for sexual and intimate partner violence reforms, as a fight against the lingering traces of National-Catholicism's repressive gender order. Orantes's death marked the moment at which other Spaniards also began to entertain the idea of crafting legislation to attempt to eliminate, or at least reduce, the remaining repressive social and cultural forces that feminists of all persuasions understood to be permeating—and poisoning—Spanish society.

The momentum generated from Orantes's death, and subsequent deaths like it,[3] culminated in the Cortes passing *Ley Orgánica de Medidas de Protección Integral contra la Violencia de Género*, or Organic Law for Integral Protection Measures against Gender Violence (henceforth LOMPIVG), on December 28, 2004, which explicitly stated that the legislation's goal was to remedy remaining imbalances between the sexes. Yet the path to passing the LOMPIVG was riddled with complications, as was the final version of the bill itself, and its subsequent impact.

First, Spaniards intent on solving the nation's intimate partner violence crisis did so in a time of protracted cultural upheaval. Both institutional and independent feminists' prevailing understanding of intimate partner violence was that it happened because of larger sociocultural forces at work: a nationwide tacit acceptance of discrimination against women and belief in female inferiority, given voice and political power through the Franco regime's policies. Conservatives—the Spanish political Right—chafed at this characterization and, as such, throughout the 1990s they clashed with progressives—the Left, along with and often including feminists—over how to define intimate partner violence. Was intimate partner violence a crime committed by dysfunctional individuals, or was it a symptom of "machismo," a term Spaniards generally used as shorthand for aggressive shows of male dominance, including those that had been encouraged by National-Catholicism? Conservatives favored labeling the crime "family" or "domestic" violence to signal their belief in the first interpretation, while progressives, who ultimately won the rhetorical battle, favored the term "gender violence" to denote that social conditions enabled men to abuse.

Relatedly, conservatives and progressives already sparred over how to shape the nation's family and religious values in the post-Franco era. Conversations about the intimate partner violence crisis necessarily took place within this larger debate, as defining and punishing the crime also required defining which family and romantic partnerships were affected, and under which circumstances, and how those partnerships should evolve or end as a result of the abuse. Labeling the crime "gender violence" had unintended consequences, however, and further complicated the debate over ways of legislating it. The term "gender violence" implied that only women were victims and only men were abusers, and in consequence also foreclosed the option of applying newly strengthened intimate partner violence protections to families other than traditional families. This was especially significant in the early 2000s as the Spanish debate about legalizing gay marriage overlapped with the debate about intimate partner violence protections. Even as legislators demonstrated their willingness to expand definitions of family to encompass same-sex partnerships, they created stronger intimate partner violence protections applicable only to families consisting of a (male) husband and a (female) wife. Moreover, as feminist terminology like "gender equality" and "gender violence" gained currency and activists came closer to attaining their vision of women's rights, conservatives began to appropriate feminist rhetoric—such as the term "gender violence"—to argue for restrictions on women's rights.

Moreover, tension between ideologically opposed feminist groups also affected the debate surrounding the LOMPIVG. The professionalization of feminism that took place with the creation of the *Instituto* had marginalized independent feminists and their grassroots activism. Both feminist factions supported legislation to resolve Spain's intimate partner violence crisis, but institutional feminists had greater access to resources, including data that helped them understand the scale and scope of the problem. In addition, institutional feminists had political leverage and social standing that allowed their inquiries and their denunciations to take root and that opened the way for their organizations to lead the legislative process. Independent feminists, on the other hand, struggled throughout the 1990s to rebuild networks, both domestic and international, that had eroded with the shift to professionalized feminism. In some ways, these differences allowed institutional feminists and independent feminists to play complementary roles advocating the increased criminalization of intimate partner violence: institutional feminists involved themselves with the political particulars, while independent feminists participated in community activism that saw the establishment of crisis centers, safe houses, and marches. Sometimes institutional and independent feminists' efforts overlapped: they occasionally worked together to gain media attention, or to gain local and regional resources for abused women. Yet the two groups of feminists still found themselves at odds over who the LOMPIVG ought to protect. While the legislation was undoubtedly an achievement, independent feminists objected to the new law and its perhaps inadvertently problematic exclusions of LGBT couples and men who suffered abuse. Institutional feminists, meanwhile, defended the law as written and worked to secure its passage.

Lastly, the late 1990s and early 2000s saw Spaniards once again grappling with the legacy of Franco-era traumas. Parties debating policies and legislation to protect victims of intimate partner violence did so in a moment of intense attention to *other* instances of violence visited upon Spaniards, including renewed attention to the Franco regime's mass executions (and subsequent mass burials) of Republican soldiers, sympathizers, and political dissidents, as well as terrorist bombings by ETA and, in the early 2000s, by Islamic extremists. Commentators and politicians used the same language to parse these forms of violence and their resulting traumas as they did to discuss intimate partner violence. Politicians also made explicit connections between all of these kinds of violence, for instance equating the trauma experienced by victims of intimate partner violence with that experienced by victims of ETA's terrorism, and positing that government assistance for both sets of victims should come from the same funds.[4]

In all cases, Spaniards merged discussion of Franco and his legacy with debates about solutions to the epidemic of intimate partner violence. Conversations about Franco's legacy were not new, and indeed feminists of all persuasions had argued for decades that women's problems persisted precisely because Spanish society had inadequately dealt with the lingering social and cultural effects of Francoist ideologies. What was new to the 1990s and early 2000s was a willingness to attribute Spain's social ills directly to Franco and to tackle them head-on, and this came out clearly in Spanish society's wrestling with how to define intimate partner violence, how to understand what its prevalence meant for their nation, and how to determine an appropriate legal response. The terms of both popular and political discourse reflected this preoccupation as Spaniards universally derided policies they opposed as "fascist" or "Francoist" or "totalitarian" measures that threatened to plunge Spain back into "backwardness" and "oppression." There seemed to be consensus that "Francoist" was a slur encompassing a wide variety of moral ills with dire consequences for post-Franco society, and indeed the term soon became a catch-all denoting all manner of horrible fates for Spanish democracy, but what actually constituted "backwardness" and "oppression" remained, and still remains, up for debate. Significantly, the debate occurred through conversations about women's rights, conversations that have become repositories for the confusion and complications that continue to surround efforts to define Spanish democracy and delineate its boundaries.

Discovering and Defining a Social Problem: Legal and Rhetorical Battles over Intimate Partner Violence Before and Following Orantes

Orantes's shocking murder highlighted Spain's long-standing problem with intimate partner violence; it also underscored that violence against women remained socially acceptable in late-twentieth-century Spanish society, as it had been for decades, and that the legal consequences, though more punitive than in the past, remained insufficient. Orantes's murder occurred in 1997, but her abuse stretched back four decades to 1957 and Francoism's heyday. Orantes recounted in the *TeleCinco* interview that Parejo had first beat her three months after their wedding, an incident that met with a mixed response from her new in-laws. While her father-in-law hit and admonished his son, Orantes's mother-in-law was furious with her husband for interfering. Marriage, she believed, was a private matter, and whether Parejo hit Orantes or kissed her, it was no one's business. Society, Orantes explained, held the same perception. She had not reported the abuse to the authorities "because at that time it was not done."[5]

Social stigma and perception of intimate partner violence as an infrequent, isolated problem made it difficult for women like Orantes to receive help and contributed to the violence becoming so widespread in Spain by century's end that it constituted a public health crisis. Several factors led to this. First,

Franco-era Spanish society had not perceived intimate partner violence as a systemic social problem, at least in part because media representations of intimate partner violence obscured its prevalence and effects. At mid-century, newspapers published reports of intimate partner violence crimes only rarely, and then only in local editions and only in especially gruesome or shocking cases. Even when periodicals did publish information on a particular incident, they blamed it on the abuser's jealous rage, alcoholism, or temporary insanity. In these cases, intimate partner violence was considered a crime of passion. In addition, labeling intimate partner violence a "crime of passion" excused men from responsibility: insanity, alcohol, a woman breaking his heart—all of these motives placed the blame for a man's violent attacks elsewhere, and sometimes on the abused woman herself.[6] Moreover, even if Orantes had reported her early abuse, she would have found little, if any, legal support. Under the Franco regime there were no laws criminalizing intimate partner violence. Divorce was also illegal, so women had no escape from or recourse against marital abuse.

Public perception of intimate partner violence began to change in the late Franco years and during Spain's transition to democracy as feminist demands and international scrutiny of Spanish culture and politics drew attention to the regime's repression. The executions of political dissidents and ETA's acts of retaliation carried headlines worldwide, but the oppression of women did, too. Along with their struggle for political representation and abortion access, feminists' early demands—all of which international newspapers eagerly reported—also included stronger criminalization of violence against women.

Practically speaking, however, these changes had limited impact. As with other forms of violence and female oppression, feminists connected violence against women to larger, ongoing social problems within Spain. In a 1978 *New York Times* article, a Barcelona feminist identified as Inma asserted that rape had a broader definition than forced intercourse, and that it pointed more generally to a machismo in Spanish society that violently oppressed women: "rape is not only the aggression that takes place in the street," she stated. "It is all the aggression that occurs against women, from the insults on the sidewalk to the disguised rape that takes place in marriage."[7] Feminists were angry that victims and not rapists suffered social stigma—in one particularly sad case, a child victim of rape was expelled from school because administrators feared that she would be a bad influence on her peers. They also railed against cultural commentary that treated rape as a joke, as when a Barcelona newspaper printed popular cartoonist Chumy Chumez's quip: "When I learn that someone has raped a fourteen-year-old girl, I'm envious, truly. I know that this may not sit well with some people, but I say what I think. To me, rape seems a good thing from eight to fourteen."[8] Perhaps unsurprisingly given this social context, feminist statistics showed that 80 percent of rapes in Spain went unreported and that even when women did report rapes, criminal investigations were rarely productive.[9]

Though sexual violence, unlike intimate partner violence, *was* criminalized, it was legally classified as a misdemeanor and carried negligible penalties. Moreover, the legal definition of "rape" also made prosecuting the crime a challenge. A 1978 *New York Times* article for instance recounted the story of one woman who, though she reported her rape and a medical exam revealed semen in her vaginal canal, was determined to have an intact hymen, which meant that under Spanish law she was still a virgin and so had not, in fact, been raped.[10] In addition, sexual violence was still only criminalized outside of marriage: marital rape only became illegal in 1989, and the terms of Spanish rape law were such that even then, Spain's Supreme Court ruled in 1992, to qualify as rape a spousal sexual assault had to be violent, indicating that the victim had not been able to freely choose whether to engage in sexual activity.[11]

The legal separation of intimate partner violence and sexual violence had important consequences for how both were legally defined, evident in part by the much later criminalization of marital rape, as well as by the fact that intimate partner violence protections did not explicitly extend to women who had been raped by their partners until the 2000s. In 1978, the legal environment surrounding rape was sufficiently ill-defined that the mother of four- and six-year-old daughters who had been raped by their father "faced the possibility of contempt of court" for refusing his requests for visitation.[12] That rape stained the reputation of victims, that culturally speaking rape was a joke, that family affairs were considered private, that divorce was illegal, that men retained the right to full custody under Spanish law, even as abusers and rapists—each of these factors affected this mother's inability to get legal separation from her abuser and protect her children from abuse. Orantes's own sad fate in the 1990s seems similar, though she was divorced: she also could not fully escape her marriage or prevent visitations, despite her husband's history of abuse and despite her fears that he was, or would soon be, raping their daughters.

Feminists fought these injustices with anti-rape campaigns and campaigns to raise awareness of intimate partner violence, and included stronger protections for intimate partner violence victims in their platforms along with demands for citizenship reforms, legal divorce, and access to contraception and abortion. Spanish feminists also used the international connections they had labored to forge through their work for abortion reform to strengthen their calls for intimate partner violence reform, and they made explicit connections between their work and feminists' efforts in other nations, arguing that "the problem of battering that our sisters in England, Germany, Denmark, and the Netherlands are fighting against has similar conditions and characteristics in our country."[13] They were especially taken with the American model of rape crisis centers, and also participated in a number of international conferences where they made contact with women from nations with better developed anti-rape and anti-intimate partner violence laws, from whom they could learn how to lobby their governments and how to set up autonomous services. Of course, Spanish feminists had to adapt these lessons to Spain's cultural and political circumstances. The negligible criminalization of intimate partner violence in Spanish law proved particularly troublesome, as did the difficulties women had in escaping their abusive husbands since divorce was illegal, and regulations that made it nearly impossible for feminists to found non-governmental rape crisis centers.[14]

In 1983, when control of the Spanish government passed to the Socialist Party and President Felipe Gonzalez founded the *Instituto de la Mujer*, abortion and divorce reforms were either, as Chapter 2 discussed, in process or already cemented and left no room for institutional feminists to influence negotiations. As such, institutional feminists moved to make rape and intimate partner violence reform the cornerstone of their platform once they had the ability to participate in government policymaking. In 1986 the *Instituto* participated in a *Cortes*-sponsored task force investigating the mistreatment of women. The *Instituto*'s first action was compiling statistics about the rates of intimate partner violence in Spain, a tricky proposition given that at the time there had been few studies on intimate partner violence and women who had been abused did not self-report for reasons ranging from fear to having so normalized their abuse that they did not recognize it as intimate partner violence. In short, in Spain as in many other places, abuse was under-reported.[15]

These efforts soon benefitted from Spain's contemporaneous entry into the EEC, which gave the *Instituto* access to statistics on intimate partner violence in other nations, permitting comparisons that showed Spanish levels to be on par with the rest of Europe, though with lower levels of criminalization and government involvement. EEC membership, combined with Spain's status as a signatory on the UN's Convention on the Elimination of All Forms of Discrimination Against Women (CEDAW) and its participation in the UN's series of World Conferences on Women, gave institutional feminists more leverage to lobby for the kinds of reforms that they wanted and that other nations similarly struggling against intimate partner violence had already implemented.

And in the decade before Orantes's death, the landscape of intimate partner violence activism had indeed begun to change. Feminist agitation and international intervention combined with new media depictions of intimate partner violence to make acts of abuse seem less isolated.[16] In the legal arena, Penal Code reforms passed in 1989 classified repeated physical abuse against domestic partners and dependents as an offense punishable by one to six months in jail.[17] Lawmakers also expanded the definition of rape to include oral and anal rape as well as vaginal rape. More significantly, these laws at last criminalized rapes occurring within marriage and other romantic relationships though notably, such assaults remained outside the legal definition of intimate partner violence, so women experiencing sexual violence within relationships could not access protections meant for victims of intimate partner violence. The Cortes strengthened intimate partner violence laws in 1995 as well, increasing penalties for abusers from a one-to-six month jail term to a required jail sentence of six months to three years.[18] At the same time, and foreshadowing a shift in the government's legislative strategy, Spanish media began reporting on women's experiences of intimate partner violence, focusing on the emotional trauma that abused women bore and not on the motivations of their abusers.[19]

Yet for all this change, it was Orantes's death in 1997 that truly opened doors for activists seeking solutions to Spain's intimate partner violence problem. Indeed, the murder was to intimate partner violence reform what Bilbao had been to abortion's legalization: the resulting media frenzy helped the public understand intimate partner violence as a public health problem; it paved the way for perception of intimate partner violence as a symptom of a larger social burden that women bore; and it catalyzed support for further legal changes that feminists demanded. This helped make the problem's pervasiveness visible and also helped frame intimate partner violence as simultaneously exceptionally violent yet, in contrast with 1970s narratives, heartbreakingly widespread. Media still portrayed intimate partner violence as a spectacle, but now the public was being prompted to interpret that spectacle as a sign of social dysfunction rather than as individual tragedy. A statement by Archbishop Elias Yanes, the head of the Spanish Catholic Church, further underscores just how significant Orantes's murder was in Spain's evolving understanding of the intersections between culture and violence, as well as how complex the debate over intimate partner violence legislation was becoming. Despite his organization's historical alliance with the conservative right, Yanes proclaimed that ending intimate partner violence involved "fighting machismo."[20] Given that Yanes himself was generally sympathetic to deeply conservative parties and causes, his statement appears more an indication of the Spanish Church's changing position on the origins of intimate partner violence than an expression of personal progressive political beliefs.[21]

Late twentieth-century Spanish society, including the Spanish Church, may have become receptive to the notion of a link between intimate partner violence and machismo, but the nation's politicians and government officials nevertheless were unable to reach consensus about the source of the violence or how to use the state's resources to prevent it. In the months after Orantes's death the *Cortes* and the *Instituto* both proposed ways to tackle the problem, but a gulf remained between the two bodies' interpretations of the problem and the solutions they proposed. First, in 1998 the *Cortes* amended the Penal Code of 1995 by passing new legislation that focused on providing assistance to women abused by their romantic partners, as opposed to prior interventions that focused on either punishing the abusers or halted family violence only when it affected children and/or the elderly.[22] Though the *Cortes*'s new focus on specifically female victims constituted a major shift in how politicians legislated questions of intimate partner violence, it was a far cry from recognizing feminist arguments, like those the *Instituto* made, that intimate partner violence disproportionately affected women, and that the Spanish state too was complicit in abetting these crimes by having done little historically to combat toxic notions of gender that ultimately fueled this abusive behavior.

That same year, the *Instituto* issued its Action Plan Against Intimate Partner Violence 1998–2000, which opened: "Spanish society has become increasingly aware not only of the seriousness of violence against women, but the true extent of this problem behavior. In the present day, violence against women has moved beyond being a private concern and is now regarded as an assault on society itself, an attack on the essence of democracy."[23] The Plan, in other words, was the *Instituto*'s effort to frame intimate partner violence as a problem that plagued society as a whole, not just individual women. In addition, strategically, the *Instituto* linked combating intimate partner violence with the ideal of democracy itself, a strategy that consequently put the Plan's opponents in the uncomfortable position of appearing to be anti-democracy.

The Action Plan was ultimately both a suggestion for new legislation focusing on intimate partner violence and a powerful denunciation of the government's refusal to engage in debate about the relationship between violence and machismo. The fact that the government had received 18,535 complaints of intimate partner violence in 1997 alone, the Plan's text argued, indicated that such abuses remained a significant problem. And the ninety-one Spanish women who had been murdered by their male partners so far that year proved that existing statutes designed to protect victims were ineffective. The Action Plan provided an outline for new legislation: the government should recognize that psychological abuse could be as damaging as physical; it should provide restrictions on the contact abusers had with victims; it should provide victims with more resources so they could escape their abusers. The Action Plan, in other words, called for correctives to Spain's legal code so the conditions leading to Orantes's death could not be replicated.[24]

It also provided an outline for how Spaniards should understand the problem of intimate partner violence. Intimate partner violence, according to the *Instituto*, was a failure not just of the government's inadequate enforcement of legislation and statues; it was a failure of transition-era legislation mandating equality of the sexes. For how, the document asked, could men and women be equal if men continually, and on such a large scale, deprived women of their right to live without abuse? The *Instituto* argued that such equality was impossible under the present conditions and that the government needed to also undertake measures such as educating children about gender equality and working to ban media advertisements that reinforced sexist and misogynistic stereotypes. From their perspective the government had a responsibility to institute stricter intimate partner violence laws to protect individual women from individual men, but also had a duty to protect all women from the discrimination they faced in a society that led men to feel that such abuse was justified, acceptable, and excusable.[25]

The government adopted the *Instituto*'s Action Plan, promising to follow the organization's recommendations, but this caused confusion and anger in the *Cortes* when politicians debated the extent to which the plan was useful for shaping new intimate partner violence legislation. Maria Carme Solsona i Piñol, an MP from Barcelona representing the Catalan center-right party *Convergència i Unió*, argued that it was useless. In her opinion, the government's adoption of it represented the governing Popular Party's attempts to shunt the problem of intimate partner violence aside:

> … the Action Plan against intimate partner violence that they present us today, which in principle was going to be an emergency plan to combat violence against women, is also the product of the government's hurry to pursue a problem that has caused a certain alarm in society and not a serious policy concern with putting in motion measures destined to eradicate the problem of gender violence … Of the 57 actions that the plan proposes, a simple analysis confirms that fewer

than ten percent are concrete measures that can be implemented; how the rest will be developed in the short or long term is unknown. I reiterate that, from our perspective, this seems a mere declaration of intentions, they seem more objectives than concrete actions, because many of them limited themselves to "insisting," "elaborating," "disseminating," and other rather vague terms.

In short, Solsona believed that officials adopted the Action Plan as a way to look like they were working for change while in actuality doing very little to help sufferers of intimate partner violence. To this end, she also questioned the structure of the government's financial commitment to the Action Plan, arguing that as adopted it failed to provide emergency budget support and, moreover, did not provide sufficient funds to implement the *Instituto*'s recommendations.[26]

PP representative Maria Jesus Sainz Garcia hit back against Solsona's claims, arguing that the Action Plan represented a marked departure from the previous government's failed policies and was, in fact, a true commitment to change:

> Let us recall ... that the previous administration, the Socialist administration, only created two equality plans, which lacked any section dealing specifically with family violence, and featured a mere six measures, all of these far less concrete than those in [our gender] violence plan, and of which only two came to anything. It may perhaps be difficult for this group to accept that the Partido Popular's administration had to arrive for the third plan to contain a section devoted specifically [to gender violence] and for the creation, for the first time, of a plan that emerged not in reaction to some truly bloody event, but as a result of a very clear commitment ... We believe that, as a result, the plan marks a watershed in government policy, a real commitment to a politics of equality and solidarity ...[27]

In reality, the impact of *Cortes*'s adoption of the Action Plan, unanimously passed in June 1999, fell somewhere between Solsona and Sainz Garcia's assertions. The PP's Action-Plan-inspired legislation did advance Spanish intimate partner violence policy, in that it offered solutions for victims in addition to punishments for abusers, and that it acknowledged, if implicitly, that it was most often women who suffered intimate partner violence. To this end, the policy pledged to provide "more and better protection for victims of such appalling behavior," and to criminalize "psychological violence exercised on a routine basis." It also introduced restraining orders for victims that made it easier for them to evict their abusive domestic partners.[28]

But, to the great disappointment of the *Instituto* and some independent feminists, the 1999 law stopped far short of what the *Instituto* envisioned in its Action Plan. Sexist and objectifying media representations of women and the call for more comprehensive education to combat gender inequality, for example, were discussed in committee but did not make it to the floor for the *Cortes* to debate. The law also continued to normalize the perception that sexual violence was not intimate partner violence. Normalization of the latter as purely physical violence had consequences for those women experiencing other forms of domestic abuse, evident in the ways that victims of intimate partner violence self-identified and the low rates at which they reported their abuse. Indeed, a 2003 survey of abused women showed that only 18 percent of those who had experienced sexual abuse in their relationships considered themselves victims of intimate partner violence, as compared to 80 percent who experienced physical abuse, and found that sexual intimate partner violence was the least reported form.[29] The study's authors felt the discrepancy large enough to urge further investigation into the incidence of marital rape, though they noted the difficulties of gathering accurate intimate partner violence statistics and making the crime fully visible to a public receiving messages from media and government agencies that intimate partner violence consisted of physical (and, increasingly, psychological) abuse.[30]

Feminists had succeeded in achieving criminalization of marital rape and spreading acceptance of the idea that committing to a relationship did not mean *a priori* consent to sexual acts—but they had not managed to move the government to classify sexual violence as intimate partner violence or to include it as a concern in negotiations for intimate partner violence legislation. Still more concerning for feminists was the 1999 law's silence concerning the origins of intimate partner violence and its roots in Franco-era misogyny. The law was rendered in sterile legalese that gave no sign of the issue's complexity and, though its text and tenets perhaps flirted with the idea of framing intimate partner violence as a larger social problem, the legislation ultimately treated it as a mundane matter of criminal law.

In 1999, at least, the *Instituto* failed to gain legislative concessions for its broader agenda of attacking Franco-era gender norms and the machismo it felt continued to affect Spanish social customs. However, it still moved the needle of public opinion on the causes of intimate partner violence. Media representations of the crime's true extent, the Catholic Church's response to Orantes's death, and the terms in which *Cortes* debated legislation to curb intimate partner violence all show that Spaniards were becoming more comfortable with thinking of the crime as one with gendered elements and which revealed underlying problems in Spanish society and women's experiences within it. Moreover, the Socialist opposition in the *Cortes*, the

PSOE, increasingly championed intimate partner violence legislation along the lines of what both institutional and independent feminists demanded. In 2000 and again in 2002, the PSOE sponsored comprehensive laws to fulfill feminist demands for intimate partner violence legislation that included social reform, though the ruling PP blocked them.[31]

This shift in perception of intimate partner violence in the late twentieth and early twenty-first centuries meant that even conservative politicians began committing themselves to legislation that described—even if it did not treat—intimate partner violence as a social problem. As feminist activism grew increasingly vocal and a new rash of high-profile murders took place in early 2003,[32] the *Cortes*, with the backing of the majority PP, unanimously passed the Order for the Protection of Victims of Intimate Partner Violence in July 2003. The law's explanatory preamble declared:

> Violence in the family and in particular gender-based violence is a serious problem in our society that demands a comprehensive and coordinated response by all public authorities. The situation giving rise to these forms of violence transcends the home to become a scourge that affects and involves all citizens. It is therefore essential to devise new and more effective legal instruments, technically well-articulated, that tackle from the outset any conduct that could, in the future, escalate into something more serious.[33]

In this new law, the Spanish government acknowledged that violence in the family was often "gender-based," with women suffering the most from abuse inflicted by their male partners. Later in the law's text, references to "supranational organizations (UN, Council of Europe, EU institutions)" underscore the influence that international bodies had on the legislation's architects. CEDAW's General Recommendations of 1992, for instance, made early use of the term "gender-based violence" to describe violence against women for the fact of being women, and violence that might be used against women because of the perception of women's inferiority.[34]

Lastly, the *Cortes*'s passage of a law describing intimate partner violence as "a scourge that affects and *involves* all citizens [emphasis added]" stressed that the prevalence of this kind of abuse was society's problem, with every Spaniard both impacted by and complicit in the perpetuation of such crimes against women. Legislators, by also introducing the law as an answer to the "serious problem in [Spanish] society" posed by "violence exerted in the family and, in particular, gender violence," also hinted at this violence's origins in the machismo that feminists continually decried. Yet the law itself did not provide for broad social reform of the kind feminists wanted, nor were its framers willing to entertain legal solutions for overhauling social structures perpetuating machismo, instead choosing to focus on deterring abuse by devising novel ways of punishing abusers.[35]

The 2003 law was thus at odds with how Spanish society increasingly perceived intimate partner violence. Before 1997, violence that women experienced in their intimate relationships was private: it was not publicly discussed, and the legal system treated incidents as a series of individual crimes. Orantes's death marked a turning point, and blurred the distinction between perceiving this violence as a private matter or as a public one: society talked about violence as a social problem even as legislation dealt with abuse as unique, isolated, individualized cases. Politicians and activists struggled with this disconnect between the legal and cultural perceptions of intimate partner violence, which played out in a rhetorical battle over what to call the crime of domestic abuse. To be clear, these parties did not have different definitions of what constituted intimate partner violence, but rather different opinions about how to legally assign responsibility and help victims. The term each party used to name the violence became an indicator of the strategy they promoted for eradicating it.

On the one hand, the term "gender violence," which feminists and the PSOE borrowed from European Union and United Nations contexts, reflected progressives' belief that domestic abuse was caused by persistent patriarchal repression. On the other, accepting the implication that society caused "gender violence" was at odds with the conservative push to legally categorize domestic abuse as a matter of individual criminality. For this reason, the PP and the Catholic Church used the terms "family violence" and/or "intimate partner violence" instead of "gender violence": each of these referred to the same physical crime, but carried different implications about its causes and the appropriate legal way of managing it.

Conservatives' rhetorical choice to call violence against women "family violence" or "domestic violence" stripped the crime of its gendered nature, "blurring the patriarchal component of violence in the more 'neutral' and less feminist concept of 'family violence,' in which roles of perpetrators and victims are not clearly defined." This, political scientist Emanuela Lombardo has argued, displaced blame for such abuse away from society's patriarchal foundations and onto society vaguely defined, while at the same time making violence against women more personal and individual. Conservative measures to combat the violence followed from these assumptions, such that legislation passed by the PP "privilege[d] individual rather than structure oriented actions. Measures [we]re not designed for men in general to change their attitudes. Rather, they tend to be targeted at individual women (and men) rather than at the dismantling of the patriarchal structures that provoke and maintain male domination over women."[36]

Use of the terms "family violence" and "domestic violence," at least legally speaking, also had another, more subtle consequence: it allowed proponents on the political Right to sidestep the question of Franco's legacy. These terms left less room for an alternative and possibly socially radical reading, allowed the PP and the Catholic Church to continue their doublespeak by rhetorically wrestling with the meaning of Francoism, and its possible impact on gender relations, without doing so during the parliamentary process in a concrete and legally binding way. This was likely due, at least in part, to the Catholic Church's reticence to support legislation that could disrupt nuclear family structures. The legislation that the PSOE and feminists wanted would make it easier for women to divorce their husbands—something to which the church was categorically opposed. Divorce had, of course, been legal in Spain since 1981, but it was still difficult to obtain and carried steep social costs for individuals who sought it out. Indeed, as Orantes herself discovered, securing a divorce from one's partner did not necessarily (or even often) come with the legal or financial means to disentangle one's life from a former partner's.

The Catholic Church had a vested interest in maintaining these complications. In its eyes, divorce should be granted in only the most severe intimate partner violence cases: in the Church's opinion, violent battering should be punishable by law, but was not a valid reason for women to secure separations. Indeed, the church argued that for the state to allow intimate partner violence to precipitate a divorce, the perpetrator should first be shown to have a mental disorder causing his aggression—which the use of violence against a partner did not itself prove.[37] In the Church's view, retooling the legal structure to view such aggression as motivated by society, rather than by mental illness, would undermine its fundamental understanding of intimate partner violence, and would also tear asunder established family structures. The Church thus found itself committed to condemning patriarchal family structures and speaking out against the evils of machismo as well as rejecting that these factors played a role in the prevalence of intimate partner violence.

From Domestic to Gender Violence: The Contentious Reframing of a Francoist Legacy in Twenty-First-Century Spain

The early 2000s saw a reinvigoration of intimate partner violence reform efforts, led by the *Instituto* and made possible by the Socialist PSOE's return to power. The Organic Law for Integral Protection Measures against Gender Violence

(LOMPIVG) of December 28, 2004, was a bold restating of the problem Spain faced: it recast intimate partner violence not as an isolated problem, but rather as a sign of large rents in Spain's social fabric. This law was the heir to decades of feminist work for increased protections for victims and punishments for abusers, but its conception, its formulation, and the debates it sparked did not happen in a vacuum, either. Rather, debate about the LOMPIVG occurred amidst a backdrop of uncertainty about Spain's democratic future and as Spanish society experienced collective traumas due to terrorism and mass violence. These factors necessarily impacted how Spaniards debated, formulated, and perceived the effects of the LOMPIVG both for individual citizens and for society as a whole.

Some of these traumas literally unearthed Franco-era skeletons: in the early 2000s Spaniards from across the country campaigned for the exhumation of Civil War-era mass graves.[38] This, along with new rumblings of discontent about labor used to build, and burial practices at the Francoist Civil War cemetery *Valle de los Caídos* (Valley of the Fallen) pushed discussion about the horrors of Francoism to the fore. Other sources of collective trauma, including the Basque terrorist group ETA's then-ongoing campaign of political bombings, highlighted the complicated relationship between the Spanish central government and regions seeking greater autonomy, reminded Spaniards of the deep interconnections between their nation and international politics, and increased fear and political tensions.[39] And in the deadliest terrorist attack in Spanish history, Islamic extremists bombed the Atocha train station in Madrid in March 2004, killing 191 and injuring almost 2,000.

These violent incidents, combined with social traumas lingering from forty years of Francoist repression, as well as from more contemporary anxieties like those raised by Ana Orantes's murder, shocked the Spanish public and influenced the tenor of debate about intimate partner violence and the legal remedies offered to victims. Activists supporting intimate partner violence legislation labeled Spain's intimate partner violence crisis a problem of "domestic terrorism," a choice that conjured images of both private and public abuses—the former literally in the domestic realm, the home, and the latter affecting the functioning of an entire nation. Feminists like the members of the institutional *Federación de Mujeres Progresistas* (or FMP) felt it an apt comparison, as they, along with independent feminists, believed negligent government officials were affected by the same discriminatory tendencies that also influenced the actions of abusive men. This rhetoric was not confined to the feminist sector either: major newspaper *El Mundo* echoed the phrasing "domestic terrorism" in a 2004 online information page containing facts about intimate partner violence and its prevention that was aimed at both female victims and other interested members of society.⁴⁰ This page included a comparison between independent and institutional feminists' positions about the LOMPIVG, which ran, as did the rest of the information page, under the header "domestic terrorism" and contained an image depicting a female figure inside what appears to be the crosshairs of a rifle sight.⁴¹ Politicians advocating for terrorist victims' rights similarly made comparisons between the trauma that society suffered due to terrorism and what women abused by domestic partners experienced, even suggesting that funds set aside by the Spanish government to assist victims of terrorist attacks by ETA or radical Islamic groups should help women seeking to escape abusive partners.⁴²

In December 2004, the *Cortes* passed the Organic Law for Integral Protection Measures against Gender Violence, a comprehensive gender violence law that once again redefined intimate partner violence while also restructuring penalties for abusers and providing additional avenues of assistance for those abused. For the first time, under the LOMPIVG, Spanish law defined intimate partner violence as the byproduct of long-standing social inequalities that placed women in an inferior position to men. More broadly, and perhaps more significantly, it was also the Spanish government's first step toward redefining the concept of discrimination, its origins, and its impact on women. Indeed, a later law, the Law for the Effective Equality of Men and Women, or Equality Act of March 2007, built on the foundation laid by the LOMPIVG by declaring, as feminists had argued for decades, that "full recognition of formal equality before the law, even though it [was] undoubtedly ... a decisive step, has turned out to be insufficient."⁴³ Both the LOMPIVG and the Equality Act represented a long-awaited change. As noted earlier, both institutional and independent feminists had spent decades lobbying for increased criminalization of intimate partner violence, and increased protections for abused women. This was in addition to their still longer fight to raise awareness of and end discrimination against women, as well as in addition to protests dating back to the transition period about how the equality clause of the Constitution, and subsequent amendments, fell short of guaranteeing equality of the sexes.

A confluence of factors made these laws possible. First was the election of a PSOE government that had a history of championing women's rights. Socialist deputies had supported divorce and abortion reform laws in the early post-Franco democratic period, continued to introduce intimate partner violence legislation throughout the 1990s and early 2000s, and pioneered a gender quota system for the party's MPs that became enshrined in Spanish law in 2007.⁴⁴ Its political platform in 2004 was similarly progressive, and made intimate partner violence reform the party's priority. Incoming Prime Minister José

Luis Rodríguez Zapatero, voted in following a PP electoral collapse prompted by the party's badly mismanaged public response to the 2004 Atocha bombing, promised to open his legislative agenda with a comprehensive gender violence law like those the PSOE had repeatedly introduced over the prior five years, and which the PP had vetoed. In addition, as discussed above, and as underscored by the PSOE's return to power, the Spanish public increasingly desired dramatic change in how their nation criminalized intimate partner violence and was open to thinking of the crime as rooted in historical inequalities that affected primarily women.

Unlike ratification of the Constitution and the legalization of abortion, the LOMPIVG was also a great feminist achievement, at least for institutional feminists. Passage of the law reflected nearly two decades of research, public awareness campaigns, and lobbying by the *Instituto de la Mujer*. In addition, as discussed in Chapter 3, the evolution of feminist networks that placed the *Instituto de la Mujer* in diplomatic relationships with intragovernmental bodies and other women's ministries also gave institutional feminists recourse to international recommendations on women's rights. In this instance, Spanish institutional feminists were able to successfully leverage international recommendations defining intimate partner violence as a larger social problem for legislative change within Spain.

International organizations' recommendations in fact provided the foundation for the LOMPIVG's new definition of intimate partner violence as well as for the legal solutions that the LOMPIVG provided. Indeed, the text of the law attributed its legal reasoning to international sources. Its opening section quoted the United Nations' definition of violence against women as "a manifestation of historically unequal power relations between women and men," while the subsequent section stated that the LOMPIVG "aim[ed] to meet the recommendations of international organizations." The following sentence listed eight international resolutions, reports, and treaties upon which the LOMPIVG was based. These included the Convention on the Elimination of Discrimination Against Women (CEDAW), the United Nations' Declaration on the Elimination of Violence against Women, resolutions from the Beijing World Conference on Women, a resolution from the World Health Organization, and a resolution from the United Nations' Human Rights Commission, among others.[45]

Drawing from these sources, and in a dramatic shift from prior intimate partner violence laws, the LOMPIVG named intimate partner violence a symptom of Spain's endemic discrimination against women. Such violence was, according to the LOMPIVG, "a brutal symbol of inequality persisting in [Spanish] society" and "an obstacle to the achievement of the objectives of equality." As such, it was "no longer a private concern" but rather "a clear cause of social alarm." Statements about intimate partner violence serving as a symptom of discrimination were not just confined to one sentence or one section of the LOMPIVG, but rather repeated throughout. The law's introductory and explanatory material acknowledged again and again, and in a variety of phrasings, that the prevalence of intimate partner violence was but one manifestation of discrimination against women, and that such discrimination prevented Spain from realizing true equality. For the first time, Spanish law unambiguously attributed the prevalence of intimate partner violence not to individual men, but to flaws within Spanish society that allowed the perpetuation of discrimination and inequality.[46]

Creation of the LOMPIVG also initiated a shift in how Spanish law understood discrimination more generally by explaining how the existence of intimate partner violence prevented women from exercising the rights guaranteed them by the Spanish Constitution. The LOMPIVG's second paragraph invoked the Constitution to imply that the existence of intimate partner violence violated "Article 15" of the document, which guaranteed "the right of everyone to life and to physical and moral integrity, without under any circumstances being subjected to torture or inhuman or degrading treatment or punishment." A subsequent section was more explicit: "Public authorities cannot be oblivious to gender violence, which constitutes one of the most flagrant attacks on fundamental rights such as freedom, equality, life, security and non-discrimination proclaimed in our Constitution." This, in combination with its stance that intimate partner violence represented inequalities in Spanish society, positioned the crime as a manifestation of flaws in Spanish culture that needed correction in order for women to gain the full equality offered by the Constitution.[47]

Later laws built on the LOMPIVG's conception of discrimination by extending the idea of corrections necessary for equality beyond intimate partner violence. The Equality Act, for example, explained that there existed instances in which "inequality ... [could not] be remedied by the mere formulation of the principle of legal or formal equality." For instance, it described intimate partner violence cases where judges and government officials neglected to intervene on behalf of abused women even when Spanish law provided for such intervention. The Equality Act mandated that "all public authorities reverse" inequalities like these, and moreover "ensure[d] constitutional legitimacy" for "the formulation of ... unequal right[s] in women's favor." Its premise was that women's struggles to realize their legal rights to equality had been neglected: Spanish society had been too intent on creating legislative reform to recognize that such reform would not help women without concurrent cultural change. It also posited that inequalities "in women's favor" could balance out long-standing inequalities in men's favor, and therefore actually give women the equality to which they were legally entitled. To this end, the Equality Act included provisions such as those mandating that businesses over 250 employees implement gender mainstreaming, provided greater maternity and paternity leave so that childbearing would do less harm to women's careers, and enshrined into law the quota system for political parties that the PSOE had practiced for decades. This represented a new legal approach to guaranteeing women's equality: instead of merely stating that men and women were equal under the law, the Equality Act advocated and indeed required social changes so women could actually achieve it.[48]

Significantly, though the Spanish government's redefinition of intimate partner violence and discrimination was revolutionary for Spain, organizations from which it drew guidance were less impressed. First, the LOMPIVG provided a narrower definition of gender violence than international recommendations suggested. Where the UN used the term "gender-based violence" to encompass a whole host of crimes against women, of which intimate partner violence was only one, Spain restricted its definition of "gender violence" to intimate partner violence. The LOMPIVG thus conflated the two, leaving no room for gender violence to include other forms of violence against women like sex trafficking, female genital cutting, or coerced sex work. CEDAW noted the oversight at its July 2004 meeting, calling it "regrettable that [Spain's proposed] new Organic Law targeted only intimate partner violence" and encouraging Spain to broaden its approach before the bill's passage later that year.[49]

Moreover, the LOMPIVG's narrow definition of intimate partner violence also excluded LGBT couples and men abused by female partners. The law specifically stated: "[t]he purpose of this Law is to act against violence that, as a manifestation of discrimination, the situation of inequality and the power relations of men over women, is exercised over them by those who are or have been their spouses or of those who are or have been linked to them by similar relationships of affection, even without cohabitation," a definition which, by specifying its application to violence exercised because of male-on-female power differentials, explicitly excluded same-sex couples.[50] Prior intimate partner violence legislation *had* protected gay couples, yet when the LOMPIVG strengthened the existing statutes it only extended the new protections to women. Feminists' desire to align Spain with mainstream Western European political ideals regarding women's rights—

in this case, by terming intimate partner violence "gender violence" and defining it as male violence directed against women which aligned Spain's position on the issue with that of international bodies like the EU and the UN—had the unintended consequence of stalling progress on LGBT rights within Spain.

Independent feminists similarly opposed the LOMPIVG. An *El Mundo* internet forum published in June 2004 presented arguments from both institutional and independent feminists about the desirability of the LOMPIVG, which was at that time still under debate. First, independent feminists, represented by *Mujeres para Democracía* (MD), objected to how the federal government sought to legislate intimate partner violence abuses. Echoing their own complaints from two decades earlier of an *Instituto*-led effort to monopolize the fight for women's rights in Spain, these feminists argued that the federal government had overstepped its bounds by not consulting more closely on the LOMPIVG with Spain's Autonomous Communities, many of which already had intimate partner violence legislation that they feared the LOMPIVG might overwrite or conflict with. Perhaps remembering the chaos and frustrations that had arisen in the 1980s from the *Instituto*'s decentralized structure, institutional feminists, represented by FMP president Enriqueta Chicano, dismissed independent feminists' concerns. Instead, she argued that the scope of the intimate partner violence crisis necessitated "comprehensive measures that [would] have an effect on powers ... delegated to municipalities and Autonomous Communities, [measures that] unless they possess legal weight will be impossible to enforce."[51]

Independent feminist critics of the LOMPIVG also objected to its contents. Where institutional feminists defended the law as having "pedagogical value" for society and as helping to facilitate a social evolution, independent feminists condemned it for lacking practical solutions. The law, they argued, had "insufficient protective measures" and ignored the possibilities offered by technology like tracking bracelets for abusers, it created legal "ghettos" for women by hearing intimate partner violence cases in specialized courts, it still "lack[ed] measures to expedite separation and divorce proceedings," and its accompanying budget was short on both funding and detail. More damningly, MD declared the LOMPIVG unconstitutional and "barbaric" because of its exclusion of abused men and gay couples.[52]

Institutional feminists won the battle over the LOMPIVG: it passed in December 2004, went into effect in January 2005, and remains in effect—though as shown in the next chapter, the law subsequently faced a long series of obstacles and its impact still fell far short of feminists' hopes even a decade after its passage. Yet the debate between feminist factions was another revealing glimpse of how women's rights activists fought for the right to define and protect women's rights. Feminist factions used the same rhetoric—speaking of gender inequalities, female oppression, *machista* society—to advance their different and at times competing agendas. Independent feminists displayed intersectional tendencies and institutional feminists remained focused solely on the plight of straight women.

Remarkably, after the LOMPIVG's passage feminists also began to face competition from conservative activists who appropriated feminist rhetoric as a way of pushing not for liberation of women, but rather for restrictions on women's rights. Whereas Spanish feminists saw and continue to see intimate partner violence reform as existing within a spectrum of women's rights reforms that constrain abusive men and prove liberating for women, Catholic conservatives have espoused a rather different view. The PP, in conjunction with the Catholic church and *Foro Español de la Famili*a, the Spanish equivalent of Focus on the Family, has sought to curtail women's rights, especially the right to abortion, and they have done so by framing abortion as a form of gender violence and as something that hurts women in part because, they claim, it is *not* liberating.

In a series of 2008 interviews, including a speech given on behalf of the PP to the Congress of Deputies (the lower house of Spanish Parliament), Benigno Blanco, the president of the Spanish Forum on the Family, argued that legalized abortion "ha[d] become a form of gender violence."[53] In his opinion, abortion was bad for all parties. He asserted that legalizing abortion gave women the sole power to decide whether to end a pregnancy or not, a process which would render men "not responsible for [their] sexual conduct," and so give men license to misbehave sexually. But the real problem, in Blanco's eyes, was not the effect legalizing abortion had on men. Instead, he was concerned that putting the decision in women's hands encouraged men to treat women badly—in his estimation legalized abortion was "a *machista* solution" that would create a culture encouraging men to behave irresponsibly and to harm women in the process. Blanco's rhetoric played to men's fears of liberated self-determining women while also claiming to be sensitive to women's vulnerability, emotional and otherwise.

Conclusion

There is little that is clear-cut about gender, intimate partner violence, and sexual violence legislation in Spain in general, and the 2004 Gender Violence Law in particular. On the one hand, the law is a product of international pressures that operated during the late 1970s and early 1980s, and which have continued to operate in subsequent decades through the political and legislative conduits of Spain's ties to international bodies such as the UN and EU. Notably, the consequence-laden base assumption underlying discourse in late twentieth- and early twenty-first-century Spain regarding the origins and nature of Spanish gender violence—that violence springs from a deficient society and culture—owed much to CEDAW documents, and CEDAW influence continued thereafter, as when the organization condemned the insufficiency of Spain's 1989 Penal Code reform.

On the other hand, the way in which Spaniards adapted and internalized this concept, and the consequences that have resulted, reflect anxieties and impulses, as well as a history, that is particular to Spain. Spanish society for the most part accepted CEDAW doctrine that culture was and remains a prevailing factor in enabling pervasive trends of violence against women. Such adoption proved easy for a people eager to move past its dictatorial past, the act itself serving as a way for Spain to self-represent as post-Francoist, as a means of finding redemption. As the issue of intimate partner violence reform grew less controversial over the years—that is, as all segments of society came to recognize it as a problem and to call for reform or legislation to help abused women—rhetoric surrounding more specific changes became highly charged, again in ways that point to Spain's unique Francoist legacy. It was (and still is) generally agreed in Spain that gender violence is a social problem, but few have agreed on the solution, and in debating this question, groups spanning the political spectrum have invoked the fearful specters of Franco, totalitarianism, and fascism, warning especially that their opponents' proposals will lead to repression and—naturally—Francoist backsliding. Spaniards have certainly internalized the notion that gender violence is a cultural problem to be solved, and that domestic abuse harms not just the individual but society as a whole. But Spain's wish to move past the legacy and history of Francoism is just as sharply manifest.

As Spanish authorities in the 1990s and 2000s accepted that intimate partner violence was a cultural problem, they also moved to integrate intimate partner violence legislation into measures focused on eliminating discrimination, again drawing upon CEDAW theories, and to implement a number of programs that reflected the United Nations' strategy of gender mainstreaming in the workplace as a means of fomenting the social changes necessary to ensure the elimination of gender-based discrimination.

Yet, once again, practical application of these European Union—and United Nations-authored measures in Spain—produced complications, as, albeit unintentionally, reforms helped obscure both the nature of intimate partner violence and the blame for its perpetuation. Legislation and popularly circulating social perceptions have combined to obscure sexual violence as a problem, starting with the separate legal classifications of rape and intimate partner violence in the 1970s. That discursive construction of intimate partner violence in Spain long focused on battery to the exclusion of other forms of violence, including rape, but also psychological abuse, made it difficult at best for Spanish society and abused women alike to define the extent of the nation's domestic abuse problem and to fully understand the ways in which women have experienced intimate partner violence. Unsurprisingly, this invisibility has only preserved Spain's domestic abuse problem, despite government and feminist intentions and efforts to the contrary. Moreover, in this labyrinth of layered, multiple interpretations of and definitions for a collection of insufficiently fixed terms including "gender violence," "intimate partner violence," "sexual violence," "maltreatment," "discrimination" and, of course, "feminism," perhaps most corrosive is that conservatives who desire a return to Franco-era norms have found ways to manipulate "feminist" rhetoric to support policies undermining feminist demands and, indeed, the legislative advances that have occurred.

5

Conclusions

"La Lucha Continúa," the Struggle Continues*

On International Women's Day 2018, in an effort jointly organized by Spain's labor unions and feminist organization Comisión 8M, 5.3 million female laborers and hundreds of thousands of additional supportive women and men participated in marches and work strikes across the country in an effort to draw attention to women's inequality in Spain.[1] An accompanying manifesto circulated by 8M, and reprinted or excerpted by various major international as well as domestic periodicals, listed organizers' demands and justifications for such spectacle.[2] Activists pointed to domestic problems like the rate of abuse against women by their domestic partners, which they described as a form of "male chauvinist violence" persisting in great part due to the state's negligence prosecuting the crime; they bemoaned the pay gap between men and women, which national newspapers reported was 13 percent; they insisted on the recalculation of state pensions so domestic care work qualified; and they requested that the government fully implement a law it had passed in 2007, which guaranteed equality in education. To protest these issues and more, women participating in International Women's Day events pledged to engage in a broadly conceived strike—not just in the union-sponsored "labor strike" for which they would stop

---

*Through the first decades of the twenty-first century, variations of the phrase "La lucha continua", or "the struggle continues," have appeared near-continuously in feminist statements, as well as outside accounts of feminist action, feminist-inspired legislation, and the fight for women's rights in general. In context, the phrase carries at least two meanings, which are not exclusive of one another: first, that the feminist struggle for women's rights remains far from over; and second, that feminism remains active in this fight and continues to amass victories. For such usage, see for example, Enrique Stuyck, "La lucha feminista continua despues del 8-M," *El Periódico de Catalunya*, March 11, 2020, https://www.elperiodico.com/es/entre-todos/participacion/la-lucha-feminista-continua-despues-del-8-m-198748 [accessed December 20, 2022]; "Feminismo 2022: La lucha continúa—Tribuna de Cristina Narbona, Presidenta del PSOE y vicepresidenta primera del Senado", *psoe.es*, March 10, 2022, https://www.psoe.es/actualidad/entrevistas-actualidad/feminismo-2022-la-lucha-continua/ [accessed December 20, 2022]; "Y el 9 qué? El 9 la lucha continúa," *UGTComunicaciones.es*, March 9, 2020, https://www.ugtcomunicaciones.es/wordpress/y-el-9-que-el-9-la-lucha-continua/ [accessed December 20, 2022].

work for several hours in the mid-afternoon, but also a "care strike" wherein they would stop domestic work for the day and a 24-hour "consumption strike" that would stop female buying activity.[3]

The manifesto also made clear that, as much as ever, Spanish activists continued to see themselves as part of a global community of female activists and their allies. International Women's Day, as they saw it, was truly international. Spanish women partly planned to march in solidarity with women from other countries who would also be participating in similar marches and strikes.[4] An article that ran the following day in the leading left-leaning Spanish national newspaper *El País* drew parallels between the 8M demonstration and the historic Icelandic women's strike of 1975, which had led to Icelandic society reimaging how it could better enshrine women's equality and incorporate women into all aspects of Icelandic life. *El País* interpreted these parallels as deliberate and understood the 8M demonstrations as Spanish feminists' attempts to force a similar moment in Spain.[5] Moreover, though some of 8M's demands targeted uniquely Spanish social, political, and economic ills, others transcended national boundaries. Indeed, meeting some of these demands, such as a call for the Spanish government to ratify International Labor Organization (ILO) Convention 189, would require the nation's politicians to engage with international networks as well. Others, including a plea for global leaders to take the threat of climate change seriously, expanded not only the range of marchers' activism on a global scale, but also its scope, identifying as a feminist issue something that affects the entire world's population.

Yet the strike as organizers conceived it, and as news outlets reported it, was not necessarily the strike as most Spaniards themselves understood it. Journalists who asked women's opinions about the protest received a range of answers about what women thought the protests were for, whether they intended to participate and why or why not, and what they hoped the strike would accomplish. Some, like twenty-year-old university student Carmen Blanco, expressed unqualified support and a clear idea of their desired outcomes. Blanco planned to participate because she wanted greater representation of women in university life as well as "a broader approach to sex education, one that is feminist, that talks about consent, that will teach men that no means no and that silence does not necessarily mean yes."[6] Others did not define how they thought "inequality" manifested, or seemed ambivalent about the strikes. For example Valencian pop star Bebe, who had on previous occasions denied being a feminist, voiced "support [for] the movement and the feminist struggle," albeit with reservations. Bebe's primary concern was that the strike might alienate men, who she believed activists needed to include if they were to meet with success.[7] And an *El País* article about eight women who did not plan to attend the strike found that they either wanted to participate but could not afford to take time off, or believed that the planned protests and strikes were not the right method for addressing inequality. The majority of responses, whether they agreed with the strikes or not, reflected the latter belief.[8]

Politicians, too, differed in their degree of support which, significantly, broke down not by gender identity or religious belief, but rather by political party affiliation. Left-wing parties supported feminism and the marches, while conservative parties waffled on feminism and criticized the marches. Female politicians from the *Partido Popular* (PP) and from *Ciudadanos*, both right of center, refused to support the strike, while male members of the center-left *Partido Socialista Obrera Español* (PSOE) and the anti-capitalist *Podemos* echoed feminist activists' own rhetoric calling for autonomy. Nor did political parties' support hinge on the opinions of the Catholic Church. Despite the long-standing association between conservative political parties and Catholicism, official religious response within Spain varied and does not seem to have influenced parties' decisions to support or disavow the strike. Though at least one member of the episcopal hierarchy, the notoriously retrograde Bishop of San Sebastián, condemned the strike, at least three others supported it, with another Basque bishop, the prelate of Bilbao, even suggesting that the Virgin Mary herself would have marched.[9]

Left-wing political parties *Podemos* and PSOE, as well as some Independent politicians and government administrative officials, supported the marches, the strike, and the messaging behind the day's protests. In Barcelona, mayor Ada Colau of the *Podemos*-affiliated *Barcelona En Comú* party, and independent Parliamentary delegate Manuela Carmena vowed to strike. "Of course I will strike," said Colau, asserting that she felt "a double responsibility as a woman … and as a politician" to represent those who "would like to strike and will not be able to due to precariousness, exploitation, or fear." Carmena similarly expressed that she felt it important to strike because, as a public official, she could use her position to point out "social inequalities" that might otherwise go unobserved.[10] Echoing long-standing rhetoric of Spanish feminists who demanded greater autonomy, *Podemos* MP David Llorente tweeted that male support of the strike was "supporting women to be protagonists."[11] And right-leaning national newspaper *ABC* reported that female leaders and politicians in Toledo, in the central Spanish region of Castilla-La Mancha, also spoke in support of the strike, including the director of the region's government-sponsored *Instituto de la Mujer*, or women's bureau, Areceli Martín, who asserted that the inequality women experienced did not "arise by spontaneous generation," but rather from "a thousand-year old cultural construction" that she hoped the strike could help overturn.[12]

Meanwhile, right-wing parties insisted that they supported women's demands for equality, but either refused to endorse the strike or pledged their support while also equivocating about the strike's real meaning and its impact. The most common critiques centered on what conservatives interpreted as the strike's attacks on men and on feminists' misguided attempt to exclude men from the political decision-making process regarding women's rights. The *Partido Popular* was perhaps the most vocal in this equivocation, with party leader and Galician regional president Alberto Núñez Feijóo seeming to agree that women faced discrimination and touting his region, Galicia's, successes correcting the problem. Yet he also asserted that "[t]o think that [the strike] has been a political manifestation is, in my opinion, a lack of respect and a grave error towards women with different ideologies and thoughts who have told us that equality has not yet been achieved or that conciliation is not only a policy, but an attitude."[13] He implied that the strike divided men and women and called for greater cooperation between the sexes, with the Galician government issuing a statement that read, in part, "[r]eal equality is not going to be achieved by going against each other, but by going against the problem."[14] Miguel Tellado, general secretary of the PP in Galicia, condemned the strike in harsher terms, calling it "macho" and "elitist," while *Ciudadanos*' representative on the Madrid City Council, Begoña Villacís, who asserted in the days before the strike that "a large majority of women [did] not feel represented" by the protests, later addressed the 8M crowd to boos.[15]

These parties also argued that, contrary to feminists' claims, they had in fact made great progress working for women's rights within Spain. Indeed, Tellado asserted that not only was the strike the domain of "feminist elites, but not real women with daily problems," but that women striking in his region improperly understood the political situation surrounding their rights. Galicia, he argued, boasted Spain's smallest gender wage gap because of the combined efforts of his party and the PP. Similarly, PP's official position was that "there [was] no problem of recognition of rights, but of transferring the recognized rights to the day to day [relationships] of women and men."[16] In other words, though these parties agreed that Spanish society perhaps had more work to do to enforce policies guaranteeing women's rights, they rejected feminist protestors' demands for more legislation. This position ultimately won the day. Despite the historic nature of the strike and the groundswell of support for activists and their demands, the Spanish government's official response was to refuse new policy goals and to restate that its intention was simply to continue with political agendas they already had planned.[17]

The strike and the tensions surrounding it represent one of the latest flare-ups of a whole array of social, cultural, political, and semantic struggles with profound bearing not just on the lives and experiences of women in Spain, but also more generally on the trajectory and basic nature of Spain's democratic political culture. Rhetoric surrounding the strike—what did participating women feel they were striking for? Were these women feminist, and who qualifies as a feminist? Who supported the strike, and why, and under what circumstances?—is and has been a crucial part of the complex battle over defining feminism in twenty-first-century Spain.

Moreover, the strike also underscores that renegotiation of women's rights has historically sprung up and continues to surface at moments of intense political turmoil in Spain, including the transition from democracy to dictatorship in the early 1930s with the fall of the Second Republic and the rise of the Franco dictatorship, and then the transition from dictatorship to democracy sparked by Franco's death in November 1975. Indeed, 2018's strike coincided with a renewed period of dissatisfaction with the Spanish democracy. This dissatisfaction was marked by ongoing unrest in Spain and a moment of constitutional crisis exacerbated by Prime Minister Mariano Rajoy's low approval ratings and difficulties forming coalitions, his attempts to alter some constitutional agreements and also ignore calls for agreed-upon renegotiation of constitutional tenets, and the Catalan crisis. In this vein, the scheduled demonstrations were a response to what feminists and progressive activists interpret as the failure of Spain's democratic government to protect constitutionally guaranteed women's rights and a failure to enforce legal statutes guaranteeing women's autonomy and safety. Notably, despite having been in effect for well over a decade the Organic Law for Integral Protection Measures against Gender Violence (LOMPIVG) of 2004 had not stopped 988 women in Spain from being murdered by their current or former partners, nor did it prevent an average of 166,000 reported cases of gender violence per year as of 2019.[18]

"Is This the Modern and Progressive Spain?": Political Advances and Setbacks in the Spanish Women's Rights Struggle after 2007

The Socialist-led government that had sponsored the LOMPIVG lasted until 2011 and oversaw the passage of several other pieces of landmark women's rights legislation. Perhaps most notably, the Zapatero administration saw a new and wide-ranging Gender Equality Law passed in 2007. Under this law, which featured an extensive preamble that amply detailed the many ways the law intentionally reflected EU gender equality directives, every branch and level of government was called upon to ensure that women and men have equal access to education, to the labor market, to career advancement, and to the full range of Spain's public services, particularly social insurance programs. On paper, the law's provisions covered a dizzying array of public and private aspects of Spain's socio-political fabric: it called on the state and regional governments to promote access to gainful work opportunities for women in rural areas; it required RTVE to use only non-sexist language in its programming and recruit women to positions of responsibility in the national broadcasting service; and, in order to promote a more equitable division of household responsibilities, it instituted a legally guaranteed period of paternity leave for new fathers. However, like the *Instituto de la Mujer*'s Action Plan Against Intimate Partner Violence (1998), in practice this law's stipulations were in many instances so vaguely worded as to be toothless: article 14, for instance, nebulously charged authorities with "cooperat[ing] ... [among themselves] ... in applying the principle of equal treatment and opportunity," and, "establish[ing] measures to ensure proper mediation of men and women's work and personal/family life, and encourage shared responsibility for care of the family and the home."[19]

Meanwhile, as has previously been noted in this book's introduction, after the arrest of fourteen individuals in Barcelona late that same year—2007— on charges of having participated in an illegal abortion ring, the PSOE also proposed a reform to existing abortion restrictions that led to a new law expanding abortion rights in 2010. Not only did this new law allow women to demand an abortion for any reason before the fourteenth week of pregnancy, as noted previously, but it also allowed minors to get abortions without parental notification if their safety was at stake.[20] However, instead of quelling tensions about abortion's legality that the Barcelona trial made visible, the loosened restrictions stoked controversy between those, like feminists, who wanted further liberalization, and conservatives, who wanted restrictions greater even than what had existed before the 2010 law came into effect.

Conservatives and conservative organizations like *Hazte Oír*, which reported regularly on international events and maintained relations with like-minded organizations abroad, saw themselves as part of an international anti-abortion community and mobilized these connections in their response to the 2010 abortion law. In particular, *Hazte Oir* and other organizations like Spanish Right to Life organized and participated in anti-abortion marches that either relied on international attendees or formed part of larger days of action that coincided with other marches happening in cities around the globe. Gádor Joya of Right to Life, for example, concluded his 2010 remarks charging President Zapatero with a disregard for human life by calling on fellow anti-abortion activists to participate in an international March for Life; news reports noted the number of international participants that such marches in Madrid drew.[21]

In line with this foreign-facing strategy, conservatives also eagerly followed a series of cases on which the European Court of Human Rights (ECHR) was ruling at the time, including a landmark case in 2010 when three Irish women sued Ireland because they believed the nation's restrictive abortion laws violated their human rights. British and Irish anti-abortion groups were especially vocal in their opposition to the women's case, and Spanish anti-abortion groups translated and published their comments for Spanish readership. Consideration of which articles and content they chose to reprint, and the additional commentary they provided, provides still further insight into Spanish conservatives' approaches to the abortion struggle in the wake of the setback they had just faced domestically. On the one hand, they believed that an ECHR ruling in favor of the women "would be a step towards establishing an internationally recognized 'human right' to abortion," and worried that such a decision would undermine the court's authority as "a ruling in favor of abortion would make nonsense of the aim of the Court which is to uphold and enforce the rights of all human beings."[22] They were consequently greatly relieved when the ECHR instead ruled against the plaintiffs. Anti-abortion activists interpreted this ruling as justification for their continued opposition against Zapatero's newly passed abortion law. As one internet commenter wrote, echoing the words of Spanish Forum on the Family president Benigno Blanco from two years prior, "What a setback for feminists—they, who had it all so well organized and manipulated. Sorry, it cannot be stated more clearly. There is NO human right to abortion. This shows the insanity of the new Spanish law that recognizes abortion as a right, which is a real atrocity."[23]

This was more than just good news for conservatives—it was ammunition. Conservatives battled their pro-choice foes at home and abroad using such decisions by international bodies, along with the actions of NGOs as tools in their fight against abortion. But conservatives also mobilized international arguments in a more subtle way: appropriation. From the late 2000s through the 2010s, Spanish conservatives have drawn on anti-abortion arguments made by other independent activists. Some of this influence has been more explicit—conservative groups have, for instance, often translated and directly quoted from

American websites and prominent twentieth-century American feminists who opposed abortion.[24] Some of this influence has been less direct, as when Spanish conservatives have echoed American and European talking points in such a way that the connections between activists are lost or obscured. This is only reinforced by the specifically Spanish context in which conservatives have made their arguments: no matter the parallels to rhetoric pervasive in other nations, conservatives in Spain have strategically tailored anti-abortion arguments for their primary audience, the Spanish public.

One of the most often-argued positions that Spanish conservatives deployed at this time stressed the dangers that abortion posed to women. Anti-abortion activists articulated this in two ways. First, they detailed the health consequences of receiving abortions—consequences that extended not just to the mother and fetus, but to the whole of society. One article circulated by *Hazte Oír* in 2008, for example, argued that abortions done to save a woman's mental health had the opposite effect: it claimed that "80 percent of women who undergo an abortion suffer from depressive symptoms," and stressed that "the frequency of … suicide attempts is 40 percent." It also listed other signs of "Post-Abortion syndrome," including "disorders of sex (40 percent), drug abuse, particularly among adolescents (30), behavioral disturbances (60) and irritability (70)."[25] Similarly, in December 2008 the President of the Institute for Family Policy voiced concerns about Zapatero's new abortion law, stating that it "would be a disaster … in which all of society (which is deprived of a child and is faced with mothers with psychological problems) loses."[26]

A second frequently used argument held that abortion was dangerous to women because of the control it gave authorities over her body and her life. In this vein, the director of the Life Foundation in Spain, Manuel Cruz, had argued in 2007 that the government's allowing legalized abortion for a rape victim was "akin to 'raping her anew,'" and that family members helping her obtain the procedure were participants in her violation.[27] In his 2010 response to Spain's newly passed abortion law, Gádor Joya equated abortion to slavery, saying that "within 10, 20, or 30 years" abortion might "be considered by a majority of society, as evil and painful as today we see slavery."[28] Joya also claimed the government was hiding findings about the negative effects of the morning-after pill, which he considered abortive, and as such were experimenting on and endangering women by allowing them to take a "hormonal bomb."[29] Rajoy's Minister of Justice, Alberto Ruiz-Gallardón, in fact defended the PP's proposed restrictions on abortion in 2010 by asserting that a woman who received an abortion was a "victim."[30] Lastly, opponents of abortion used a strategy akin to Benigno Blanco's invocations of Francoism's long shadow, claiming that the procedure constituted "structural gender violence on women," with the government, and not women's romantic partners, as the abusive party—in other words, a leveraging of rhetoric appropriated from feminists and the Left to advance their own conservative agenda via fearmongering.[31]

Meanwhile, amid all of this conservative pushback, the economic crisis of 2008 had already greatly complicated the task of governing for the PSOE, and in the general election held one year after the socialists' controversial abortion law, in November 2011, a disillusioned and economically battered Spanish public voted overwhelmingly for the PP, giving party leader Mariano Rajoy a record-breaking absolute majority and handing the PSOE its worst election defeat since the 1970s.[32] For their part, notwithstanding the context of global recession in which the election took place, Rajoy and his party interpreted the result as a mandate to tackle more than the nation's economic troubles—they also initiated a rollback of feminist policies, beginning with abortion.

Rajoy, along with his Minister of Justice Alberto Ruíz Gallardón, vowed to reinstitute restrictions on abortion enshrined in Spain's original law in 1985 legalizing the procedure. The proposed restrictions proved deeply unpopular and ultimately the PP's attempt to pass them failed when, in 2014, Rajoy withdrew the proposal for "lack of consensus" after considerable public outcry; Ruiz-Gallardón, the restrictions' chief proponent, subsequently resigned.[33] With that said, the PP did manage more restrictions in 2015, passing a law requiring minors that get parental consent for abortions.[34]

The PP also expanded the *Instituto de la Mujer*'s responsibilities, and in doing so compromised the body's ability to fulfill its original mission of working to end discrimination against women. Long an autonomous body, the PP's changes made the *Instituto* subordinate to the State Secretariat for Social Services and Equality and the Equal Opportunities General Management. In addition to handing administration of the *Instituto* to these other bodies, the PP also merged it with the *Dirección General para la Igualdad de Oportunidades* and altered its mission from focusing on discrimination against women to working toward the elimination of all kinds of discrimination: "on the grounds of birth, sex, racial or ethnic origin, religion or ideology, sexual identity, sexual orientation, age, disability, or any other personal or social condition or circumstance."[35] As an independent feminist report to the European Commission noted, the "extended scope" of the new body had the potential to "less[en] attention paid to issues of gender equality."[36]

Feminists protested both of these changes, but opposition to the Rajoy's proposed abortion restrictions had staying power. In the days leading up to the International Women's Day marches in 2018, politicians and commentators attributed the demonstrations' size and popularity in part to the lasting feminist outcry to Rajoy and Gallardón's thwarted abortion restrictions. One PSOE spokesman, Ángeles Álvarez, voiced just this sentiment in the days before the 2018 event. He proclaimed that feminist demonstrations against Rajoy and Gallardón's abortion restrictions "marked a before and after in the women's movement in Spain"—in other words, that feminist ire about abortion created a turning point that made the 2018 International Women's Day possible.[37] Similarly, an *El País* commentator positing reasons why the march had a historic turnout also pointed to the PP's 2010 proposal to restrict abortion, also arguing that feminist demonstrations against the law were important for mobilizing opposition not only to Rajoy's policies, but to discrimination against women in general.[38]

Abortion, however, was not the only feminist issue motivating activists in the women's march. 8M brought feminists' diverse complaints about labor regulations, abortion restrictions, sexual assault and rape legislation, and intimate partner violence under one umbrella while continuing to also advocate not solely individual pieces of intervention but rather a society-wide reckoning with systemic, structural discrimination faced both by Spanish women and women across the globe.

In addition to their ardent defense of abortion rights, Spanish feminists remained concerned about the prevalence of intimate partner violence (IPV) within Spain—this even as IPV in Spain has been on the decline overall in the early twentieth century and Spain's rate of IPV is either level with or lower than most other European countries. In the days before the 2018 International Women's Day marches, Castellón feminist group *Femme Força* created a public art installation titled "Art Against Domestic Violence." The installation consisted of a "makeshift graveyard by the sea" containing 739 crosses, one for each Spanish woman who had been murdered by a domestic partner since 2007. That *Femme Força* termed this "sexist violence" illustrates one reason why feminists found its continuation troubling: they understood it as a reflection of a larger unsavory dynamic between men and women in Spanish society.[39]

Moreover, though, according to *El País*, overall rates of IPV declined from 2012 to 2014, both 2016 and 2017 saw increases in the number of reported incidents.[40] Purificación Causapié, member of the Madrid City Council, in fact promoted the International Women's Day marches by arguing that one reason to support the demonstrations was to bring attention to IPV, mentioning specifically that "every 40 minutes a woman makes a report for having suffered gender violence in Madrid."⁴¹

In addition, though feminist activists had been calling for a change to Spanish rape laws since the end of the Franco dictatorship, as noted in Chapter 4, a verdict in the high-profile *La Manada* case also brought conversation about rape and sexual assault to the forefront of feminist political issues on the eve of the strike. The *La Manada* trial galvanized twenty-first-century institutional and independent feminists alike to fight anew for change in the legal definition of rape, accompanied by largest and most visible extended feminist demonstration since the Bilbao Abortion trial in the early days of Spain's democratic transition. Twenty-first-century activists argued, as their predecessors had, that rape laws needed to change to reflect that not all rapes fit the profile of violent sexual offenses. The *La Manada* case perfectly encapsulated feminists' arguments.

On the night of July 7, 2016 in Pamplona, Spain, revelers packed the streets to celebrate the town's famous San Fermín festival, known as a raucous party to which people travel from across the globe. Rape and sexual assault are common at San Fermín; multiple such crimes are reported every year, so many that a group of Basque feminists called *Gora Iruñea* roams the city during the festival, threatening violence against men seeking to take advantage of women enjoying the party. Feminist organizations routinely demonstrate at San Fermín and protest on behalf of the festival's female sexual assault victims.⁴²

This particular year five male friends calling themselves *La Manada* or "the wolfpack" planned to attend the festival and find a woman who would have group sex with them. They took their mission seriously, even "practicing" their plan on a woman in the weeks prior to the festival. At the festival itself, they found an intoxicated young woman, attempted to convince her to have sex with them in an alley, and then herded her into the hallway of a hotel, where they took turns penetrating her before stealing her phone, leaving her alone and distraught. The men delighted in what they considered to be their conquest, the girl informed local police of her rape, and authorities duly filed criminal charges.⁴³

In 2016, however, the rape accusation hit a new nerve with feminists frustrated that their long-standing cry for attention to the rate of sexual assault was not addressed by new government policy protecting victims and providing stricter punishments. When the accusations against *La Manada* and details of the case became public, feminists across Spain immediately responded in support of the victim, participating not just in demonstrations both in San Fermín and across Spain, but also on social media platforms like Twitter. Women rallied around the victim, calling for "sororidad," a term that references both sisterhood and solidarity, and insisting that female protesters were now "the wolfpack" come to rally around its victimized member.[44] Protests were so large and so visible that international media from around Europe ran stories in addition to Spain's own.[45] Public opinion clearly showed substantial support for the victim, and an overwhelming belief that *La Manada* were guilty.[46] However, the "wolfpack's" victim was also forced to endure a degree of public scrutiny that bordered on harassment: footage of the assault that the woman's assailants had taken on their mobile phones was released by the media without her permission, her identity was revealed before the trial—again without permission—and a private investigator hired by one of the accused trailed her, seeking to prove that she had quickly gone back to living a normal, seemingly untraumatized life, and so cast doubt on the veracity of her claims.[47]

La Manada went to trial in 2018 and were sentenced to nine years of prison time for the lesser charge of sexual abuse rather than rape. The presiding panel of judges based this decision on the fact that under Spanish law, as noted in Chapter 4, a rape sentence required the use of violence when the crime was committed. Moreover, even this far more conservative verdict was contested, as only two of the panel's three judges agreed that *La Manada* had committed sexual abuse. The third judge called for a near-complete acquittal, believing that the only convictable offense committed was one count of minor larceny, since one of the five men had stolen the victim's phone after the assault. The victim, this judge insisted, had seemed quiet and compliant in the footage her assailants had taken on their mobile phones, and that the men likewise did not seem to have physically intimidated her or hurt her during the assault. Even a conviction for sexual abuse, he reasoned, required the objective exercise of forcible coercion, not merely that one or both parties perceive the situation to be coercive.[48]

Feminists exploded in protest, both on and offline, when the verdict was announced. Online, an assortment of hashtags including #*Sororidad* (Women's Solidarity) and #*HermanaYoSíTeCreo* (Sister I Do Believe You) trended across Spain and abroad.[49] Offline, outraged protesters descended upon the courthouse. In addition, the verdict was announced just days before the annual International Women's Day march—the 2018 march described at the beginning of this chapter. Unsurprisingly, the organizers added a slate of demonstrations focused on the issue of rape and sexual assault against women.

8M and other feminist demonstrations were not the only sign that the electorate was tiring of PP leadership and its accompanying social and cultural legislation: elections in 2015 and 2016, though they enabled Prime Minister Mariano Rajoy and his party to continue governing, were disastrous for the

PP. Though the PP was the largest party in the 2015 general election, it did not win an absolute majority, and the fragmented nature of the results—with smaller parties winning more seats than anticipated—meant that it needed to form a coalition in order to govern. Its inability to do so led to another general election in 2016, in which the PP was able to form a governing coalition with the right-wing *Ciudadanos* or "Citizens" (C's) party. Political upheaval continued, however, and a vote of no confidence due to corruption scandals and the PP's handling of the Catalan crisis toppled Rajoy's government shortly after 8M; Rajoy also resigned from both the leadership of his party and political life in general in July 2018.[50]

Before the PSOE formed a governing coalition with *Unidos Podemos* (UP) in November 2019, Spain had four general elections in five years. Spanish elections had been affected by wildly swinging public opinion and support for diverse parties that manifested in part as a pendulum of support swinging between conservative and progressive parties. The 2019 elections in particular revealed how divided the political public had become, and the results demonstrated both the power of Spain's growing far-right and the precariousness of leftist politics, embodied in Vox's astonishing electoral gains and in the fact that though PSOE and UP formed a coalition, it has been famously tense and occasionally acrimonious.[51]

Conclusion

The 2018 International Women's Day protests in Spain serve as a lens through which we can examine long-standing tensions and understand their continuing manifestation in twenty-first-century Spanish politics and society. In recent Spanish history, moments of political tension—including but not limited to the descent into dictatorship, the transition to democracy, and 2018's uncertainty about the continued strength of the post-Franco government—have been accompanied by a period of renewed debate about women's role in society, the rights women should have, and the extent to which the government should become involved in relations between the sexes.

The intersection between Spaniards' struggle to process living in a post-fascist society and debates about women's rights and gender discrimination has influenced the shape of Spain's democracy over the past half-century since Generalissimo Francisco Franco's death and continues to do so today. Yet the sustained murmur of conversation about feminism and women's rights does not mean that Spanish feminists have been successful in achieving the rights they have desired. Nor does the seeming legislative progress. Instead, non-feminist actors and/or well-meaning male allies have co-opted both the label of feminist and, at times, feminist rhetoric, to push for restrictions on women's rights or on the passage of ostensibly "feminist" legislation that was more limited than what feminists themselves desired or were willing to recognize as feminist. In addition, since the beginning of Spain's modern feminist movement in the last years of the Franco regime, feminists themselves have lacked consensus about what it means to be feminist and about which demands qualify as feminist. The 2018 International Women's Day protests in Spain serve as one of the most recent lenses through which we can examine these long-standing tensions and understand their continuing manifestation in twenty-first-century Spanish politics and society.

Moreover, the independence crisis that raged especially forcefully in Catalonia from 2010 through the PSOE's return to power in 2019, and which remains ongoing, highlights that these tensions exist beyond the boundaries of feminist issues and debates over women's rights. Instead, debates about women's issues have reflected and continue to reflect larger political hot spots within the Spanish nation. All of this is to say, the process of constructing democratic citizenship—its structures, its responsibilities, its protections—has continued to the present day and remains ongoing. Just as scholars like Victor Pérez Díaz has argued that Spain's democratic transition lasted beyond the Constitution's ratification,[52] so I contend that the process of defining the very character of democracy in Spain remains a work in progress. This book's chapters each highlight a small segment of how this process has been negotiated to date.

Seccion Femenina, as shown in the first chapter, worked throughout the midcentury to create a version of female citizenship that could both satisfy their desires for autonomy and participation in public life while also hewing to their antifeminism and National-Catholic ideology. Significantly, the legal structures for women's economic and labor rights that the *Seccion Femenina* helped usher in during the late years of the Franco regime were, for their time, progressive though Pilar Primo de Rivera, her colleagues, and Francisco Franco himself would certainly have rejected that label.

As the Franco regime came to its close, Chapter 2 argues, feminists battled for legislative concessions including equal citizenship, but also decriminalization of adultery, legalization of divorce, and legalization of abortion. These reforms did make their way into Spanish legislation, though feminists themselves could claim little responsibility for it. Moreover, feminists struggled for common ground and battled each other over whether the democratic order outlined in Spain's new proposed Constitution was even worth working for (as double militants felt) or whether feminists needed to promote their causes untethered to such a flawed, and seemingly still Francoist-tinged, government structure (as single militants argued). Ultimately, feminists' lack of input into the final versions of the Constitution and subsequent ostensibly feminist legislative victories widened these divisions, and encouraged more radical activists to continue battling for a form of democracy that could meet their demands.

These struggles—between Spain's ideologically diverse feminists as much as against a Spanish state and society that too often either ignored or sought to coopt the cause of women's rights—only continued as the nation's new democratic order established itself in the century's closing decades. Increasingly, the third chapter reveals, Spain's feminists sought to internationalize these various conflicts, liaising with foreign bodies like the United Nations and the European Union in an effort to use outside pressures to shape Spain's changing political culture and social order. Meanwhile, as both this and Chapter 4 underscore, feminists' internal conflicts grew more acerbic as the 1980s passed into the 1990s and then into the new millennium. The national government's official *Instituto de la Mujer*, founded in 1983 and soon home to Spain's double militant (now "institutional") feminists, quickly became an especially active flashpoint. Indeed, institutional feminists' successes eventually so embittered Spain's single-militant grassroots feminists that they came to reject all such officially sanctioned feminisms, abroad as well as at home, for having made what they deemed a Faustian alliance with the patriarchy.

And meanwhile, as the fourth chapter shows, though feminists achieved a landmark victory in 2004 with the passage of a groundbreaking law that reconceived the crime of domestic partner abuse as a symptom of deep-seated and explicitly gendered problems in Spanish society, both the lead-up to and aftermath of the new law saw these activists still at loggerheads with one another and with powerful social and government figures. Radical feminists rejected the 2004 law—an *Instituto* initiative—for phrasing that excluded same-sex couples from its protections; feminists as a whole contended with pushback from conservatives who, in a curious inversion, began to use feminists' own rhetoric on Spain's gender violence epidemic to press new attacks on abortion rights.

Recent conflicts—only the latest in a long series of battles fought over all of the issues cited above, as well as others—are still more broadly part of not just a war over "culture" or women's bodies, but for claim over the very essence of contemporary Spanish national identity, whose mythic foundations include a sacralized Constitution of 1978 and the notion that, under this new political framework, Spain has fully shed its Francoist ghosts and developed into a democratic Western European paragon. This contest is far from decided. The shakiness of those foundations and, relatedly, the degree to which the complaints that feminists have long voiced about the Spanish Constitution remain unaddressed, have most recently been underlined by the crisis over Catalan independence that came sharply to a head in late 2017.

This crisis stems in no small part from the asymmetric structure of the modern Spanish state, in which some regions have greater autonomy than others, as well as a continued perception that the Spanish state is built on a Francoist foundation from which it has inherited an unreconstructed centralism and hostility to true progress. These are frustrations (as efforts to coordinate between regional *Institutos* faltered) and fears (which fueled radical feminists' hostility toward the *Institutos*) that marked Spanish feminism during and after the transition, and which remain unresolved. It is telling how closely a common Catalanist quip, which accuses the 1978 Constitution's architects of having sold them the document as a point of departure ("*punt de partida*") when they and the Spanish political right always intended it to be an end point ("*punt i final*"), echoes single militant refrains.

And yet, this sound bite notwithstanding, the Constitution was for Spanish feminists as for Catalonia's secessionists an end point they refused to accept, and so has instead proven a point of departure indeed—if not for a socially progressive consensus, then at least for an ongoing struggle over the very definition of Spain and Spanish modernity that continues into the present and threatens to tear the nation apart culturally, socially, and even geopolitically.

Notes

Introduction

1 Paco Rego, "Denuncia: el magnato del aborto," *El Mundo*, December 2, 2007, https://www.elmundo.es/suplementos/cronica/2007/632/1196550001.html [accessed December 20, 2022]; Celia Maza and Darío Menor, "España se convierte en el 'coladero' europeo de los abortos ilegales," *La Razón*, December 2, 2007, https://www.larazon.es/historico/espana-se-convierte-en-el-coladero-europeo-de-los-abortos-ilegales-KJLA_RAZON_27997/ [accessed December 20, 2022]; Charlie Torres, "Cuando la información se convierte en propaganda," *Soitu.es*, September 15, 2008, http://www.soitu.es/participacion/2008/09/15/u/charlie_torres_1221474903.html [accessed December 20, 2022]; and Matthew Cullinan Hoffman, "Full Abortions Shown on Spanish Television—First in History," *LifeSite*, December 14, 2007, https://www.lifesitenews.com/news/full-abortions-shown-on-spanish-television-first-in-history/ [accessed December 20, 2022].

2 "Zapatero se muestra ahora dispuesto a reformar la Ley del aborto," *20 Minutos*, December 17, 2007, http://www.20minutos.es/noticia/322944/0/zapatero/ley/aborto/ [accessed May 15, 2007]; "Zapatero pide que se revea la ley del aborto," *La Nacion*, December 18, 2007, http://www.lanacion.com.ar/972099-zapatero-pide-que-se-revea-la-ley-del-aborto [accessed May 15, 2012].

3 "En España no se explota ni se discrimina pero Zapatero quiere inventor un derecho al aborto," Hazte Oir, February 4, 2010, http://www.hazteoir.org/node/27752 [accessed May 15, 2012].

4 "Arsuaga: 'Si el PSOE está mejor de lo que parece, España está peor de lo que nos temíamos,'" Hazte Oir, July 23, 2010, http://www.hazteoir.org/node/31880 [accessed May 15, 2012].

5 Sandie Holguín, "'National Spain Invites You': Battlefield Tourism during the Spanish Civil War," *American Historical Review* 110, no. 5 (December 2005): 1400.

6 The Falangist party was explicitly fascist, but there is debate among Spanish historians about whether Franco and his *Movimiento Nacional* were. For more on this debate, see Stanley G. Payne, *Fascism in Spain, 1923–1977* (Madison, WI: University of Wisconsin Press, 1999); Paul Preston, *The Politics of Revenge: Fascism and the Military in 20th-Century Spain* (New York: Routledge, 2003); and Ismael Saz Campos, "Fascism, Fascistization and Developmentalism in Franco's Dictatorship," *Social History* 29, no. 3 (August 2004): 342–57, https://www.jstor.org/stable/4287107.

For more on the patriarchal gender hierarchy established under Franco, see Aurora G. Morcillo, *True Catholic Womanhood: Gender Ideology in Franco's Spain* (DeKalb, IL: Northern Illinois University Press, 1999); Aurora G. Morcillo, *The Seduction of Modern Spain: The Female Body and the Francoist Body Politic* (Lewisburg, PA: Bucknell University Press, 2010); Inbal Ofer, *Señoritas in Blue: The Making of a Female Political Elite in Franco's Spain* (Toronto: Sussex Academic Press, 2010); Kathleen Richmond, *Women and Spanish Fascism: The Women's Section of the Falange 1934–1959* (New York: Routledge, 2003); Carmen Martín Gaite, *Courtship Customs in Postwar Spain (Usos amorosos de la postguerra española)*, trans. Margaret E. W. Jones (Lewisburg, PA: Bucknell University Press, 2004); Gloria Nielfa Cristóbal, ed., *Mujeres y Hombres en la España Franquista: Sociedad, Economía, Política, Cultura* (Madrid: Complutense, 2003); and Lourdes Benería, *Mujer, economía y patriarcado en la España de Franco* (Barcelona: Cuadernos Anagrama, 1977). For more detail about Spanish religious history, particularly the regime's ties to the Catholic Church, see William J. Callahan, *The Catholic Church in Spain, 1875–1998* (Washington, DC: The Catholic University of America Press, 2012).

7 "La legislación social de la España de Franco: Texto íntegro del 'Fuero del Trabajo' (Del «Boletín Oficial» de la Provincia de Barcelona)," *La Vanguardia Española*, March 10, 1939, http://hemeroteca.lavanguardia.com/preview/1939/03/10/pagina-3/33122377/pdf.html [accessed March 27, 2018].

8 María Ángeles Moraga García, "Notas sobre la Situacion Jurídica de la Mujer en el Franquismo," *Feminismo/s* 12 (2008): 236.

9 Morcillo, *True Catholic Womanhood*, Chs. 1–2, especially pp. 33, 40, 42, 44, 69; Rafael Abella, *La vida cotidiana durante la guerra civil: la España nacional* (Barcelona: Editorial Planeta, 1973), 213–14; Pilar Folguera Crespo, "*El Franquismo. El Retorno a la Esfera Privada (1939–1975)*," in *Historia de las Mujeres en España*, ed. Elisa Garrido González (Madrid: Editorial Síntesis, S.A., 1997), 529–30; John Hooper, *The New Spaniards*, 2nd ed. (London, New York: Penguin Books, 2006), 126. For more on the patriarchal gender hierarchy established under Franco, see also Carmen Martín Gaite, *Courtship Customs in Postwar Spain*; Gloria Nielfa Cristóbal, ed., *Mujeres y Hombres en la España Franquista*; and Lourdes Benería, *Mujer, economía y patriarcado en la España de Franco*.

10 Abella, *La vida cotidiana bajo el régimen de Franco*, 106, 111 and Luis Alonso Tejada, *La represión sexual en la España de Franco* (Barcelona: Luis de Caralt, 1978), 31–4.

11 Morcillo, *True Catholic Womanhood*, 25–6.

12 Ibid., 25–6; Amalia Morales Villena, "*Género, Mujeres, Trabajo Social y Sección Femenina. Historia de una Profesión Feminizada y con Vocación Feminista*" (Ph.D. Diss., Universidad de Granada, 2010), 314–5; and Jessica Davidson, "Politics, Policy, and Propaganda of the Sección Femenina in Francoist Spain, 1934–1977" (Ph.D. Diss., Brandeis University, 2005), 161.

13 Lynn Savery, *Engendering the State: The International Diffusion of Women's Human Rights* (New York: Routledge, 2007), 125.
14 Sasha D. Pack, *Tourism and Dictatorship: Europe's Peaceful Invasion of Franco's Spain* (New York: Palgrave Macmillan, 2006), 39–40.
15 Julio Crespo MacLennan, *Spain and the Process of European Integration, 1957–85* (New York: Palgrave Macmillan, 2000).
16 MacLennan, *Spain and the Process of European Integration, 1957–85* and Sebastián Royo, "The Experience of Spain and Portugal in the European Union: Lessons for Latin America," *Miami European Union Centre, Working Paper Series* 2, no. 2 (2002): 8.
17 Savery, *Engendering the State*, 125.
18 United Nations President Kurt Waldheim and President of United Nations General Assembly Gaston Thorn to Generalissimo Francisco Franco, telegram, September 20, 1975, S-0907-0009-02, Correspondence Files of the Secretary General: Kurt Waldheim—with Heads of States, Governments, Permanent Representatives and Observers to the UN; Heads of States—Spain 20/12/1973–09/10/1981, United Nations Archives. This is despite Waldheim's own history of fascist sympathizing, which included membership in several National Socialist organizations, a Ph.D. dissertation seemingly in agreement with National Socialist policy, as well as wartime service for the German army. For more information, see: International Commission of Historians Designated to Establish the Military Service of Lt. Kurt Waldheim. *The Waldheim Report: Submitted February 8, 1988, to Federal Chancellor Dr. Franz Vranitzky* (Oxford: The Alden Press, 1993).
19 Pablo Martín Aceña and Elena Martínez Ruiz, "The Golden Age of Spanish Capitalism: Economic Growth without Political Freedom," in *Spain Transformed: The Late Franco Dictatorship, 1959–1975*, ed. Nigel Townson (New York: Palgrave Macmillan, 2007), 30–1 and Stanley Payne, *The Franco Regime, 1936–1975* (Madison, WI: University of Wisconsin Press, 1987), 478. This rate of growth was outstripped only by Japan.
20 Inbal Ofer, "La Guerra de Agua: Notions of Morality, Respectability, and Community in a Madrid Neighborhood," *Journal of Urban History* 35, no. 2 (January 2009): 220–35 and Antonio Cazorla Sánchez, *Fear and Progress: Ordinary Lives in Franco's Spain, 1939–1975* (Malden, MA: Wiley-Blackwell, 2010), 95–6, 115–22, 154–5.
21 Moraga García, "Notas sobre la Situacion Jurídica," 239–41, 248–9.
22 MacLennan, *Spain and the Process of European Integration, 1957–85* and Pamela Radcliff, "Imagining Female Citizenship in the 'New Spain': Gendering the Democratic Transition, 1975–1978," *Gender and History* 13, no. 4 (November 2001): 498–523.
23 Mercedes Ballesteros and Claudio de la Torre, "*Setenta y Cuatro Mujeres Candidatos en las Próximas Elecciones Inglesas*," *ABC*, March 17, 1966,

http://hemeroteca.abc.es/nav/Navigate.exe/hemeroteca/madrid/abc/1966/03/17/073.html [accessed April 8, 2018].

24 "Ayer celebraron sesión plenaria las cortes del reino—Intervención de Pilar Primo de Rivera," *La Vanguardia Española*, July 16, 1961, http://hemeroteca-paginas.lavanguardia.com/LVE07/HEM/1961/07/16/LVG19610716-004.pdf [accessed April 8, 2018].

25 Morcillo, *True Catholic Womanhood*, 7.

26 Lili Álvarez, "Feminismo y Masculinismo," *ABC*, April 9, 1963, http://hemeroteca.abc.es/nav/Navigate.exe/hemeroteca/madrid/abc/1963/04/09/015.html [accessed April 9, 2018]; Santiago Córdoba, "*Figuras de la Actualidad—Lili Álvarez*," *ABC* (Sevilla), April 9, 1964, http://hemeroteca.abc.es/nav/Navigate.exe/hemeroteca/sevilla/abc.sevilla/1964/04/09/047.html [accessed April 9, 2018]; Gonzalo Fernández de la Mora, "*«Feminismo y Espiritualidad» de Lili Álvarez*," *ABC*, March 4, 1965, http://hemeroteca.abc.es/nav/Navigate.exe/hemeroteca/madrid/abc/1965/03/04/019.html [accessed April 9, 2018]; Jorgina Gil-Delgado, "*El Feminismo de Lili Álvarez*," *ABC*, April 6, 1965, http://hemeroteca.abc.es/nav/Navigate.exe/hemeroteca/madrid/abc/1965/04/06/023.html [accessed April 9, 2018]; José Luis Pérez Cebrián, "*La Lenta Evolución de la Mujer Española*," *ABC*, October 31, 1965, http://hemeroteca.abc.es/nav/Navigate.exe/hemeroteca/sevilla/abc.sevilla/1965/10/31/023.html [accessed April 9, 2018]; and "*Lili Álvarez en F.A.E.*," *ABC*, April 13, 1967, http://hemeroteca.abc.es/nav/Navigate.exe/hemeroteca/madrid/abc/1967/04/13/094.html [accessed April 9, 2018].

27 [No Author], *La Iglesia en el Mundo de Hoy: Pablo VI*: "*En la concepción cristiana la mujer debe encontrar el reconocimiento de sus derechos humanos y civiles*," *ABC*, August 19, 1975, http://hemeroteca.abc.es/nav/Navigate.exe/hemeroteca/madrid/abc/1975/08/19/030.html [accessed April 9, 2018] and Juan Ordóñez Márquez, "*¿Mariología Antropológica?*," ABC (Sevilla), December 7, 1975, http://hemeroteca.abc.es/nav/Navigate.exe/hemeroteca/sevilla/abc.sevilla/1975/12/07/030.html [accessed April 9, 2018]. For more on Ordóñez himself, see Francisco Espinosa Maestre, "*Sobre la represión franquista en el País Vasco*," *Historia Social* 63 (2009): 59–75.

28 Monica Threlfall, "The Women's Movement in Spain," *New Left Review* 151 (1985): 52.

29 Radcliff, "Imagining Female Citizenship in the 'New Spain.'"

30 Temma Kaplan, "Female Consciousness and Collective Action: The Case of Barcelona, 1910–1918," *Signs* (1982): 545–66.

31 Mary Nash, *Defying Male Civilization: Women in the Spanish Civil War* (Denver: Arden Press, 1995).

32 Threlfall, "The Women's Movement in Spain," 47.

33 Ofer, *Señoritas in Blue*, 13.

34 Aurora Morcillo, *True Catholic Womanhood: Gender Ideology in Franco's Spain* (DeKalb, IL: Northern Illinois University Press, 2008).
35 Pamela Radcliff, *Making Democratic Citizens in Spain: Civil Society and the Popular Origins of the Transition, 1960–1978* (New York: Palgrave Macmillan, 2011).
36 Temma Kaplan, *Taking Back the Streets: Women, Youth, and Direct Democracy* (Los Angeles: University of California Press, 2004), 191.
37 For one example, see: Joni Lovenduski, *Women and European Politics: Contemporary Feminism and Public Policy* (Amherst, MA: University of Massachusetts Press, 1986). One need only consider Lovenduski's foreword to her work, *Women and European Politics*: "A motivation for writing this book is my belief that discrimination on the grounds of sex is morally wrong and politically unwise. As a member of the sex that is discriminated against I hold these views strongly. I also believe that sex equality will come about only when women make use of the full array of political weapons available to them to achieve it; that is, political activity is essential to the struggle for women's liberation. It is as a political feminist that I have chosen my subject," (xi). Monica Threlfall has also disclosed her activism in Spain's feminist movement and, more recently, the *Instituto de la Mujer* consulted Celia Valiente in their efforts to push forward their proposals and create change.
38 Gisela T. Kaplan, *Contemporary Western European Feminism* (New York: New York University Press, 1992) and Lovenduski, *Women and European Politics*.
39 Clyde Wilcox, "The Causes and Consequences of Feminist Consciousness among Western European Women," *Comparative Political Studies* 23, no. 4 (January 1991): 526.
40 Nancy F. Cott, *The Grounding of Modern Feminism* (New Haven, CT: Yale University Press, 1987).
41 Claire Duchen, *Women's Rights and Women's Lives in France 1944–1968* (New York: Routledge, 2003), 3.
42 Temma Kaplan, "Female Consciousness and Collective Action."
43 For the discussion of Spanish women, see: Jo Labanyi, "Resemanticizing Feminine Surrender: Cross-Gender Identifications in the Writings of Spanish Female Fascist Activists," in *Women's Narrative and Film in 20th Century Spain*, ed. Kathleen Glenn (New York: Routledge, 2017), 75–92; Radcliff, *Making Democratic Citizens in Spain*; Ofer, *Señoritas in Blue*; Morcillo, *True Catholic Womanhood*; Morcillo, *The Seduction of Modern Spain*; and Richmond, *Women and Spanish Fascism*. For more on non-Spanish female fascists, see: Victoria de Grazia, *How Fascism Ruled Women: Italy, 1922–1945* (Los Angeles: University of California Press, 1992); Julie V. Gottlieb, *Feminine Fascism: Women in Britain's Fascist Movement, 1923–1945* (London: I.B. Taurus, 2000); Julie V. Gottlieb, "Women and British Fascism Revisited: Gender, the Far-Right, and Resistance," *Journal of Women's History* 16,

no. 3 (Fall 2004): 108–23.; Claudia Koonz, *Mothers in the Fatherland: Women, the Family, and Nazi Politics* (New York: St. Martin's Press, 1986); and Gisela Bock, "Racism and Sexism in Nazi Germany: Motherhood, Compulsory Sterilization, and the State," *Signs* 8, no. 3 (Spring 1983): 400–21.

44 Valentine M. Moghadam, *Globalizing Women: Transnational Feminist Networks* (Baltimore, MD: Johns Hopkins University Press, 2005), 1.

45 Julio Crespo MacLennan, Spain and the Process of European Integration, 1957–85; Pack, Tourism and Dictatorship; Alejandro J. Gómez del Moral, *Buying into Change: Mass Consumption, Dictatorship, and Democratization in Franco's Spain, 1939–1982* (Lincoln, Neb: University of Nebraska Press, 2021).

46 Andrew Nagorski, Jane Friedman, Loren Jenkins, Helen Gibson, and Miguel Acoca, "Latin Women: A New Fire," *Newsweek*, July 4, 1977, 18, magazine clipping in private collection donated to author by Temma Kaplan.

47 Though colloquially this violence is often called domestic violence, that term carries political and ideological connotations in the Spanish context. Scholars often use the term Intimate Partner Violence, or IPV, which I use throughout the chapter for its neutrality.

Chapter 1

1 For information about the *Ley de derechos*, see: Julia Hudson-Richards, "'Women Want to Work': Shifting Ideologies of Women's Work in Franco's Spain, 1939–1962," *Journal of Women's History* 27, no. 2 (2015): 87–109 and Aurora G. Morcillo, *True Catholic Womanhood: Gender Ideology in Franco's Spain* (DeKalb, Ill.: Northern Illinois University Press, 1999).

2 Ángel Ruiz Ayucar, "España en la vanguardia de la dignificación del trabajo de la mujer," *Teresa: Revista para todas las mujeres*, August 1961, 23–5.

3 Miguel Ángel Ruiz Carnicer, "La idea de Europa en la cultura franquista 1939–1962," *Hispania* 58, no. 199 (1998): 679–701.

4 Morcillo, *True Catholic Womanhood*, 101; Kathleen JL. Richmond, "The Yoke of Isabella: the women's section of the Spanish Falange 1934–1959" (Ph.D. Diss., University of Southampton, 1999), 15.

5 Jessica Davidson, "Women, Fascism and Work in Francoist Spain: The Law for Political, Professional and Labour Rights," *Gender & History* 23, no. 2 (2011): 404; Morcillo, *True Catholic Womanhood*, 33; Kathleen Richmond, *Women and Spanish Fascism: The Women's Section of the Falange 1934–1959* (New York: Routledge, 2003).

6 Davidson, "Women, Fascism, and Work in Francoist Spain," 404; Morcillo, *True Catholic Womanhood*, 33; Richmond, *Women and Spanish Fascism*, 19–20.

7 Richmond, *Women and Spanish Fascism*, 17.

8 Morcillo, *True Catholic Womanhood*.

9   Pablo Martín Aceña and Elena Martínez Ruiz, "The Golden Age of Spanish Capitalism: Economic Growth without Political Freedom," in *Spain Transformed: The Late Franco Dictatorship, 1959-1975*, ed. Nigel Townson (New York: Palgrave Macmillan, 2007), 30-1 and Stanley Payne, *The Franco Regime, 1936-1975* (Madison, WI: University of Wisconsin Press, 1987), 478.
10 Hudson-Richards, "Women Want to Work," 97.
11 For more on tourism, see: Justin Crumbaugh, *Destination Dictatorship: The Spectacle of Spain's Tourist Boom and the Reinvention of Difference* (Albany, NY: State University of New York Press, 2009); Alejandro J. Gómez del Moral, *Buying Into Change: Mass Consumption, Dictatorship, and Democratization in Franco's Spain, 1939-1982* (Lincoln, Neb.: University of Nebraska Press, 2021); Sasha Pack, *Tourism and Dictatorship: Europe's Peaceful Invasion of Franco's Spain* (New York, NY: Palgrave Macmillan, 2006).
12 Charles Powell, "International Aspects of Democratization: The Case of Spain," in *The International Dimensions of Democratization: Europe and the Americas*, 2nd ed., ed. Laurence Whitehead (Oxford: Oxford University Press, 1996), 285-314.
13 Richmond, *Women and Spanish Fascism*, 11.
14 Davidson, "Women, Fascism and Work in Francoist Spain," 405.
15 Ofer, *Señoritas in Blue*, 95.
16 Richmond, *Women and Spanish Fascism*, 11.
17 "I Pleno de la nueva Legislatura: las cortes aprobaron la ley de derechos políticos, profesionales y laborales femeninos y la de seguro nacional de desempleo— Discursos de la Srta. Pilar Primo de Rivera y de los señores Herrero Tejedor, Sanz Orrio y Bilbao," *A.B.C. (Sevilla)*, July 16, 1961, 23-4 and María del Rosario Ruiz Franco, "Nuevos horizontes para las mujeres de los años 60: la ley de 22 de julio de 1961," *Arenal*, 2:2 (July-Dec. 1995): 264.
18 Ángel Ruiz Ayucar, "España en la vanguardia de la dignificación del trabajo de la mujer," *Teresa: Revista para todas las mujeres*, August 1961, 23-5.
19 "La proposición de ley sobre los Derechos Politicos, Profesionales y de Trabajo de la Mujer," *Teresa: Revista para todas las mujeres*, June 1961, 8-9.
20 Julio Crespo MacLennan, *Spain and the Process of European Integration, 1957-85* (New York, NY: Palgrave Macmillan, 2000).
21 Ángel Ruiz Ayucar, "España en la vanguardia de la dignificación del trabajo de la mujer," *Teresa: Revista para todas las mujeres*, August 1961, 23-5.
22 Anna van der Vleuten, *The Price of Gender Equality: Member States and Governance in the European Union* (Burlington, VT: Ashgate Publishing Company, 2007), 36-8.
23 Rachel A. Cichowski, "Women's Rights, the European Court, and Supranational Constitutionalism," *Law and Society Review* 38, no. 1 (September 2004): 501.
24 Treaty establishing the European Economic Community (Treaty of Rome), Article 119, March 25, 1957, EUR-Lex: Access to European Union Law database, https://eur-lex.europa.eu/legal-content/EN/TXT/?uri=CELEX:11992E/TXT [accessed April 16, 2018].

25 Richmond, *Women and Spanish Fascism*, 86–8 and Ofer, *Señoritas in Blue*, 94–5.
26 David Brydan, *Franco's Internationalists: Social Experts and Spain's Search for Legitimacy* (Oxford, UK: Oxford University Press, 2019).
27 Richard Gunther, José Ramón Montero Gilbert, and José Ignacio Wert, *The Media and Politics in Spain: From Dictatorship to Democracy* (Barcelona, Spain: Institut de Ciències Polítiques i Socials, 1999).
28 van der Vleuten, *The Price of Gender Equality*, 36–40.
29 Eve C. Landau and Yves Beigbeder, *From ILO Standards to EU Law: The Case of Equality Between Men and Women at Work* (Leiden The Netherlands: Martinus Nijhoff Publishers, 2008); Torild Skard, "Gender in the Malestream—Acceptance of Women and Gender Equality in Different United Nations Organisations," *Forum for Development Studies* 36 (2009): 160; van der Vleuten, *The Price of Gender Equality*, 35–9.
30 In Western Europe, Scandinavian nations were a rare exception to this. Boasting the longest history of women's equality of any region in Europe, Scandinavia has historically not only had a relatively large number of women in politics (with the percentages of women MEP in Scandinavian countries ranging as high as 12% in 1949 and 17% in 1966), but has also had such strong protections for women's rights that the region did not develop the vocal feminist movements or require the establishment of women's rights centric government ministries that other nations found necessary for resolving discrimination against women. Norway, for instance, enacted an equal pay law in 1908. For discussion of the development of women's rights throughout Europe, see: Gisela Kaplan, *Contemporary Western European Feminism* (New York, NY: New York University Press, 1992).
31 Neal M. Rosendorf, *Franco Sells Spain to America: Hollywood, Tourism and Public Relations as Postwar Spanish Soft Power* (New York, NY: Palgrave Macmillan, 2014), 97. Regarding the transformation of female university life in Spanish universities, Pamela Radcliff notes that female students "reached 22–24 percent of the college population by the early 1960s and [doubled] in absolute numbers between 1950 and 1960." For more information, see: Pamela Beth Radcliff, *Modern Spain: 1808 to the Present* (Hoboken, NJ: Wiley Blackwell, 2017), 247.
32 For more information on the founding of the Women's Bureau and its work in the early twentieth century, see: Nancy F. Cott, *The Grounding of Modern Feminism* (New Haven, CT: Yale University Press, 1987).
33 Gráinne de Búrca, "The Road Not Taken: The European Union as a Global Human Rights Actor," *American Journal of International Law* 105, no. 4 (2011): 651.
34 Antonio Moreno Juste, "The European Economic Community and the End of the Franco Regime: the September 1975 Crisis," *Cahiers de la Méditerranée*, 90 (June 2015): 25–45.
35 Ronald Janse, "The Evolution of the Political Criteria for Accession to the European Community, 1957–1973," *European Law Journal* 24, no. 1 (2018): 66–8.

36 "La mujer en el mundo de hoy: El tema del Congreso Internacional que prepara la Seccion Femenina," *Teresa: Revista para todas las mujeres*, November 1969, 8–9.
37 "En marcha el primer Congreso Internacional de la Mujer," *Teresa: Revista para todas las mujeres*, January 1968, 7.
38 Gómez del Moral, *Buying Into Change*, 3.
39 "En marcha el primer Congreso Internacional de la Mujer," *Teresa: Revista para todas las mujeres*, January 1968, 7.
40 "La mujer en el mundo de hoy: Congreso Internacional de Madrid," *Teresa: Revista para todas las mujeres*, July 1970, 5.
41 Ibid., 6.
42 "El viaje de Pilar Primo de Rivera a hispanoamerica," *Teresa: Revista para todas las mujeres*, September 1969, 4–5.
43 Congreso Internacional de la Mujer, Madrid, 7 al 14 de junio de 1970: Memoria, (Madrid: Editorial Almena, 1972), 177–98.
44 Kristen Ghodsee, "Revisiting the United Nations Decade for Women: Brief Reflections on Feminism, Capitalism and Cold War Politics in the Early Years of the International Women's Movement," *Women's Studies International Forum* 33, no. 1 (2010): 4.
45 Temma Kaplan, *Taking Back the Streets: Women, Youth, and Direct Democracy* (Los Angeles: University of California Press, 2004), 176–202; Elena Díaz Silva, "El Año Internacional de La Mujer En España: 1975," *Cuadernos de Historia Contemporánea* 31 (2009): 319–39; and Martin Klimke and Joachim Scharloth, *1968 in Europe: A History of Protest and Activism, 1956–1977* (New York: Palgrave Macmillan, 2008).
46 Jill M. Bystydzienski, *Women Transforming Politics: Worldwide Strategies for Empowerment* (Bloomington, IN: Indiana University Press, 1992), 7.
47 Morcillo, *True Catholic Womanhood*, 119.
48 Radcliff, *Making Democratic Citizens in Spain*, 145–8 and Morcillo, *True Catholic Womanhood*, 119.
49 During the late years of the Franco regime, authorities detained and imprisoned a number of women, many of whom were feminists, either for suspected ties to ETA or to communist organizations, both of which were illegal, or because of their husbands' illegal political activities. Lídia Falcón and Eva Forest are two of the most prominent of these women (Forest imprisoned for suspicion of carrying out an ETA attack, Falcon implicated by Forest for a similar crime) and both published memoirs of their time in Spanish jail. In subsequent interviews about her experience, as detailed by Alejandro Torrús in an article for *Público*, Falcón described the full extent of her torture and "recall[ed] that after the interrogations, she had to have five surgeries to try to repair the damage from the tortures to her shoulders, stomach and uterus." Forest's writings are decidedly more upbeat—her book is a collection of letters to her family—though she does describe the isolation of solitary confinement and her fears of facing the death

penalty for a crime she did not commit. Ordinary women were also imprisoned and tortured under Franco. From September 2016 to January 2017, the El Born Centre de Cultura i Memòria in Barcelona held an exhibit exploring citizens' experiences of torture in the late Franco years; many of the published excerpts in the exhibition guide came from women who were savagely beaten and recounted their experiences for the exhibit. Additionally, torture did not stop during or after the transition to democracy. Writing in 1985 scholar Hylah Jacques reached the conclusion that, despite Spain's transition to democracy, state violence continued and was levied primarily against "leftists and social activists," including feminists and their demonstrations; Chapter 2 of this book also describes at least one such instance of this type of violence, one in which policemen drove trucks into a crowd of feminist demonstrators demanding abortion's legalization.

For more information, see: Eva Forest. *From a Spanish Jail* (Baltimore, Maryland: Penguin Books, 1975); M. Edurne Portela, "Writing (in) Prison: The Discourse of Confinement in Lidia Falcón's *En El Infierno*," *Arizona Journal of Hispanic Cultural Studies* 11 (2007): 121–36; Hylah M. Jacques, "Spain: Systematic Torture in a Democratic State," *Monthly Review* 37 (November 1985): 57–63; Alejandro Torrús, "Billy el Niño, mientras torturaba a Lidia Falcón: 'Ya no parirás más, puta,'" *Público*, February 26, 2015, http://www.publico.es/politica/billy-nino-torturaba-lidia-falcon-ya-no-pariras-mas-puta.html [March 18, 2018]; and "De tortures i d'impunitats (1960–1978), Això Em Va Passar," online exhibition guide, El Born Centre de Cultura i Memòria, http://elbornculturaimemoria.barcelona.cat/aixo-em-va-passar-de-tortures-i-dimpunitats-1960-1978 [accessed April 16, 2018].

50 Radcliff, *Making Democratic Citizens in Spain*, 135–6 and Monica Threlfall "Gendering the transition to democracy: reassessing the impact of women's activism," in *Gendering Spanish Democracy*, ed. Monica Threlfall, Christine Cousins, and Celia Valiente (New York: Routledge, 2004), 22.
51 Díaz Silva, "El Año Internacional de La Mujer En España," 322–3 and Threlfall "Gendering the transition to democracy," 19.
52 Anny Brooksbank Jones, *Women in Contemporary Spain* (Manchester, UK: Manchester University Press, 1997), 4–6.
53 Monica Threlfall, "The Women's Movement in Spain," *New Left Review* 151, no. May/June (1985): 48.
54 Threlfall "Gendering the Transition to Democracy," 22.
55 Díaz Silva, "El Año Internacional de La Mujer En España," 322.
56 Mujeres Democraticas de España, "Primera Reunion General de Las Mujeres Democráticas de España," meeting minutes, 1970, Colleccions Moviments Socials, Organitzacions de dones, Folder C 46–1: Mujeres Democraticas de España, Fundació Cipriano García Arxiu Històric de CCOO de Catalunya, Barcelona, Spain.

57 "El Año Internacional de la Mujer, en marcha," *Teresa: Revista para todas las mujeres*, August 1974, 16.
58 "Quedo oficialmente inaugurado: Año Internacional de la Mujer," *Teresa: Revista para todas las mujeres*, March 1975, 4.
59 "Treinta y dos paises estudian la integracion de la mujer," *Teresa: Revista para todas las mujeres*, November 1974, 6.
60 "Resumen de la intervencion de Carmen Salinas en el plenario de la conferencia mundial sobre A.I.M.," *Teresa: Revista para todas las mujeres*, August 1975, 16, 59.
61 "Quedo oficialmente inaugurado: Año Internacional de la Mujer," *Teresa: Revista para todas las mujeres*, March 1975, 4.
62 Ibid.
63 Arvonne Fraser, *UN Decade for Women: The Power of Words and Organizations* (Alexandria, VA: Alexander Street, 2012), https://search.alexanderstreet.com/view/work/bibliographic_entity%7Cbibliographic_details%7C2476931 [accessed April 16, 2018].
64 Ghodsee, "Revisiting the United Nations Decade for Women," 5.
65 Ibid., 3–5.
66 United Nations Department of Public Information, *The United Nations and the Advancement of Women, 1945–1996*, The United Nations Blue Books Series, vol. 6 (New York: Department of Public Information, 1995), 34.
67 Arvonne S. Fraser, "Becoming Human: The Origins and Development of Women's Human Rights," *Human Rights Quarterly* 21, no. 4 (November 1999): 898.
68 Fraser, "Becoming Human," 895.
69 Ghodsee, "Revisiting the United Nations Decade for Women," 5.
70 Isabel Perez, "Año Internacional de la Mujer: Regreso la representacion española en la conferencia de mejico," *ABC* (Madrid), July 5, 1975, http://hemeroteca.abc.es/nav/Navigate.exe/hemeroteca/madrid/abc/1975/07/05/046.html [accessed February 5, 2018].
71 Fraser, "Becoming Human," 893.
72 United Nations. *Report of the World Conference of the International Women's Year, Mexico City, 19 June—2 July 1975*, E/CONF.66/34 (New York: United Nations, 1976), 90.
73 Ibid., 44.
74 Ibid., 90.
75 Ibid.,173. The sole Spanish vote at the WCOW was in favor of a controversial resolution stating "Zionism is a form of racism and racial discrimination." It received sixty-six ayes, three nays, thirty-five abstentions and was repealed by the UN General Assembly in 1991 by a vote of 111/25/13.
76 "Carola Ribed de R. de Valcarcel: Habla sobre El Año Internacional de la Mujer," *Teresa: Revista para todas las mujeres*, January 1976, 4.

77 "Resumen de la intervencion de Carmen Salinas en el plenario de la conferencia mundial sobre A.I.M.," *Teresa: Revista para todas las mujeres*, August 1975, 14.
78 "Programa-Manifiesto de la Plataforma de Organizaciones de Mujeres de Madrid," February 20, 1975, catalogued in a document collection on the personal website of Amparo Moreno Sardà, www.amparomorenosarda.es/node/86 [accessed April 13, 2018].
79 "Manifiesto a la Opinion Publica Aprobado por la II Asamblea de Mujeres de Barcelona," March 1975, catalogued in a document collection on the personal website of Amparo Moreno Sardà, www.amparomorenosarda.es/node/87 [accessed April 13, 2018].
80 Movimento Democratico de Mujeres, "Declaratio de la IV Reunion General del Movimento Democratico de Mujeres," August 31, 1975, Colleccions Moviments Socials, Organizaciones de dones, Folder C46-2: Movimento Democrático de Mujeres (MDM), Fundació Cipriano García Arxiu Històric de CCOO de Catalunya, Barcelona, Spain.
81 "Carmen Salinas habla para Teresa de la conferencia mundial sobre el año internacional de la mujer celebrada en mejico," *Teresa: Revista para todas las mujeres*, August 1975, 14.

Chapter 2

1 Paloma Saavedra and Regina Bayo, Mujeres del Mundo, "En el Mundo," *Vindicación Feminista*, July 1976, 55-6.
2 Ibid., 55-6.
3 In fact, Carlism as an ideology was born directly out of an act of discrimination against women: Carlists rejected Queen Isabella II's reign as illegitimate, citing Salic law that barred even first-born daughters from the royal succession, and thereafter supported an ideologically far more conservative line of pretenders. And again, though they often disagreed with regime policies, hungered for a return to absolute monarchy (rather than dictatorship), and despised Falangism, Carlists consistently supported Franco through the regime's existence. In sum, they seemed to run counter to everything the women's rights movement of the 1970s championed. See José Alvarez Junco and Adrian Shubert, *Spanish History since 1808* (Arnold, 2000) and Stanley G. Payne, *Fascism in Spain, 1923-1977* (Madison, WI: University of Wisconsin Press, 1999). For the Carlists' ties to the Catholic Church and further information about its ideologies, see: William James Callahan, *The Catholic Church in Spain, 1875-1998* (Washington, D.C.: Catholic University of America Press, 2000).
4 Paloma Saavedra and Regina Bayo, Mujeres del Mundo, "En el Mundo," *Vindicación Feminista*, July 1976, 55-6.

5   Pamela Beth Radcliff, "Imagining Female Citizenship in the 'New Spain': Gendering the Democratic Transition, 1975–1978," *Gender and History* 13, no. 4 (November 2001): 498–523; Julio Crespo MacLennan, *Spain and the Process of European Integration, 1957–85* (New York, NY: Palgrave Macmillan, 2000); and Celia Valiente, "Spain at the Vanguard in European Gender Equality Policies," in *Gender Politics in the Expanding European Union: Mobilization, Inclusion, Exclusion*, ed. Silke Roth (New York: Berghahn, 2008), 101–17.
6   Javier Tusell, *Spain: From Dictatorship to Democracy, 1939 to the Present*, trans. Rosemary Clark (Malden, MA: Wiley-Blackwell, 2011), 289.
7   Federación de Organizaciones Feministas del Estado Español, "Declaración Programatica de la Federación de Organizaciones Feministas del Estado Español," January 23, 1977 catalogued in a document collection on the personal website of Amparo Moreno Sardà, www.amparomorenosarda.es/node/85 [accessed February 9, 2018].
8   Monica Threlfall, "Explaining Gender Parity Representation in Spain: The Internal Dynamics of Parties," *West European Politics* 30, no. 5 (November 1, 2007): 1080, https://doi.org/10.1080/01402380701617464.
9   Radcliff, "Imagining Female Citizenship in the 'New Spain,'" 509; Monica Threlfall, "The Women's Movement in Spain," *New Left Review* I, no. 151 (1985): 52; Monica Threlfall, Christine Cousins, and Celia Valiente, Gendering Spanish Democracy (Routledge, 2004), 34; Valiente, "Spain at the Vanguard in European Gender Equality Policies," 5.
10 Radcliff, "Imagining Female Citizenship in the 'New Spain.'"
11 Pamela Beth Radcliff, *Making Democratic Citizens in Spain: Civil Society and the Popular Origins of the Transition, 1960–78* (New York, NY: Palgrave Macmillan, 2011), 129–30.
12 Kathleen Richmond, *Women and Spanish Fascism: The Women's Section of the Falange 1934–1959* (New York, NY: Routledge, 2003), 128.
13 Radcliff, *Making Democratic Citizens in Spain*, 139.
14 Luis Suárez Fernández, *Cronica de la Sección Femenina y su tiempo 1934–1977* (Madrid: Asociación Nueva Andadura, 1993).
15 Congreso Internacional de la Mujer, Madrid, 7 al 14 de junio de 1970: Memoria (Madrid: Editorial Almena, 1972).
16 Threlfall, Cousins, and Valiente, *Gendering Spanish Democracy*, 26. This source also suggests that the first Catalan Women's Conference, in May 1976, drew 4,000, but that was less typical (p28); Begoña Mendia Ibarrola, "Historia del Movimento Feminista." Undated, but sources used suggest that this was written after 1984. Made available to this author by Temma Kaplan.
17 Radcliff, "Imagining Female Citizenship in the 'New Spain,'" 516.

18 Anny Brooksbank Jones, *Women in Contemporary Spain* (New York, NY: Manchester University Press, 1997).
19 Richmond, *Women and Spanish Fascism*, 127.
20 Ibid., 161, footnote 18.
21 Conversations with Merce Otero, archivist at *Ca La Dona Centre de Documentació*, Barcelona, Spain, July 13, 2014.
22 *Telva*, March 1975.
23 *Interviu*, January 1977. *Hola!*, May 1976.
24 *Teresa* archive, Biblioteca Nacional de España, Madrid
25 *Vindicación Feminista*, Num. 1, July 1976.; *Opción* 1, December 1976, Ca la Dona Centre de Documentació, Barcelona, Spain.
26 Conversations with Merce Otero, archivist at *Ca La Dona Centre de Documentació*, Barcelona, Spain, July 13, 2014.
27 "Editorial: O Juguem Totes O Estripem La Baralla!," *dones en lluita* Vol. 9, January/February 1979, 2, *dones en lluita* folders, Ca la Dona Centre de Documentació, Barcelona, Spain.
28 "Balance de Situacion," 1981, *dones en lluita* folders, Ca la Dona Centre de Documentació, Barcelona, Spain.
29 L. Falcon, "La Razon de la Sinrazon que con la Razon se entiende: La Ofensiva Contra El Feminismo," *Vindicacion Feminista*, January 1977, 17.
30 Radcliff, "Imagining Female Citizenship in the 'New Spain,'" 510.
31 Ibid., 518 and Celia Valiente, "Gendering Abortion Debates: State Feminism in Spain," in *Abortion Politics, Women's Movements and the Democratic State*, ed. Dorothy McBride Stetson (New York: Oxford University Press, 2001), 146.
32 Temma Kaplan, *Taking Back the Streets: Women, Youth, and Direct Democracy* (Los Angeles: University of California Press, 2004), 194.
33 "Resoluciones y Conclusiones de las I Jornadas por la Liberacion de la Mujer," resolution approved on December 8, 1975 and conclusions approved February 14, 1976, catalogued in a document collection on the personal website of Amparo Moreno Sardà, www.amparomorenosarda.es/node/88 [accessed April 13, 2018].
34 For general information on feminist double militancy in a non-Spanish context, see: Karen Beckwith, "Beyond compare? Women's movements in comparative perspective," *European Journal of Political Research* 37, no. 4 (June 2000): 442–6.
35 Begoña Mendia Ibarrola, "Historia del movimento feminista: Curso de extension universitaria—ciclo mujer y sociedad," undated but produced after 1984, 4, in private collection donated to author by Temma Kaplan. Appears to be an early draft of a similar, later document: Begoña Mendia Ibarrola, "Apuntes para una historia del movimiento feminista en el estado español (75–92)," July 1992, unpublished document belonging to the collection of the Centro de Documentación de Mujeres, http://cdd.emakumeak.org/recursos/2160 [accessed April 13, 2018].

36 Ibarrola, "Historia del Movimento Feminista."
37 Federación de Organizaciones Feministas del Estado Español, "Declaración Programatica de la Federación de Organizaciones Feministas del Estado Español," January 23, 1977 catalogued in a document collection on the personal website of Amparo Moreno Sardà, www.amparomorenosarda.es/node/85 [accessed April 13, 2018].
38 "Conclusiones de las I Jornades Catalanes de la Dona," May 31, 1976, catalogued in a document collection on the personal website of Amparo Moreno Sardà, www.amparomorenosarda.es/node/89 [accessed April 13, 2018].
39 "Nacimiento, trayectoria y disolucion del grup de mujeres de ANCHE (Barcelona)," April 15, 1977, catalogued in a document collection on the personal website of Amparo Moreno Sardà, www.amparomorenosarda.es/node/93 [accessed April 13, 2018]. Asociación de Comunicación Humana y Ecología (The Association for Human Communication and Ecology), or ANCHE, was legally an organization for female engineers, but the group had extensive involvement in feminist efforts.
40 For more information, see: Laura Desfor Edles, *Symbol and Ritual in the New Spain: The Transition to Democracy after Franco* (Cambridge, UK: Cambridge University Press, 1998); Omar G. Encarnación, *Democracy Without Justice in Spain: The Politics of Forgetting* (Philadelphia: University of Pennsylvania Press, 2014); and Tusell, *Spain*.
41 Paloma Cruz Pepa-García, "Acerca del Movimiento Feminista," *Triunfo*, December 24, 1977.
42 Ibid.
43 "La unio per l'alliberament de la dona por una constitucion democratica," *dones en lluita*, January 1978, 10, *dones en lluita* folders, Ca la Dona Centre de Documentació, Barcelona, Spain.
44 Organización Comunista de España (Bandera Roja), "mujer: la constitución está contra nosotras, no a la constitucion," undated pamphlet circulated before ratification of the 1978 Constitution, Fons D'Orgnitzacions Politiques, Folder C6-2a: OCE Bandera Roja, Fundació Cipriano García Arxiu Històric de CCOO de Catalunya, Barcelona, Spain.
45 Lidia Falcon, "La constitucion: las españolas ni fu ni fa, el pene sigue siendo rey," *Vindicacion Feminista*, July 1978, 17.
46 There were 26,632,180 registered voters, 17,873,271 voted (67.11% of Spain's registered voters), and 91.81% of those voters voted YES for the referendum. Gobierno de España, Ministerio del Interior, Consulta de Resultados Electores, "Referendum / December 1978," http://www.infoelectoral.mir.es/infoelectoral/min/busquedaAvanzadaAction.html [accessed April 16, 2018].

Interestingly, and highlighting the long life of leftist dissatisfaction with the Constitution, in 2018 some Catalan pro-secession outlets expressed doubt about the integrity of this electoral consensus, drawing in part on a 1978 *El País* article that very cautiously questioned some aspects of the census used to draw up the electoral rolls for the referendum vote. For more information on these accusations, see: "'El País' admitía en 1978 que el referéndum de la Constitución se hizo sin censo," *El Nacional*, June 17, 2007, https://www.elnacional.cat/es/politica/pais-referendum-constitucion-1987-censo_167052_102.html [accessed April 18, 2018]; "La constitució espanyola es va votar en 78 amb un ces falsejat, amb més d'un milió persones més, i alterat vint dies abans," *VilaWeb*, June 19, 2017, https://www.vilaweb.cat/noticies/la-constitucio-espanyola-es-va-votar-al-78-amb-un-cens-falsejat-en-mes-dun-milio-de-persones-i-alterat-vint-dies-abans/ [accessed April 18, 2018]; and Editorial, "Incompetencia y caos," *El País*, December 7, 1978, https://elpais.com/diario/1978/12/07/opinion/281833202_850215.html [accessed February 9, 2018].

47 Radcliff, "Imagining Female Citizenship in the 'New Spain,'" 509.
48 Montserrat Amat Roca, "Man and Woman: The Same, But Different," *La Vanguardia Española*, December 1, 1976, http://hemeroteca.lavanguardia.com/preview/2005/04/26/pagina-5/33635857/pdf.html [accessed February 9, 2018].
49 José Luis Calleja, "Manifestación Feminista," *ABC*, May 17, 1978, http://hemeroteca.abc.es/nav/Navigate.exe/hemeroteca/madrid/abc/1978/05/17/003.html [accessed February 9, 2018].
50 Diez de Rivera's appointment in fact made international news, and she was included in a *Newsweek* write-up of prominent women assuming political positions worldwide: Andrew Nagorski, Jane Friedman, Loren Jenkins, Helen Gibson, and Miguel Acoca, "Latin Women: A New Fire," *Newsweek,* July 4, 1977, 18, magazine clipping in private collection donated to author by Temma Kaplan. For more on Carmen Diez de Rivera and her political career, see: Ana Romero, *Historia de Carmen: memorias de Carmen Díez de Rivera* (Barcelona: Planeta, 2002) and Ana Romero, *Carmen, Suárez, y El Rey: El Triángulo de la Transición* (Barcelona: Planeta, 2013).
51 Paul Preston, *Juan Carlos: Steering Spain from Dictatorship to Democracy* (New York: W.W. Norton & Company, 2004), 371, 379–85. Preston mentions Diez de Rivera's role in governing several times, including mentioning that Spain's King Juan Carlos was attracted to her, that she was aristocratic, and that she had famous successes negotiating difficult political situations like the PCE's legalization.
52 Francisco Umbral, "La Musa de la Reforma," *El País*, January 30, 1977, https://elpais.com/diario/1977/01/30/sociedad/223426807_850215.html [accessed February 9, 2018].
53 Mária Angeles Sanchez, "Carmen Díez de Rivera, directora del Gebinete de Presidencia," *Blanco y Negro,* July 31, 1976, http://hemeroteca.abc.es/nav/Navigate.exe/hemeroteca/madrid/blanco.y.negro/1976/07/31/022.

html and http://hemeroteca.abc.es/nav/Navigate.exe/hemeroteca/madrid/blanco.y.negro/1976/07/31/023.html [accessed February 9, 2018].
54 Nagorski et al, "Latin Women: A New Fire," 18.
55 Ibid. Ironically this ban was nullified only four months later with the political negotiations of the Moncloa Pacts, though the stigma of women allying with feminist causes remained.
56 Ana Romero, "Carmen Díez de Rivera: musa de Suárez, jamás amante," *El Mundo*, March 30, 2014, http://www.elmundo.es/loc/2014/03/29/5335b4ca268e3e93408b457d.html and Beatriz Miranda, "Justicia histórica para Carmen Díez de Rivera," *Sin noticias de Dior* (blog), *El Mundo*, July 30, 2014, http://www.elmundo.es/blogs/elmundo/sinnoticiasdedior/2014/07/30/justicia-historica-para-la-musa-carmen.html [accessed February 9, 2018].
57 Celia Valiente, "The Women's Movement, Gender Equality Agencies and Central-State Debates on Political Representation in Spain," in *State Feminism and Political Representation*, ed. Joni Lovenduski (New York: Cambridge University Press, 2005), 178. This became national law requiring political parties' electoral lists to be at least 40 percent women for all elections, starting in 2007 (*Anteproyecto de Ley Orgánica de Igualdad entre Mujeres y Hombres*).
58 There were twenty-one women in the Congress of Deputies and six in the Senate. Of the twenty-one women elected to the Congress of Deputies, *Grupo Parlamentario de Unión de Centro Democrático* (GUCD) had 171 representatives, seven of which (or 4.1%) were women. *Grupo Parlamento Socialista del Congreso* (GS) had 108 representatives, seven of which (or 6.5%) were women. *Grupo Parlamentario Comunista* (GCO) had twenty-two representatives, three of which (or 13.6%) were women. *Grupo Parlamentario de Alianza Popular* (GAP) had sixteen representatives, one of which (or 6.3%) was a woman. *Grupo Parlamentario Socialistes de Catalunya* (GSC) had nineteen representatives, two of which (or 10.5%) were women. For information about female delegates to the Congress of Deputies, see: http://www.congreso.es/portal/page/portal/Congreso/Congreso/Diputados/Diputadas%20en%20activo?_piref73_1333086_73_1333081_1333081.next_page=/wc/cambioLegislatura&tipoBusqueda=completo&idLegislatura=0 [accessed April 16, 2018]. For information on female Senators, see: http://www.senado.es/web/conocersenado/temasclave/presenciamujeres/listasenadoras/index.html [accessed April 16, 2018].
59 Tusell, *Spain*, 396.
60 Threlfall, "Explaining Gender Parity Representation in Spain," 1080.
61 Rosa Cusó, "Feminismo de UCD, O a la caza de los votos de la mujer," *dones en lluita*, October 1978, 4, *dones en lluita* folders, Ca la Dona Centre de Documentació, Barcelona, Spain.
62 Radcliff, "Imagining Female Citizenship in the 'New Spain,'" 509.

63 Threlfall, Cousins, and Valiente, *Gendering Spanish Democracy*; Radcliff, "Imagining Female Citizenship in the 'New Spain'"; Jones, *Women in Contemporary Spain*.
64 Radcliff, "Imagining Female Citizenship in the 'New Spain,'" 509.
65 Lidia Falcon, "La constitucion: las españolas ni fu ni fa, el pene sigue siendo rey," *Vindicacion Feminista*, July 1978, 17.
66 *Constitución Española, Boletín Oficial del Estado núm. 311*, December 29, 1978, pgs. 29313–424, https://www.boe.es/buscar/doc.php?id=BOE-A-1978-31229 [accessed 16 April 2018].
67 Organización Comunista de España (Bandera Roja), "mujer: la constitución está contra nosotras, no a la constitucion," undated pamphlet circulated before ratification of the 1978 Constitution, Fons D'Orgnitzacions Politiques, Folder C6-2a: OCE Bandera Roja, Fundació Cipriano García Arxiu Històric de CCOO de Catalunya, Barcelona, Spain.
68 "La Asamblea de Mujeres de Vizcaya ante la CONSTITUCION," pamphlet, November 1978, in private collection donated to author by Temma Kaplan.
69 Spanish law first required in 1988 that 25 percent of the party's deputies and representatives be women, and then raised the number to 40 percent in 1997 through the Constitutional Act 3/2007 of 22 March for effective equality between women and men. *Ley Orgánica 3/2007, de 22 de marzo, para la igualdad efectiva de mujeres y hombres, Jefatura del Estado (Spain), Boletín Oficial del Estado núm. 71*, March 23, 2007, pgs. 12611–45, http://www.boe.es/buscar/doc.php?id=BOE-A-2007-6115 [accessed February 9, 2018].
70 Eva y Elisenda, "Sobre Violaciones," *dones en lluita*, February 1978, 5, *dones en lluita* folders, Ca la Dona Centre de Documentacio, Barcelona, Spain.
71 Comision Pro-Derecho al Aborto, "Derecho al Aborto," *Tribuna Feminista* no. 1, 1983, 5–6, *Tribuna Feminista* folders, Ca la Dona Centre de Documentació, Barcelona, Spain.
72 Coordinadora de Catalunya pel Dret a l'Avortament, "Avortament Sense Restriccions! Les Dones Decidim! Manifest," undated illustration, Colleccions Moviments Socials, Organizaciones de dones, Folder C46-8: Coordinadora de Catalunya pel Dret a l'Avortament, Fundació Cipriano García Arxiu Històric de CCOO de Catalunya, Barcelona, Spain.
73 Comision Pro-Derecho al Aborto, "Derecho al Aborto," *Tribuna Feminista*, October 1984, 9, *Tribuna Feminista* folders, Ca la Dona Centre de Documentació, Barcelona, Spain.
74 Encuentros Feministas Estatales Por el Derecho al Aborto, Minutes of the Ponencia Comision Aborto Madrid, December 6–9, 1981, unpublished document belonging to the collection of the Centro de Documentación de Mujeres, http://cdd.emakumeak.org/recursos/2303 [accessed April 13, 2018].
75 Conversation with Mercè Otero, archivist at *Centre de Documentació de Ca la Dona*, Barcelona, Spain, July 6, 2014. The ad campaign that the *L'eix Violeta* poster

played on was the controversial "No Undesired Pregnancy" campaign discussed on page 122.

76 L'eix Violeta, "Póntelo, Pónselo, L'anticoncepció és un dret, l'avortament també," undated poster, Fons Ca la Dona, Cartells Donació Mercè Otero Vidal, Centre de Documentació de Ca la Dona, Barcelona, Spain.

77 Coordinadora de Catalunya pel Dret a l'Avortament, "Avortament Sense Restriccions! Les Dones Decidim! Manifest," undated illustration, Colleccions Moviments Socials, Organizaciones de dones, Folder C46-8: Coordinadora de Catalunya pel Dret a l'Avortament, Fundació Cipriano García Arxiu Històric de CCOO de Catalunya, Barcelona, Spain and a conversation with Mercè Otero, archivist at *Centre de Documentació de Ca la Dona*, Barcelona, Spain, July 6, 2014. The same illustration was also printed in *dones en lluita*, June 1983, 42.

78 Teresa Ortiz-Gómez and Agata Ignaciuk, "The Family Planning movement in Spain during the democratic transition," unpublished paper presented at the Health Activist Symposium, Yale University, October 22-3, 2010; Merike Blofield, *The Politics of Moral Sin: Abortion and Divorce in Spain, Chile and Argentina* (New York: Routledge, 2006), 77; and María R. Sahuquillo, "Abortion: A trip back in time," *El Pais*, May 8, 2013, online, http://elpais.com/elpais/2013/05/08/inenglish/1368013670_006955.html [accessed February 9, 2018].

79 Ana Maria Prata Amaral Pereira, "Women's Movements, the State, and the Struggle for Abortion Rights: Comparing Spain and Portugal in Times of Democratic Expansion" *(1974-1988)* (Ph.D. Diss., University of Minnesota, 2007), 115, ProQuest Dissertations Publishing. Ironically, as of 2008 abortion laws in the UK were more restrictive than in Spain and UK abortion clinic workers advised women who could no longer obtain legal abortions in the UK to travel to Spain for the procedure: Sofia Strid, *Gendered Interests in the European Union: The European Women's Lobby and the Organisation and Representation of Women's Interests* (Örebro, Sweden: Örebro University, 2009), 111.

80 Sahuquillo, "Abortion: A trip back in time."

81 Figure 10.1 from an article economists Facundo Alvaredo and Emmanuel Saez published historical income level in Spain suggests that the average income in Spain in 1980 was approximately 11,317 (in 2010 euros) and that income level held relatively steady in the years before and after. With the help of an online calculator, I converted 11,317 2010 euros into 1980 pesetas, choosing to use the "labor earnings" section under their Income and Wealth comparison section https://www.measuringworth.com/calculators/spaincompare/relativevalue.php [accessed February 9, 2018]. This calculation told me that the average income in Spain, in pesetas, in 1980 was 258,000, or 21,500 pesetas per month. For more information, see: Facundo Alvaredo and Emmanuel Saez, "Income and Wealth Concentration in Spain from a Historical and Fiscal Perspective," *Journal of the*

European Economic Association 7, no. 5 (2009): 5, using the Excel tables linked in footnote 5.
82 Sahuquillo, "Abortion: A trip back in time."
83 Rebecca Howard Davis, *Women and Power in Parliamentary Democracies: Cabinet Appointments in Western Europe, 1968–1992* (Lincoln, NE: University of Nebraska Press, 1997), 6.
84 Conversation with Carles Gomez-del-Moral, Barcelona, Spain, June 10, 2016.
85 Blofield, *The Politics of Moral Sin*, 77.
86 Pereira, "Women's Movements, the State, and the Struggle for Abortion Rights," 119.
87 "Spanish Court Suspends Abortion Trial in Bilbao," *New York Times*, October 27, 1979, http://www.nytimes.com/1979/10/27/archives/spanish-court-suspends-abortion-trial-in-bilbao.html [accessed 9 February, 2018].
88 Monica Threlfall, "Feminist Politics and Social Change in Spain," in *Mapping the Women's Movement: Feminist Politics and Social Transformation in the North*, ed. Monica Threlfall (New York: Verso, 1996), 121.
89 Comisión Permanente (96ª) de la Conferencia Episcopal Española, "La vida y el aborto: Declaración del Episcopado sobre la despenalización del aborto," February 5, 1983, Conferencia Episcopal Española, Colección Documental Informática: Documentos oficiales desde 1966, http://www.conferenciaepiscopal.nom.es/archivodoc [accessed April 16, 2018].
90 Conversations with Merce Otero, July 13, 2014.
91 Generalitat de Catalunya, Departament de Sanitat i Assistència Social, "L'amor és cec, però tu cal que hi vegis clar," poster, 1980, Fons Ca la Dona, Cartells Donació Mercè Otero Vidal, Centre de Documentació de Ca la Dona, Barcelona, Spain.
92 Merike Blofield, "Women's Choices in Comparative Perspective: Abortion Policies in Late-Developing Catholic Countries," *Comparative Politics* 40, no. 4 (July 2008): 409, www.jstor.org/stable/20434093. Blofield argues that feminists must characterize abortion as a public health issue and get the public to accept that before there is reform, and in Spain feminists certainly did make that argument. However, as this chapter argues, this was one politically expedient strategic argument among many that feminists made to draw attention to the issue—PSOE in fact made it a cornerstone of the abortion debate though for feminists it seemed more a tangential issue, after bodily autonomy.
93 Davis, *Women and Power in Parliamentary Democracies*, 6.
94 Blofield, "Women's Choices in Comparative Perspective," 78 and Gisela T. Kaplan, *Contemporary Western European Feminism* (New York, NY: New York University Press, 1992), 202.
95 Blofield, *The Politics of Moral Sin*, 78 and Pereira, "Women's Movements, the State, and the Struggle for Abortion Rights," 119.

96 "Italy Legalizes Abortion Despite Vatican Opposition," *New York Times*, May 19, 1978, newspaper clipping in private collection donated to author by Temma Kaplan.
97 Pereira, "Women's Movements, the State, and the Struggle for Abortion Rights," 119.
98 Colin Francome, *Unsafe Abortion and Women's Health: Change and Liberalization* (London, UK: Routledge, 2016), 44.
99 Richard Gunther, Giacomo Sani, and Goldie Shabad, eds., *Spain after Franco: The Making of a Competitive Party System* (Los Angeles: University of California Press, 1988).
100 Pereira, "Women's Movements, the State, and the Struggle for Abortion Rights," 137.
101 Coordinadora de Organizaciones Feministas del Estado Español, "Tribunal Contra Las Agresiones al Derecho Aborto," December 13, 1986, pg. 27, Fons Ca la Dona, Box 81: Avortament i dret al propi cos [1979–92], Centre de Documentació de Ca la Dona, Barcelona, Spain.
102 Pereira, *Women's Movements, the State, and the Struggle for Abortion Rights*, 176.
103 Ibid., 165.
104 Blofield, *The Politics of Moral Sin*, 69–70.
105 Valiente, "Spain at the Vanguard in European Gender Equality Policies," 107–9.
106 Callahan, *The Catholic Church in Spain, 1875–1998*, 567. For more information about particularly leftists' disappointment with the 1978 Constitution and their desired church-state relations in the new democracy, see: Tusell, *Spain*; Richard Gunther, "Spain: the very model of the modern elite settlement," in *Elites and Democratic Consolidation in Latin American and Southern Europe*, eds. John Higley and Richard Gunther (New York: Cambridge University Press, 1992), 45–7, 58–9; Robert Agranoff, "Federal Evolution in Spain," *International Political Science Review* 17, no. 4 (October 1996): 387–9; Montserrat Gibernau, "Spain: a Federation in the Making?," in *Federalism: The Multiethnic Challenge*, ed. Graham Smith (New York: Routledge, 1995), 245–54; and Juan J. Linz, "Church and State in Spain from the Civil War to the Return of Democracy," *Daedalus* 120, no. 3 (Summer 1991): 159–78. Tusell discusses the "laborious" process of negotiating the Constitution and coming to consensus as well as the ultimate wide-spread "disenchantment" Spaniards felt with the final product (297). Multiple scholars have noted that the socialist representative on the drafting council withdrew from the negotiations at one point, expressing dissatisfaction with their direction. Indeed, as Gunther noted, leftists typically wanted something akin to the Constitution of the Second Republic—they wanted, at the very least, *a* Republic, and they wanted greater distancing between church and state (45–7). They also wanted, as scholars like Agranoff and Guibernau have discussed in detail, regions like the Basque Country

and Catalunya to become autonomous communities as had been the case in the 1930s rather than Spain being a rigid and formal federal state. Leftists for the most part achieved this latter goal, but the others, and particularly the wish for separation of church and state, remained unmet. This was the case even though, as Gunther has asserted, some church officials also pushed for disentanglement between the two institutions because they wanted the church to have greater autonomy. In any case, despite Juan Linz's contention that the 1978 Constitution created greater and more formal separation between church and state than had the Constitution of the Second Republic, leftists, and especially extreme leftists, certainly did not feel that way, and a significant part of their disenchantment was because of the church-state ties that remained.

107 Cristina Palomares, *The Quest for Survival After Franco* (Portland, OR: Sussex Academic Press, 2006).

108 Pereira, "Women's Movements, the State, and the Struggle for Abortion Rights," 166 and Valiente, "Gendering Abortion Debates," 241.

109 Valiente, "Gendering Abortion Debates," 235, 238–41.

110 Ibid., 236.

111 Ibid., 239–40 and Threlfall, "Feminist Politics and Social Change in Spain," 124. Valiente in particular discusses single militant objections to what they interpreted as the *Instituto's* compromises while working for abortion reform. These "radical" feminists, as Valiente termed them, felt that the *Instituto* "and the socialist government would always promote measures that were far behind what radical feminists wanted, that is, abortion on demand performed in the public health system and free of charge."

112 Pereira, "Women's Movements, the State, and the Struggle for Abortion Rights," 168–9 and Valiente, "Gendering Abortion Debates," 235.

113 Periera, "Women's Movements, the State, and the Struggle for Abortion Rights," 171–2 and Valiente, "Gendering Abortion Debates," 233–4.

114 Ley Orgánica 9/1985 de reforma del articulo 417 bis del Código Penal, Jefatura del Estado (Spain), Boletín Oficial del Estado núm. 166, July 12, 1985, pg. 22041, www.boe.es/buscar/doc.php?id=BOE-A-1985-14138 [accessed February 9, 2018].

115 Belén Cambronero-Saiz, María Teresa Ruiz Cantero, Carmen Vives-Cases and Mercedes Carrasco Portiño, "Abortion in Democratic Spain: The Parliamentary Political Agenda 1979–2004," *Reproductive Health Matters* 15, no. 29 (May 2007): 86.

116 Marina Calloni, "Debates and Controversies on Abortion in Italy," in *Abortion Politics, Women's Movements, and the Democratic State*, ed. Dorothy McBride Stetson (New York: Oxford University Press, 2001), 185. Interestingly, feminists in that nation also insisted that legislators had ignored their demands and delivered far less than they had requested.

117 "Dossier: Movimento feminista en España," page 4 of special insert, 1981 section, *Tribuna Feminista*, 1983, *Tribuna Feminista* folders, Ca la Dona Centre de Documentació, Barcelona, Spain.
118 Ibid.
119 "8 de Març Dia de les Dones Manifestació 19 h Plaça Universitat," poster, March 8, 1986, Fons Ca la Dona, Cartells Donació Mercè Otero Vidal, Centre de Documentació de Ca la Dona, Barcelona, Spain.
120 Coordinadora de Organizaciones Feministas del Estado Español, "Tribunal Contra Las Agresiones al Derecho Aborto," December 13, 1986, pg. 27, Fons Ca la Dona, Box 81: Avortament i dret al propi cos [1979–92], Centre de Documentació de Ca la Dona, Barcelona, Spain.
121 Valiente, "Gendering Abortion Debates," 236, 238–43.

Chapter 3

1 For example, a number of speeches and pamphlets collected from an independent feminist gathering in Valencia in October 1983 addressed this topic, as did several issues of Basque feminist magazine Lanbroa: IV Jornadas Estatales de Feministas Independientes, Valencia, October 29, 1983. Document belonging to the gray literature collection of: "WOMEN'S DOCUMENTATION CENTER. EMAKUMEEN DOKUMENTAZIO ZENTROA", http://cdd.emakumeak.org/recursos/2387 [accessed February 9, 2018]; Lanbroa No. 4, December 1994, Donació Merce Otero Vidal, Ca La Dona Centre de Documentació, Barcelona, Spain; Lanbroa No. 5, March 8, 1995, Donació Merce Otero Vidal, Ca La Dona Centre de Documentació, Barcelona, Spain.
2 Valentine M. Moghadam, *Globalizing Women: Transnational Feminist Networks* (Baltimore, MD: Johns Hopkins University Press, 2005).
3 Comissió de dones 8 de març, "Manifiesto Por La Igualdad, En la ciudad de Valencia, a 8 de Marzo, Día Internacional de la Mujer, del año 1996," in "Lluna creixent o de l'afirmació personal," in Moviment Ara que tenim feminista 20 Anys: II Jornades feministes al pais Valencia, October 31, 1997, page 48, Document belonging to the gray literature collection of: "WOMEN'S DOCUMENTATION CENTER. EMAKUMEEN DOKUMENTAZIO ZENTROA", http://cdd.emakumeak.org/recursos/2389 [accessed February 9, 2018].
4 The Women's Campaign Against Fascist Spain, "Fascismo y Machismo," *Red Magazine*, December 31, 1975, 3–5, magazine in private collection donated to author by Temma Kaplan.
5 La Otra Historia, "Así nacio el feminismo," *Opción*, December 1976, 45–7, Ca la Dona Centre de Documentación, Barcelona, Spain.

6   La Otra Historia, "Así nació el feminismo (3)," *Opción*, February 1977, 84–7 and La Otra Historia, "Las historias excepcionales de tres españolas: Asi nació el feminismo (4)," *Opción*, March 1977, 86–90.
7   La Otra Historia, "Así nació el feminismo (3)," *Opción*, February 1977, 84.
8   Ibid., 86.
9   Mercedes Montoya, "La mujer china avanza por el camino socialista," *Vindicación Feminista*, January 1977, 50–1; Alicia Fajardo, "Italia: Las mujeres se movilizan contra la violencia," *Vindicación Feminista,* June 1978, 20–1; Lidia Falcón, "Etiopia: La agonia del ultimo reino biblico," *Vindicación Feminista*, April 1977, 24–8; and Comité de Solidaridad con la lucha del Pueblo Chileno, "Lucha antifascista de la mujer chilena," *Vindicación Feminista*, September 1978, 9.
10 Boletin de Suscripcion, *Vindicación Feminista*, in each issue, page variable.
11 *dones en lluita*, October 1981.
12 Margarita, "mujeres palestinas en la lucha armada," *dones en lluita*, November 1982, 4–6.
13 "La prostitución en Nicaragua," *dones en lluita*, May 1982, 12–6.
14 Celia Shalon and Karen Welch, "El movimiento de liberacion de la mujer in Gran Bretaña," *dones en lluita*, June 1983, 14–21.
15 "Medio Mundo," *Opción* no. 1, December 1976, 17–8.
16 For examples, see: "Dossier: El aborto una cuestión aún pendiente," *dones en lluita*, March 1983, 13–33; "Dossier: Aborto," *Tribuna Feminista,* October 1984, special insert; Alicia Fajardo, "El aborto en Italia ya no es delito," *Vindicacion Feminista*, March 1977, 48–53; Alicia Fajardo, Cronica/Italia, "Ley del aborto: estafa, parlamentarismo e ingenuidad," *Vindicacion Feminista*, August 1977, 27–30.
17 Paloma Saavedra and Regina Bayo, Mujeres Del Mundo, "En el Mundo," *Vindicación Feminista*, July 1976, 55–6.
18 "Investigaciones de mujeres e investigaciones feministas: Internacional," *Tribuna Feminista*, 1983, 8.
19 Begoña San Jose, "America Latina: Las Feministas Dominicanas … Caliente, Caliente," *Tribuna Feminista*, October 1984, 10.
20 "A modo de introduccion al tema del sexismo en la lengua," *Tribuna Feminista*, July 1985, 9.
21 These symbols are still widely used during feminist protests in Spain. During the International Women's Day strike on March 8, 2018, for example, demonstrators marched while holding up the diamond hand symbol. *The New York Times* published a photograph of the Bilbao demonstrators showing hundreds of women simultaneously making the gesture: Elisabetta Povoledo, Raphael Minder, and Yonette Joseph, "International Women's Day 2018: Beyond #MeToo, With Pride, Protests and Pressure," *The New York Times*, March 8, 2018, https://www.nytimes.com/2018/03/08/world/international-womens-day-2018.html [accessed March 27, 2018].

22 National Abortion Campaign (British), "Abortion Internationally," pamphlet, 1978, Fons Ca la Dona, Box 81: Avortament i dret al propi cos [1979–92], Folder 81,1: Recursos i informatius avortament i dret propius, Donació de Marcela Güell, Centre de Documentació de Ca la Dona, Barcelona, Spain.
23 The Women's Campaign Against Fascist Spain, "Fascismo y Machismo," *Red Magazine*, December 31, 1975, 3–5, magazine in private collection donated to author by Temma Kaplan.
24 El Colective "Consulterios" del Movimente Italiano de Liberación de la Mujer (MLD), "Como evitar al embarazo," pamphlet, 1975, Fons Ca la Dona, Box 81: Avortament i dret al propi cos [1979–92], Folder 81,2: metódes autoconceptius, Centre de Documentació de Ca la Dona, Barcelona, Spain.
25 Vocalia de Mujeres del Carmela, "El examen ginecologio," undated pamphlet, Fons Ca la Dona, Box 81: Avortament i dret al propi cos [1979–92], Folder 81,4: recursos informatius & salut 1234, Donació Maria Olivara, Centre de Documentació de Ca la Dona, Barcelona, Spain and Vocalia de Mujeres del Carmela, "Infecciones vaginales y cura alternativa," undated pamphlet, Fons Ca la Dona, Box 81: Avortament i dret al propi cos [1979–92], Folder 81,4: recursos informatius & salut 1234, Donació Maria Olivara, Centre de Documentació de Ca la Dona, Barcelona, Spain. Notation inside the back cover referencing these specific editions implies that the organization translated and edited other editions as well.
26 "Infecciones vaginales y curas alternativas (Reproduccio del folleto publicado por la Vocalia de Mujeres del Carmelo)," *dones en lluita*, May 1982, 48.
27 Conversations with Merce Otero, archivist at Ca La Dona Centre de Documentació, Barcelona, July 13, 2014.
28 El Colective "Consulterios" del Movimente Italiano de Liberación de la Mujer (MLD), "Como evitar al embarazo," pamphlet, 1975, Fons Ca la Dona, Box 81: Avortament i dret al propi cos [1979–92], Folder 81,2: metódes autoconceptius, Centre de Documentació de Ca la Dona, Barcelona, Spain.
29 Jones, *Women in contemporary Spain*, 7; National Abortion Campaign (British), "Abortion Internationally," pamphlet, 1978, Fons Ca la Dona, Box 81: Avortament i dret al propi cos [1979–92], Folder 81,1: Recursos i informatius avortament i dret propius, Donació de Marcela Güell, Centre de Documentació de Ca la Dona, Barcelona, Spain; Gruppo Femminista per la Salute della Donna (Italian), Series of three pamphlets, "L'Autovisita," "Visita Ginecologica," "Infezioni Vaginali," May 1979, Fons Ca la Dona, Box 81: Avortament i dret al propi cos [1979–92], Folder 81,4: Recursos informatius & salut 1234, Donació Isabel Martínez, Centre de Documentació de Ca la Dona, Barcelona, Spain; and Stimezo (Dutch feminist organization), "Abortius uit het wetboek strafrecht," pamphlet, April 1980, Fons Ca la Dona, Box 81: Avortament i dret al propi cos [1979–92], Folder 81,1: Recursos i informatius avortament i dret propius, Donació de Marcela Güell, Centre de Documentació de Ca la Dona, Barcelona, Spain.

30 Stimezo, "El aborto en las clinicas holandeses," pamphlet, 1983, Fons Ca la Dona, Box 81: Avortament i dret al propi cos [1979–92], Folder 81,1: Recursos i informatius avortament i dret propius, Centre de Documentació de Ca la Dona, Barcelona, Spain. Abortion was legalized in the Netherlands in November 1981 and the law came into effect in November 1984.

31 National Abortion Campaign (British), "Abortion Internationally," pamphlet, 1978, Fons Ca la Dona, Box 81: Avortament i dret al propi cos [1979–92], Folder 81,1: Recursos i informatius avortament i dret propius, Donació de Marcela Güell, Centre de Documentació de Ca la Dona, Barcelona, Spain.

32 International Campaign for Abortion Rights, "Minutes of the Third International Planning Meeting of the International Campaign for Abortion Rights (ICAR)," December 9, 1978, Fons Ca la Dona, *dones en lluita* folder, Centre de Documentació de Ca la Dona, Barcelona, Spain.

33 Coordinadora de Organizaciones Feministas del Estado Español, "Tribunal Contra Las Agresiones al Derecho al Aborto," December 13, 1986, Fons Ca la Dona, Box 81: Avortament i dret al propi cos [1979–92], Folder 81,5: Avortament i dret a pel propis, Centre de Documentació de Ca la Dona, Barcelona, Spain.

34 See: Temma Kaplan, "Women's Rights as Human Rights: Women as Agents of Social Change," in *Women, Gender, and Human Rights: A Global Perspective*, ed. Marjorie Agosín (New Brunswick, NJ: Rutgers University Press, 2002), 199 and Donna J. Sullivan, "Women's Human Rights and the 1993 World Conference on Human Rights," *American Journal of International Law* 88, no. 1 (January 1994): 152, https://doi.org/10.2307/2204032. The breakout moment of feminists' turn toward "gendering" human rights was in 1993, at the UN conference for Human Rights in Vienna, Austria. Conference shows the confluence of these two trends— activists' calls for women's inclusion in human rights policy, and their insistence that every policy area wrestle with how to incorporate women's rights. Female delegates had long sought an opportunity to expand the definition of human rights to apply specifically to women as well as men, and to recognize that abuses against women were human rights violations. In light of the brutality and sexual violence in the former Yugoslavia, female activists pushed the Commission on Human Rights to recognize that rape was a war crime, and to prosecute accordingly, as well as to expand the Charter on Human Rights to define rape, violence against women and girls, and infringement on women's bodily autonomy as violations of human rights. This was contentious. Indeed, Temma Kaplan describes that women forced their way into plenary sessions in an effort to raise awareness for their cause. In one particular instance, women marched into a closed session in order to present a petition with 300,000 signatures to have their voices heard. In the end, The Vienna Declaration and Programme of Action is where we see the emergence of "women's rights are human rights" slogan. Sullivan argues that this Programme of Action

"identifies particular examples of gender-specific abuses as human rights violations and calls for integration of women's rights throughout United Nations activities. Most strikingly, the conference crystallized a political consensus that various forms of violence against women should be examined within the context of human rights standards and in conjunction with gender discrimination."

35 Valentine M. Moghadam, *Globalizing Women*.
36 Elisabeth Jay Friedman, "Gendering the Agenda: The Impact of the Transnational Women's Rights Movement at the UN Conferences of the 1990s," *Women's Studies International Forum* 26, no. 4 (July-August 2003): 313.
37 Office of the Special Adviser on Gender Issues, *Gender Mainstreaming: An Overview* (New York: United Nations, 2002), 1, www.un.org/womenwatch/osagi/pdf/e65237.pdf [accessed February 9, 2018].
38 Kenneth Cmiel, "The Recent History of Human Rights," *The American Historical Review* 109, no. 1 (2004): 117-35.
39 Torild Skard, "Gender in the Malestream—Acceptance of Women and Gender Equality in Different United Nations Organisations," *Forum for Development Studies* 36, no. 1 (2009): 1.
40 Ibid., 167.
41 Ibid., 185.
42 Mariagrazia Rossilli, ed., *Gender Policies in the European Union* (New York: Peter Lang Publishing, 2000).
43 Jane Jenson, "Writing Women Out, Folding Gender In: The European Union 'Modernises' Social Policy," *Social Politics: International Studies in Gender, State & Society* 15, no. 2 (Summer 2008): 131-53.
44 Xavier Arbós Marín, "The Federal Option and Constitutional Management of Diversity in Spain," in *The Ways of Federalism in Western Countries and the Horizons of Territorial Autonomy in Spain*, ed. Alberto López-Basaguren and Leire Escajedo San Epifano (Berlin: Springer, 2013), 375.
45 John Hooper, *The New Spaniards* (New York: Penguin Books, 2006); Víctor Pérez Díaz, *The Return of Civil Society: The Emergence of Democratic Spain* (Cambridge, MA: Harvard University Press, 1993); Alba Alonso and Maxime Forest. "Is Gender Equality Soluble into Self-Governance: Europeanizing Gender at the Sub-National Level in Spain," in *The Europeanization of Gender Equality Policies: A Sociological-Discursive Approach*, ed. Emanuela Lombardo and Maxime Forest (New York: Palgrave Macmillan, 2012), 7-8.
46 Carmen Olmeda Checa, Editorial, *Meridiana*, April 1996, 3.
47 Encantada Garcia, "Politicas de igualdad: lo que los partidos no proponen," *Meridiana*, April 1996, 17.
48 Encantada Garcia, "No todas la Instituciones son iguales," *Meridiana*, April 1996, 17.

49 Plataforma Andaluza de Apoyo al Lobby Europeo de Mujeres, "Plataforma Andaluza de Apoyo al Lobby Europeo de Mujeres," *Meridiana*, April 1997, 57.
50 Ibid.
51 Valiente, "Spain at the Vanguard in European Gender Equality Policies," 107.
52 Plataforma Andaluza de Apoyo al Lobby Europeo de Mujeres, "Plataforma Andaluza de Apoyo al Lobby Europeo de Mujeres," *Meridiana*, April 1997, 57.
53 "Comunicado de la Comisión Preparatoria para el Foro de Nairobi de Madrid," *Tribuna Feminista*, July 1985, 6.
54 Ibid.
55 Lola G. Luna and Maria Luisa Merino i Serra, "Feminismo y Poder," in "IV Jornadas Estatales de Feministas Independientes," October 29, 1983, 6. Document belonging to the gray literature collection of: "WOMEN'S DOCUMENTATION CENTER. EMAKUMEEN DOKUMENTAZIO ZENTROA", http://cdd.emakumeak.org/recursos/2387 [accessed February 9, 2018].
56 Ibid.
57 Karmele Marchante Barrobes, "El Nuevo Feminismo," in "IV Jornadas Estatales de Feministas Independientes," collected papers from feminist conference, October 29, 1983, 20. Document belonging to the gray literature collection of: "WOMEN'S DOCUMENTATION CENTER. EMAKUMEEN DOKUMENTAZIO ZENTROA", http://cdd.emakumeak.org/recursos/2387 [accessed February 9, 2018].
58 El Colectivo Lanbroa, "Analisis y Perspectivas del movimiento Feminisa en Bizkaia," *Lanbroa*, December 1994, 17.
59 Entrevisa, "Lidia Falcón, Pionera del Feminismo en el Estado Español, Fundadora del Partido Feminista Escritora," *Lanbroa*, December 1994, 32.
60 Entrevista, "Concha Fagoaga," *Lanbroa*, March 8, 1995, 7.
61 El Colectivo Lanbroa, "Analisis y Perspectivas del movimiento Feminisa en Bizkaia," *Lanbroa*, December 1994, 12.
62 Ibid., 17.
63 In her work, Radcliff has noted that similar coverage of feminists in the early transition also failed to provide "a conceptual framework that made sense of their presence" despite "significant coverage" so this was typical of Spanish perceptions of feminism. Pamela Beth Radcliff, "Imagining Female Citizenship in the 'New Spain': Gendering the Democratic Transition, 1975–1978," *Gender & History* 13, no. 3 (2001): 509.
64 Francisco Acedo, "Carmen Romero, 'estrella' del encuentro de mujeres del PSOE," *ABC*, February 9, 1986, http://hemeroteca.abc.es/nav/Navigate.exe/hemeroteca/madrid/abc/1986/03/09/023.html [accessed February 9, 2018].
65 Teresa Cardenas, "Isabel Donaire, la mayoría absoluta en el hogar de Pedro Pacheco," *ABC*, June 26, 1990, http://hemeroteca.abc.es/nav/Navigate.exe/hemeroteca/sevilla/abc.sevilla/1990/06/26/111.html [accessed February 9, 2018].

66 Clara Guzman, "'Estoy en contra del feminismo radical'," *ABC*, October 15, 1989, http://hemeroteca.abc.es/nav/Navigate.exe/hemeroteca/sevilla/abc.sevilla/1989/10/15/142.html [accessed February 9, 2018].

67 Most intellectuals and public figures interviewed for a 1990 *Blanco y Negro* article put forth similar arguments, including PP representative Maria Jesús Sainz who felt that legislative changes and women's right to vote made feminism in general less useful; journalist Rosa María Mateo, who sociologist Amando de Miguel who argued that feminism "[was] a thing of the past" and that 1990s Spanish feminism was "a caricatured fool of what it [had been]." Even the director of the *Instituto* acknowledged that she thought feminists had met their major goal of legal equality, and to the extent that they still had work do, it involved "equal opportunities at work, a true balanced distribution in the private sphere and a greater presence of women in positions of responsibility." Valenti Puig, "Veinte años después: El Feminismo Resucita,"*Blanco y Negro*, November 4, 1990, http://hemeroteca.abc.es/nav/Navigate.exe/hemeroteca/madrid/blanco.y.negro/1990/11/04/036.html [accessed February 9, 2018].

68 Valenti Puig, "Veinte años después".

69 Francisco Vázquez Graciano, "Machismo y feminismo," *ABC*, May 5, 1984, http://hemeroteca.abc.es/nav/Navigate.exe/hemeroteca/sevilla/abc.sevilla/1984/05/05/042.html [accessed February 9, 2018] and Miguel Pérez Calderón, "Feminismo y machismo," *ABC*, September 13, 1989, http://hemeroteca.abc.es/nav/Navigate.exe/hemeroteca/madrid/abc/1989/09/13/018.html [accessed February 9, 2018].

70 Almudena Guzmán, "No tememos arreglo," *ABC*, May 8, 1990, http://hemeroteca.abc.es/nav/Navigate.exe/hemeroteca/madrid/abc/1990/05/28/020.html [accessed February 9, 2018].

71 Colectivo de Coeducación de Lanbroa, "Politica Feminista en Educación," *Lanbroa*, December 1994, 34.

72 Alonso and Forest, "Is Gender Equality Soluble into Self-Governance"; Alba Alonso and Tània Verge, "Territorial Dynamics and Gender Equality Policies in Spain," in "Étudier les systèmes fédéreux à travers le prisme du genre," ed. Petra Meier, special issue, *Fédéralisme Régionalisme* 14 (2014), https://popups.uliege.be/1374-3864/index.php?id=1365 [accessed December 16, 2022].

73 Comissió de dones 8 de març, "Manifiesto Por La Igualdad, En la ciudad de Valencia, a 8 de Marzo, Día Internacional de la Mujer, del año 1996," in "Lluna creixent o de l'afirmació personal," in Moviment Ara que tenim feminista 20 Anys: II Jornades feministes al pais Valencia, October 31, 1997, 48. Document belonging to the gray literature collection of: "WOMEN'S DOCUMENTATION CENTER. EMAKUMEEN DOKUMENTAZIO ZENTROA", http://cdd.emakumeak.org/recursos/2389 [accessed February 9, 2018].

74 Alonso and Verge, "Territorial Dynamics and Gender Equality Policies in Spain," 4.

Chapter 4

1. "Entrevista íntegra a Ana Orantes días antes de su asesinato," *Informativos TeleCinco*, November 25, 2008, https://www.telecinco.es/informativos/sociedad/Entrevista-intregra-Ana-Orantes-asesinato_0_747600023.html [accessed March 3, 2018].
2. Ibid.
3. For more information, see: Consejo General del Poder Judicial (Spain), Servicio de Inspeccion, Grupo de Trabajo de Violencia Doméstica, "Informe sobre muertes violentas en el ambito de violencia doméstico en el año 2003," p.4 and Sebastián Tobarra, "La mujer asesinada por su ex marido en Barcelona lo había denunciado 54 veces," *El País*, June 12, 2003, https://elpais.com/diario/2003/06/12/sociedad/1055368805_850215.html [accessed March 3, 2018]. According to the Consejo General del Poder Judicial study on intimate partner violence, 102 women were murdered by their husbands or domestic partners in Spain in 2003 alone. Only some of these cases were publicized, like Ana Maria Fabregas, whose spouse beat her to death with a hammer.
4. For some examples, see: Diario de Sesiones de las Cortes Generales (Spain), VI Legislature, Núm. 90, Sesión núm. 16, "De los derechos de la mujer," March 9, 1998, 1860–1861, 1864, http://www.congreso.es/public_oficiales/L6/CORT/DS/CM/CM_090.PDF [accessed April 18, 2018] and Diario de Sesiones de las Cortes Generales (Spain), VI Legislature, Núm. 102, Sesión núm. 17, "De los derechos de la mujer," April 28, 1998, 2117, 2121, http://www.congreso.es/public_oficiales/L6/CORT/DS/CM/CM_102.PDF [accessed April 18, 2018].
5. "Entrevista íntegra a Ana Orantes días antes de su asesinato," *Informativos TeleCinco*, November 25, 2008, https://www.telecinco.es/informativos/sociedad/Entrevista-intregra-Ana-Orantes-asesinato_0_747600023.html [accessed March 3, 2018].
6. Sonia Aran Ramspott and Pilar Medina Bravo, "Representación de la violencia doméstica en la prensa española," *Estudios sobre el Mensaje Periodístico* 12 (2006): 11.
7. James M. Markham, "Spain's Feminist Movement Concentrating on Rape Issue," *New York Times*, May 29, 1978, newspaper clipping in private collection donated to author by Temma Kaplan.
8. Eva i Elisenda, "Sobre Violaciones," *dones en lluita*, February 1978, 5, *dones en lluita* folders, Ca la Dona Centre de Documentació, Barcelona, Spain. Chumez originally made his comment—intended to be a joke—in the February 3, 1978 edition

of Barcelona periodical *Correu Catala*; *dones en lluita* reprinted the offending paragraph.

9   Markham, "Spain's Feminist Movement Concentrating on Rape Issue."
10 Ibid.
11 Tribunal Supremo (Spain), Judgement of April 24, 1992, Pub Med Database, PMID: 12293730, https://www.ncbi.nlm.nih.gov/pubmed/12293730 [accessed April 18, 2018].
12 Markham, "Spain's Feminist Movement Concentrating on Rape Issue."
13 Conny Roggeband, "'Immediately I Thought We Should Do the Same Thing' International Inspiration and Exchange in Feminist Action against Sexual Violence," *European Journal of Women's Studies* 11, no. 2 (May 2004): 168.
14 Roggeband, "'Immediately I Thought We Should Do the Same Thing,'" 165–7.
15 Celia Valiente, "But Where Are the Men?: Central-State Public Policies to Combat Violence against Women in Post-Authoritarian Spain (1975–1999)," paper presented at the Council of Europe Seminar on Men and Violence against Women, Strasbourg, October 7–8, 1999, http://www.europrofem.org/White-Ribbon/13.institutions/3.coe/en-violence-coe/16.en-coe-oct99.htm [accessed April 16, 2018] and Celia Valiente, "Combating violence against women," in *Gendering Spanish Democracy*, ed. Monica Threlfall, Christine Cousins, and Celia Valiente (New York: Routledge, 2004), 107.
16 Ramspott and Bravo, "Representación de la violencia doméstica en la prensa española."
17 Ley Orgánica 3/1989, de 21 de junio, de actualización del Código Penal, Artículo 18, Jefatura del Estado (Spain), Boletín Oficial del Estado núm. 148, June 22, 1989, pgs. 19351–8, http://www.boe.es/buscar/doc.php?id=BOE-A-1989-14247 [accessed February 2, 2018].
18 Ley Orgánica 10/1995, de 23 de noviembre, del Código Penal, Artículo 153, Jefatura del Estado, Boletín del Estado núm. 281, November 24, 1994, pg. 34006, http://www.boe.es/buscar/doc.php?id=BOE-A-1995-25444 [accessed February 2, 2018].
19 Ramspott and Bravo, "Representación de la violencia doméstica en la prensa española," 11.
20 "Death of a Wife in Spain Brings Outcry on Intimate Partner Violence," *New York Times*, December 26, 1997, http://www.nytimes.com/1997/12/26/world/death-of-a-wife-in-spain-brings-outcry-on-domestic-violence.html [accessed March 5, 2018].
21 William J. Callahan, *The Catholic Church in Spain, 1875–1998* (Washington, DC: The Catholic University of America Press, 2012), 562. Callahan described Yanes' personal political inclinations as following in the "Herrera accidentalist tradition," a reference to Ángel Herrera Oria, one of the founders of the Catholic conservative

political party, the Confederación Española de Derechas Autónomas (CEDA) (536, fn40).
22 Ley Orgánica 10/1995, de 23 de noviembre, del Código Penal, Jefatura del Estado (Spain), Boletín Oficial del Estado núm. 281, November 24, 1995, pgs. 33987–4058, https://www.boe.es/diario_boe/txt.php?id=BOE-A-1995-25444 [accessed February 2, 2018].
23 Plan de Acción Contra la Violencia Doméstica 1998–2000, https://web.archive.org/web/20110915130459/http://www.malostratos.org/images/pdf/PLAN%20DE%20ACCION%20CONTRA%20LA%20VIOLENCIA%20DOMESTICA%201998.pdf [accessed April 18, 2018].
24 Plan de Acción Contra la Violencia Doméstica 1998–2000, https://web.archive.org/web/20110915130459/http://www.malostratos.org/images/pdf/PLAN%20DE%20ACCION%20CONTRA%20LA%20VIOLENCIA%20DOMESTICA%201998.pdf [accessed April 18, 2018].
25 Ibid.
26 Diaro de Sesiones de las Cortes Generales (Spain), VI Legislature, Núm. 102, Sesión núm. 17, "De los derechos de la mujer," April 28, 1998, 2120, http://www.congreso.es/public_oficiales/L6/CORT/DS/CM/CM_102.PDF [accessed April 18, 2018].
27 Ibid.
28 Ley Orgánica 14/1999, de 9 de junio, de modificación del Código Penal de 1995, en materia de protección a las víctimas de malos tratos y de la Ley de Enjuiciamiento Criminal, Jefatura del Estado (Spain), Boletín Oficial del Estado núm 138, June 10, 1999, pgs. 22251–3, https://www.boe.es/buscar/doc.php?id=BOE-A-1999-12907 [accessed February 2, 2018].
29 Juanjo Medina-Ariza and Rosemary Barberet, "Intimate Partner Violence in Spain: Findings from a National Survey," *Violence against Women* 9, no. 3 (March 2003): 316.
30 Medina-Ariza and Barberet, "Intimate Partner Violence in Spain," 311–2.
31 Silvia López, Elin Peterson, and Raquel Platero, *Issue Histories Spain: Series of Timelines of Policy Debates*, Quality in Gender and Equality Policies (QUING) Project (Vienna: Institute for Human Sciences, 2007), 7, http://www.quing.eu/files/results/ih_spain.pdf [accessed March 18, 2018].
32 For an example of one of these murders, see Sebastián Tobarra, "La mujer asesinada por su ex marido en Barcelona lo había denunciado 54 veces," *El País*, June 12, 2003, https://elpais.com/diario/2003/06/12/sociedad/1055368805_850215.html [accessed April 15, 2018].
33 Ley 27/2003, de 31 de Julio, reguladora de la Orden de protección de las víctimas de la violencia domestica, Jefatura del Estado (Spain), Boletín Oficial del Estado núm. 183, August 1, 2003, pgs. 29881–3, https://www.boe.es/buscar/doc.php?id=BOE-A-2003-15411 [accessed March 3, 2018].

34 United Nations Convention on the Elimination of All Forms of Discrimination against Women, General Recommendations made by the Committee on the Elimination of Discrimination against Women, General Recommendation 19, "Violence against women," Eleventh session, 1992, http://www.un.org/womenwatch/daw/cedaw/recommendations/recomm.htm#recom19 [accessed April 18, 2018].
35 Ley 27/2003, de 31 de Julio, reguladora de la Orden de protección de las víctimas de la violencia domestica, Jefatura del Estado (Spain), Boletín Oficial del Estado núm. 183, August 1, 2003, pgs. 29881–3, https://www.boe.es/buscar/doc.php?id=BOE-A-2003-15411 [accessed March 3, 2018].
36 Emanuela Lombardo, "The Influence of the Catholic Church on Spanish Political Debates on Gender Policy (1996-2004)," in *Gender, Religion, Human Rights in Europe*, ed. Kari Børresen and Sara Cabibbo (Rome: Herder, 2006), 8. Lombardo made this chapter accessible as stand-alone.pdf on her personal research website, which this author last consulted December 16, 2022, and which is accessible via https://www.researchgate.net/publication/277009466_The_Influence_of_the_Catholic_Church_on_Spanish_Political_Debates_on_Gender_Policy_1996-2004%27_in_Gender_Religion_Human_Rights_in_Europe. All references to this Lombardo text are to the pdf, not the book article, and the pages listed are cited accordingly.
37 Ibid., 7.
38 For more information about mass graves and their exhumations, see: Francisco Ferrándiz, "Cries and Whispers: Exhuming and Narrating Defeat in Spain Today," *Journal of Spanish Cultural Studies* 9, no. 2 (2008): 177–92; Francisco Ferrándiz, "Exhuming the Defeated: Civil War Mass Graves in 21st-Century Spain," *American Ethnologist* 40, no. 1. (2013): 38–54; Francisco Ferrándiz, "Mass Graves, Landscapes of Terror: A Spanish Tale," in *Necropolitics: Mass Graves and Exhumations in the Age of Human Rights*, ed. Francisco Ferrándiz and Antonius C. G. M. Robben (Philadelphia: University of Pennsylvania Press, 2015), 92–118; Judith Keene, "Review Article: Turning Memories into History in the Spanish Year of Historical Memory," *Journal of Contemporary History* 42, no. 4 (October 2007): 662–5; and Jo Labanyi, "Memory and Modernity in Democratic Spain: The Difficulty of Coming to Terms with the Spanish Civil War," *Poetics Today* 28, no. 1 (Spring 2007): 95–6.
39 For more information about the relationship between the Spanish government and ETA, see: Teresa Whitfield, *Endgame for ETA: Elusive Peace in the Basque Country* (New York: Oxford University Press, 2014).
40 Sonia Aparicido (Editor), "Terrorismo Doméstico: Un Documento de elmundo.es," *El Mundo*, special online document feature, June 2004, http://www.elmundo.es/documentos/2004/06/sociedad/malostratos/index.html [access date April 16, 2018].

41 Luis Parejo (Illustrator), "Terrorismo Doméstico: Un Documento de elmundo. es," El Mundo, special online document feature, June 2004, http://www.elmundo.es/documentos/2004/06/sociedad/malostratos/index.html [access date April 16, 2018].

42 For some examples, see: Diario de Sesiones de las Cortes Generales (Spain), VI Legislature, Núm. 90, Sesión núm. 16, "De los derechos de la mujer," March 9, 1998, 1860–1, 1864, http://www.congreso.es/public_oficiales/L6/CORT/DS/CM/CM_090.PDF [accessed April 18, 2018] and Diario de Sesiones de las Cortes Generales (Spain), VI Legislature, Núm. 102, Sesión núm. 17, "De los derechos de la mujer," April 28, 1998, 2117, 2121, http://www.congreso.es/public_oficiales/L6/CORT/DS/CM/CM_102.PDF [accessed April 18, 2018].

43 Ley Orgánica 3/2007, de 22 de marzo, para la igualdad efectiva de mujeres y hombres, Jefatura del Estado (Spain), Boletín Oficial del Estado núm. 71, March 23, 2007, pgs. 12611–45, http://www.boe.es/buscar/doc.php?id=BOE-A-2007-6115 [March 3, 2018].

44 Ibid. Spanish law first required in 1988 that 25% of the party's deputies and representatives be women, and then raised the number to 40% in 2007.

45 Ley Orgánica 1/2004, de 28 de diciembre, de Medidas de Protección Integral contra la Violencia de Género, Jefatura del Estado (Spain), Boletín Oficial del Estado núm. 313, December 29, 2004, pgs. 42166–97, https://www.boe.es/buscar/doc.php?id=BOE-A-2004-21760 [accessed March 3, 2018].

46 Ibid.

47 Ibid.

48 Ley Orgánica 3/2007, de 22 de marzo, para la igualdad efectiva de mujeres y hombres, Jefatura del Estado (Spain), Boletín Oficial del Estado núm. 71, March 23, 2007, pgs. 12611–45, http://www.boe.es/buscar/doc.php?id=BOE-A-2007-6115 [March 3, 2018].

49 United Nations, Convention on the Elimination of All Forms of Discrimination against Women, CEDAW/C/SR.650, Committee on the Elimination of Discrimination against Women, Thirty-first session, Summary record of 650th meeting, Consideration of reports submitted by States parties under article 18 of the Convention (continued), Fifth periodic report of Spain (continued), July 7, 2004, 9, https://www.un.org/womenwatch/daw/cedaw/31sess.htm#documents [accessed April 18, 2018].

50 Ley Orgánica 1/2004, de 28 de diciembre, de Medidas de Protección Integral contra la Violencia de Género, Artículo 1: Objeto de la Ley, Jefatura del Estado (Spain), Boletín Oficial del Estado núm. 313, December 29, 2004, pgs. 42166–97, https://www.boe.es/buscar/doc.php?id=BOE-A-2004-21760 [accessed March 3, 2018].

51 Nuria Labari, "20 Argumentos para una ley," *El Mundo*, special online document feature, June 2004, http://www.elmundo.es/documentos/2004/06/sociedad/malostratos/favorycontra.html [accessed April 16, 2018].

52 Ibid.
53 Carmen Morán Breña, "Begnino Blanco: 'El aborto legal es violencia de género,'" *El País*, November 11, 2008, https://elpais.com/diario/2008/11/11/sociedad/1226358002_850215.html [accessed April 16, 2018].

Chapter 5

1 Susana Urra, "Spanish unions say 5.3 million observed morning strike on Women's Day," *El Pais In English*, 8 March 2018, https://elpais.com/elpais/2018/03/08/inenglish/1520498047_423763.html [accessed March 27, 2018].
2 This *El País* article contains excerpts of coverage from international newspapers, including The Guardian (UK), Le Monde (France), la Repubblica (Italy), and the New York Times, among others. "*La primera huelga feminista en España, en los principales medios internacionales*," *El Pais*, March 9, 2018. https://politica.elpais.com/politica/2018/03/08/actualidad/1520528768_368042.html [accessed March 27, 2018].
3 *Comisión 8M*, "*Manifiesto 8M*," http://hacialahuelgafeminista.org/manifiesto-8m/ [accessed March 27, 2018] and Pilar Álvarez, "*Las mujeres exigen medidas urgentes tras el éxito del 8 de Marzo*," *El País*, March 10, 2018, https://politica.elpais.com/politica/2018/03/09/actualidad/1520621522_367555.html [accessed March 27, 2018].
4 *Comisión 8M*, "International," http://hacialahuelgafeminista.org/international/ [accessed March 27, 2018].
5 Rocío González, "*Escaso seuimiento de autónomas en la huelga del 8 de marzo*," *Cincodias: El País Economía*, 9 March 2018, https://cincodias.elpais.com/cincodias/2018/03/09/autonomos/1520582490_764679.html?rel=str_articulo#1521064890527 [accessed March 27, 2018].
6 Pilar Álvarez, "*Las mujeres exigen medidas urgentes tras el éxito del 8 de Marzo*," *El País*, 10 March 2018, https://politica.elpais.com/politica/2018/03/09/actualidad/1520621522_367555.html [accessed March 27, 2018].
7 "*Bebe, sobre el feminismo actual, 'Ahora parece eua está mal nacer hombre*,'" *ABC*, 12 March 2018, http://www.abc.es/estilo/gente/abci-bebe-sobre-feminismo-actual-ahora-parece-esta-nacer-hombre-201803081144_noticia.html [accessed March 27, 2018].
8 Paco Puentes, "*Ocho mujeres no harán huelga el 8M*," *El País*, 7 March 2018, https://elpais.com/elpais/2018/03/07/album/1520413389_137070.html?rel=str_articulo#foto_gal_8 [accessed March 27, 2018].
9 Pere Vilanova, "*El día después*," *El País*, March 11, 2018, https://elpais.com/ccaa/2018/03/09/catalunya/1520551021_231064.html [accessed March 27, 2018].

10 Elsa Garcia de Blas, "*Las políticas más influyentes ante la huelga feminista del 8 de marzo*," *El País*, March 6, 2018, https://politica.elpais.com/politica/2018/03/05/actualidad/1520245523_685055.html [accessed March 27, 2018].

11 "*7.000 personas claman en Toledo por la mujer y el respeto a sus derechos*," *ABC*, March 9, 2018, http://www.abc.es/espana/castilla-la-mancha/toledo/ciudad/abci-7000-personas-claman-toledo-mujer-y-respeto-derechos-201803082113_noticia.html [accessed March 27, 2018].

12 Ibid.

13 D.G., "*Feijóo: 'El 8-M fue un clamor que hemos de entender los gobiernos*,'" *ABC Galicia*, March 9, 2018, "http://www.abc.es/espana/galicia/abci-feijoo-clamor-hemos-entender-gobiernos-201803092030_noticia.html" [March 27, 2018].

14 Z. Rial, "Paros en empresas y un a treintenta de actos marcan el 8-M más reivindicativo," *ABC Galicia*, March 8, 2018. http://www.abc.es/espana/galicia/abci-paros-empresas-y-treintena-actos-marcan-mas-reivindicativo-201803071942_noticia.html (March 27, 2018).

15 D.G., "Feijóo: 'El 8-M fue un clamor que hemos de entender los gobiernos,'" *ABC Galicia*, March 9, 2018, http://www.abc.es/espana/galicia/abci-feijoo-clamor-hemos-entender-gobiernos-201803092030_noticia.html [March 27, 2018].; Alexis Romero, "*Rivera asegura que 'solo unas pocas' abuchearon a Villacís en la manifestación feminista*," *ABC*, March 9, 2018, http://www.abc.es/sociedad/abci-rivera-asegura-solo-unas-pocas-abuchearon-villacis-manifestacion-feminista-201803091435_noticia.html [accessed March 27, 2018]; and "*Villacís sobre 8m: 'Una mayoría de mujeres no se sienten representadas*,'" *ABC*, March 5, 2018, http://www.abc.es/espana/abci-villacis-sobre-mayoria-mujeres-no-sienten-representadas-201803041400_video.html [accessed March 27, 2018].

16 de Blas, "*Las políticas más influyentes ante la huelga feminista del 8 de marzo.*"

17 Anabel Díez, "*El Gobierno está 'muy satisfecho' con las movilizaciones de las mujeres del 8 de Marzo*," *El País*, March 9, 2018, https://politica.elpais.com/politica/2018/03/09/actualidad/1520594787_282640.html [accessed March 27, 2018].

18 *Comisión 8M*, "Manifiesto 8M," http://hacialahuelgafeminista.org/manifiesto-8m/ [accessed March 27, 2018] and Pilar Álvarez, "*Las mujeres exigen medidas urgentes tras el éxito del 8 de Marzo*," *El País*, March 10, 2018, https://politica.elpais.com/politica/2018/03/09/actualidad/1520621522_367555.html [accessed March 27, 2018]; Delegación del Gobierno para la Violencia de Género, *Folleto—Pacto de Estado contra la Violencia de Género*, https://violenciagenero.igualdad.gob.es/pactoEstado/docs/FolletoPEVGcastweb.pdf [accessed December 21, 2022].

19 Ley Orgánica 3/2007, de 22 de marzo, para la igualdad efectiva de mujeres y hombres, Jefatura del Estado (Spain), Boletín Oficial del Estado núm. 71, March 23,

2007, pgs. 12611–645, http://www.boe.es/buscar/doc.php?id=BOE-A-2007-6115 [accessed December 15, 2022].

20 *Ley Orgánica* 2/2010, *de 3 de marzo, de salud sexual y reproductiva y de la interrupción voluntaria del embarazo*, Jefatura del Estado (Spain), *Boletín Oficial del Estado núm* 55, March 4, 2010, pgs. 21001–21014, http://boe.es/buscar/doc.php?id=BOE-A-2010-3514 [accessed March 8, 2018]; "*Zapatero pide que se revea la ley del aborto*," *La Nacion*, December 18, 2007, http://www.lanacion.com.ar/972099-zapatero-pide-que-se-revea-la-ley-del-aborto [accessed February 9, 2018]; An article in *El País*' opinion pages nine years later recapped the trial and its outcome, celebrated that Zapatero had in fact loosened restrictions on abortion in response, and expressed thanks that Rajoy had not succeeded in rolling back Zapatero's policies. Berna González Harbour, "*Hay algo peor que abortar: ir al juez además de abortar*," *El País*, June 22, 2016, https://elpais.com/elpais/2016/06/22/opinion/1466615594_827779.html [accessed April 6, 2018]; "*Zapatero se muestra ahora dispuesto a reformar la Ley del aborto*," 20 *Minutos*, December 17, 2007, http://www.20minutos.es/noticia/322944/0/zapatero/ley/aborto/ [accessed February 9, 2018].

21 "En España no se explota ni se discrimina per Zapatero quiere inventor un derecho al aborto." For an example of such coverage of these marches, see: "Más de 600.000 personas claman en Madrid contra la ley del aborto", *Libertad Digital*, March 7, 2010, https://www.libertaddigital.com/sociedad/madrid-acoge-la-gran-marcha-internacional-contra-el-aborto-1276386550/ [accessed December 21, 2022].

22 "Las leyes provida, ante el inminente fallo de Estrasburgo sobe la Constitución provida irlandesa," Hazte Oir, December 16, 2010, http://www.hazteoir.org/noticia/34935-leyes-provida-inminente-fallo-tribunal-estrasburgo-constitucion-provida-irlandesa [accessed February 9, 2018].

23 http://oldsite.alliancedefensefund.org/userdocs/IrelandJudgmentPR.pdf [accessed February 9, 2018].

24 See Rosemary Oelrich Bottcher, "El aborto, traición al feminismo," September 28, 2004, https://solidaridad.net/el-aborto-traici-n-al-feminismo565/ [accessed February 9, 2018]; Susan Walders, "Duelo a una vida perdida por una rápida decisión," Feminists for Life, 2004 http://www.feministsforlife.org/espanol/duelo.htm [accessed February 9, 2018]; "Nueva Sere de Anuncios de Feministas Pro Vida," Feminists for Life, 2004 http://www.feministsforlife.org/espanol/adsespanol.htm [accessed February 9, 2018]; "Declaración feminista contra el aborto," Feminists for Life of America, http://www.vidahumana.org/vidafam/feminismo/fem_abort.html [accessed February 9, 2018].

25 "DAV: El 40% de las mujeres que abortan ha pensado en suicidarse," Hazte Oir, December 4, 2008, http://www.hazteoir.org/np/dav-40-mujeres-que-abortan-ha-pensado-en-suicidarse [accessed February 9, 2018].

26 "New law would make Spain the country with highest number of abortions in EU," Catholic News Agency, December 12, 2008, http://www.catholicnewsagency.

com/news/new_law_would_make_spain_the_country_with_highest_number_of_abortions_in_eu [accessed February 9, 2018].

27 "Life Foundation in Spain denounces Amnesty International embracing abortion," Catholic News Agency, May 23, 2007, http://www.catholicnewsagency.com/news/life_foundation_in_spain_denounces_amnesty_international_embracing_abortion/ [accessed February 9, 2018].

28 "HO y DAV prometen 'no parar hasta que la ley del aborto sea derogada,'" Hazte Oir, February 25, 2010, http://www.hazteoir.org/node/28408 [accessed February 9, 2018].

29 "DAV despide a las 'ministras del aborto', 'las dos mujeres que más daño han hecho a las mujeres,'" Hazte Oir, October 20, 2010, http://www.hazteoir.org/np/dav-despide-ministras-aborto-dos-mujeres-que-mas-dano-han-hecho-mujeres [accessed February 9, 2018].

30 Vera Gutiérrez Calvo, "El Gobierno aprueba la ley del aborto más restrictiva de la democracia," *El País*, December 20, 2013, https://elpais.com/sociedad/2013/12/20/actualidad/1387544028_883233.html [accessed February 9, 2018].

31 "Un aplauso a … Gallardón, ministro de Justicia," Foro de la Familia, March 9, 2012, http://www.forofamilia.org/noticias/un-aplauso-a-gallardon-ministro-de-justicia [accessed February 9, 2018].

32 Irene Martín and Ignacio Urquizu-Sancho, "The 2011 General Election in Spain: The Collapse of the Socialist Party," *South European Society and Politics* 17, no. 2 (2012): 347–63.

33 "*Rajoy confirma la retirada de la ley del aborto por falta de consenso*", El País, September 23, 2014, https://politica.elpais.com/politica/2014/09/23/actualidad/1411473129_685551.html [accessed February 9, 2018].

34 Vera Gutiérrez Calvo and María R. Sahuquillo, "Controversial abortion reform expected to be cleared by Cabinet," https://english.elpais.com/elpais/2013/12/20/inenglish/1387542491_176780.html [accessed February 9, 2018].

35 Ley 15/2014, de 16 de septiembre, de racionalización del Sector Público y otras medidas de reforma administrativa, Boletín Oficial del Estado núm. 226, September 17, 2014, pgs. 72340–1, https://boe.es/boe/dias/2014/09/17/pdfs/BOE-A-2014-9467.pdf [accessed November 10, 2022].

36 María-Amparo and Ballester-Pastor, "The Women's Institute is transformed into the Institute for women and equal opportunities," European network of legal experts in gender equality and non-discrimination, April 9, 2015, https://www.equalitylaw.eu/document?task=document.viewdoc&id=938 [accessed November 10, 2022].

37 "*Portavoz igualdad PSOE: España será el 8M el país de mayor movilización,*" *La Vanguardia*, 7 March 2018, http://www.lavanguardia.com/vida/20180307/441335033051/portavoz-igualdad-psoe-espana-sera-el-8m-el-pais-de-mayor-movilizacion.html [accessed April 6, 2018].

38 Monica Ceberio Belaza, "*De Gallardón a La Mancha: el porqúe del éxito arrollador del 8-M en España*," *El País*, March 18, 2018, https://politica.elpais.com/politica/2018/03/17/actualidad/1521284688_453147.html [accessed April 6, 2018].
39 "*Una playa se llena de 739 cruces contra de los crímenes machistas de los diez últimos años en España*," *ABC*, 10 March 2018, http://www.abc.es/sociedad/abci-mujer-2018-playa-llena-731-cruces-contra-crimenes-machistas-diez-ultimos-anos-espana-201803081658_noticia.html [accessed April 6, 2018].
40 Alba Moraleda, "*Aumentan las víctimas registradas de violencia machista por segundo año*," *El País*, May 31, 2017, https://politica.elpais.com/politica/2017/05/31/actualidad/1496216239_724424.html [accessed February 9, 2018].
41 Purificación Causapié, "*Sobran razones*," *El País*, February 26, 2018, https://elpais.com/ccaa/2018/02/26/madrid/1519661038_134812.html?rel=str_articulo#1521065315682 [accessed April 6, 2018].
42 Olatz G. Abrisketa and Marian G. Abrisketa, "'It's Okay, Sister, Your Wolf-Pack Is Here': Sisterhood as Public Feminism in Spain," *Signs: Journal of Women in Culture and Society* 45, no. 4 (2020): 944.
43 "El duro relato de la joven que denunció la violación múltiple de 'La Manada': "Otro me cogió por detrás, me bajó los leggins y me penetró"", *Antena3 Notícias*, November 14, 2017, https://www.antena3.com/noticias/sociedad/el-duro-relato-de-la-joven-que-denuncio-la-violacion-multiple-de-la-manada-otro-me-cogio-por-detras-me-bajo-los-leggins-y-me-penetro_201711135a0a34950cf2ebaa1678da5f.html [accessed December 21, 2022]; Pepa López, "Estos son los mensajes de Whatsapp de 'La Manada,' el grupo acusado de la violación de San Fermín 2016," *Trendencias.com*, November 14, 2017, https://www.trendencias.com/feminismo/estos-son-los-mensajes-de-whatsapp-de-la-manada-el-grupo-acusado-de-la-violacion-de-san-fermin-2016 [accessed December 21, 2022]; Ana María Ortíz, "96 segundos de vídeo: la clave del juicio a 'La Manada'," *El Mundo*, November 12, 2017, https://www.elmundo.es/espana/2017/11/12/5a075dc822601d1a3a8b458e.html [accessed December 21, 2022].
44 Abrisketa and Abrisketa, 932.
45 See, for instance, James Badcock, "Pamplona 'Wolf Pack' Gang Rape Trial Angers Spain," *BBC News*, November 28, 2017, https://www.bbc.com/news/world-europe-42149912 [accessed December 21, 2022]; "Spain: 'Wolf Pack' Gang Rape Trial Angers Protestors", *Malta Today*, November 28, 2017, https://www.maltatoday.com.mt/news/world/82608/_spain_wolf_pack_gang_rape_trial_angers_protestors#.Y6M9GS8RqN8 [accessed December 21, 2022]; Sirin Kale, "Outrage in Spain as Country Awaits the 'Wolf Pack' Gang Rape Case Verdict," *Vice.com*, November 29, 2017, https://www.vice.com/en/article/vbz4y4/outrage-in-spain-as-country-awaits-the-wolf-pack-gang-rape-case-verdict [accessed December 21, 2022]; "Fünf Männer vergewaltigten 18-Jährige—der Prozess gerät zum Justiz-Skandal", *Focus Online*, November 21, 2017, https://www.focus.de/panorama/welt/

spanien-fuenf-maenner-vergewaltigen-18-jaehrige-beweismittel-nicht-zugelassen_id_7874888.html [accessed December 21, 2022].
46 See, for instance, Jesús Diges, "Juicio en Pamplona: Rabia colectiva por un informe sobre la víctima de la violación de San Fermín," *El Periódico de Catalunya*, November 15, 2017, https://www.elperiodico.com/es/sociedad/20171115/indignacion-en-las-redes-por-un-informe-sobre-la-violacion-de-san-fermin-que-asegura-que-la-joven-no-quedo-traumatizada-6425197 [accessed December 21, 2022].
47 Jesús Diges, "Juicio en Pamplona: Rabia colectiva."
48 Abrisketa and Abrisketa; Sección Segunda de la Audiencia Provincial de Navarra, "Sentencia No. 000038/2018," https://cdn.20m.es/adj/2018/04/26/3934.pdf [accessed December 21, 2022].
49 Abrisketa and Abrisketa; Elisa García-Mingo & Patricia Prieto Blanco, "#SisterIdobelieveyou: Performative hashtags against patriarchal justice in Spain", *Feminist Media Studies* (October 2021): 1–17.
50 Juan José Mateo, "Rajoy anuncia su dimisión como líder del PP y deja en manos de su sucesor la renovación," *El País*, 5 June 2018, https://elpais.com/politica/2018/06/05/actualidad/1528193102_308542.html [accessed December 21, 2022].
51 Carlos E. Cué, "Spain's Governing Coalition Partners: 'It Can't Go on like This,'" *El Pais English*, 22 February 2021, https://english.elpais.com/politics/2021-02-22/spains-governing-coalition-partners-it-cant-go-on-like-this.html [accessed November 10, 2022.]
52 Víctor Pérez Díaz. *The Return of Civil Society: The Emergence of Democratic Spain* (Cambridge, MA: Harvard University Press, 1993).

Bibliography

Archives Consulted

Centre de Documentació de Ca la Dona (Barcelona, Spain):
 Magazine archives
 Ca la Dona Records
 March 8 Posters
 Mercè Otero Vidal Donation, Posters

Centro de Documentación de Mujeres, Movimiento Feminista de Euskadi
 (Digital Archive)

Conferencia Episcopal Española (Digital Archive)

Fundació Cipriano García Arxiu Històric de CCOO de Catalunya (Barcelona, Spain):
 Christian Associations and Movements Records
 Political Organizations Records
 Social Movements and Women's Organizations Collection

United Nations Archives (New York, NY):
 Records of the Executive Office of the Secretary General
 Records of Secretary General Kurt Waldheim

Libraries Consulted

Biblioteca Nacional de Catalunya (Barcelona, Spain)
Biblioteca Nacional de España (Madrid, Spain)

Magazines and Bulletins Consulted

¡Hola!: Semanario de amenidades
Boletín Oficial de Estado
Diaro de Sesiones de las Cortes Generales
dones en lluita: Bulleti Mensual de la Coordinadora Feminista de Barcelona
Lanbroa, Conspiración Feminista

Interviú
Meridiana: Instituto Andaluz de la Mujer
Newsweek
Opción: Revista de la mujer liberada
Red Magazine
Telva
Teresa: Revista para todas las mujeres
Tribuna Feminista
Triunfo
Vindicacion Feminista

Newspapers Consulted

20 Minutos
A.B.C.
Blanco y Negro
Der Spiegel
El País
El Mundo
La Nación (Argentina)
La Vanguardia Española
La Vanguardia
Le Monde
The New York Times
Público

Other Published Sources

Abella, Rafael. *La vida cotidiana durante la guerra civil: la España nacional.* Barcelona: Editorial Planeta, 1973.

Aceña, Pablo Martín and Elena Martínez Ruiz. "The Golden Age of Spanish Capitalism: Economic Growth without Political Freedom." In Townson, 30–46.

Agosín, Marjorie. *Women, Gender, and Human Rights: A Global Perspective.* New Brunswick, NJ: Rutgers University Press, 2002.

Agranoff, Robert. "Federal Evolution in Spain." *International Political Science Review* 17, no. 4 (October 1996): 385–401.

Alonso, Alba and Maxime Forest. "Is Gender Equality Soluble into Self-Governance: Europeanizing Gender at the Sub-National Level in Spain." In Lombardo and Forest, 192–213.

Alonso, Alba and Tània Verge. "Territorial Dynamics and Gender Equality Policies in Spain." In "Étudier les systèmes fédéreux à travers le prisme du genre," edited by Petra Meier. Special issue, *Fédéralisme Régionalisme* 14 (2014). https://popups.uliege.be/1374-3864/index.php?id=1365.

Alvaredo, Facundo and Emmanuel Saez. "Income and Wealth Concentration in Spain from a Historical and Fiscal Perspective." *Journal of the European Economic Association* 7, no. 5 (September 2009): 1143–67.

Alvarez Junco, José and Adrian Shubert, eds. *Spanish History since 1808*. London: Hodder Arnold, 2000.

Aran Ramspott, Sonia and Pilar Medina Bravo. "Representación de la violencia doméstica en la prensa española." *Estudios sobre el Mensaje Periodístico* 12 (2006): 9–25.

Arbós Marín, Xavier. "The Federal Option and Constitutional Management of Diversity in Spain." In López-Basaguren and Epifano, 375–400.

Beckwith, Karen. "Beyond Compare? Women's Movements in Comparative Perspective." *European Journal of Political Research* 37, no. 4 (June 2000): 431–68.

Benería, Lourdes. *Mujer, economía y patriarcado en la España de Franco*. Barcelona: Cuadernos Anagrama, 1977.

Blofield, Merike. *The Politics of Moral Sin: Abortion and Divorce in Spain, Chile and Argentina*. New York: Routledge, 2006.

Blofield, Merike. "Women's Choices in Comparative Perspective: Abortion Policies in Late-Developing Catholic Countries." *Comparative Politics* 40, no. 4 (July 2008): 399–419.

Bock, Gisela. "Racism and Sexism in Nazi Germany: Motherhood, Compulsory Sterilization, and the State." *Signs* 8, no. 3 (Spring 1983): 400–21.

Børresen, Kari and Sara Cabibbo, eds. *Gender, Religion, Human Rights in Europe*. Rome: Herder, 2006.

Brydan, David. *Franco's Internationalists: Social Experts and Spain's Search for Legitimacy*. Oxford, UK: Oxford University Press, 2019.

Bystydzienski, Jill M. *Women Transforming Politics: Worldwide Strategies for Empowerment*. Bloomington, IN: Indiana University Press, 1992.

Callahan, William J. *The Catholic Church in Spain, 1875–1998*. Washington, DC: The Catholic University of America Press, 2012.

Calloni, Marina. "Debates and Controversies on Abortion in Italy." In Stetson, 181–204.

Cambronero-Saiz, Belén, María Teresa Ruiz Cantero, Carmen Vives-Cases and Mercedes Carrasco Portiño. "Abortion in Democratic Spain: The Parliamentary Political Agenda 1979–2004." *Reproductive Health Matters* 15, no. 29 (May 2007): 85–96.

Carnicer, Miguel Ángel Ruiz. "La idea de Europa en la cultura franquista 1939–1962." *Hispania* 58, no. 199 (1998): 679–701.

Cazorla Sánchez, Antonio. *Fear and Progress: Ordinary Lives in Franco's Spain, 1939–1975*. Malden, MA: Wiley-Blackwell, 2010.

Cichowski, Rachel A. "Women's Rights, the European Court, and Supranational Constitutionalism." *Law and Society Review* 38, no. 1 (September 2004): 489–512.

Cmiel, Kenneth. "The Recent History of Human Rights." *The American Historical Review* 109, no. 1 (2004): 117–35.

Cott, Nancy F. *The Grounding of Modern Feminism*. New Haven, CT: Yale University Press, 1987.

Crumbaugh, Justin. *Destination Dictatorship: The Spectacle of Spain's Tourist Boom and the Reinvention of Difference*. Albany, NY: State University of New York Press, 2009.

Davidson, Jessica. "Politics, Policy, and Propaganda of the Sección Femenina in Francoist Spain, 1934–1977." Ph.D. Diss., Brandeis University, 2005. ProQuest Dissertations and Theses Global.

Davidson, Jessica. "Women, Fascism and Work in Francoist Spain: The Law for Political, Professional and Labour Rights." *Gender & History* 23, no. 2 (August 1, 2011): 401–14.

Davis, Rebecca Howard. *Women and Power in Parliamentary Democracies: Cabinet Appointments in Western Europe, 1968–1992*. Lincoln, NE: University of Nebraska Press, 1997.

de Búrca, Gráinne. "The Road Not Taken: The European Union as a Global Human Rights Actor." *American Journal of International Law* 105, no. 4 (October 2011): 649–93.

de Grazia, Victoria. *How Fascism Ruled Women: Italy, 1922–1945*. Los Angeles: University of California Press, 1992.

Delegación Nacional de la Sección Femenina del Movimiento. *Congreso Internacional de la Mujer, Madrid, 7 al 14 de junio de 1970: Memoria*. Madrid: Editorial Almena, 1972.

Díaz Silva, Elena. "El Año Internacional de La Mujer En España: 1975." *Cuadernos de Historia Contemporánea* 31 (2009): 319–39.

Duchen, Claire. *Women's Rights and Women's Lives in France 1944–1968*. New York: Routledge, 2003.

Edles, Laura Desfor. *Symbol and Ritual in the New Spain: The Transition to Democracy After Franco*. New York: Cambridge University Press, 1998.

Encarnación, Omar G. *Democracy Without Justice in Spain: The Politics of Forgetting*. Philadelphia: University of Pennsylvania Press, 2014.

Espinosa Maestre, Francisco. "Sobre la represión franquista en el País Vasco." *Historia Social* 63 (2009): 59–75.

Ferrándiz, Francisco. "Cries and Whispers: Exhuming and Narrating Defeat in Spain Today." *Journal of Spanish Cultural Studies* 9, no. 2 (2008): 177–92.

Ferrándiz, Francisco. "Exhuming the Defeated: Civil War Mass Graves in 21st-Century Spain." *American Ethnologist* 40, no. 1 (2013): 38–54.

Ferrándiz, Francisco. "Mass Graves, Landscapes of Terror: A Spanish Tale." In Ferrándiz and Robben, 92–118.

Ferrándiz, Francisco and Antonius C. G. M. Robben, eds. *Necropolitics: Mass Graves and Exhumations in the Age of Human Rights*. Philadelphia: University of Pennsylvania Press, 2015.

Forest, Eva. *From a Spanish Jail*. Baltimore, Maryland: Penguin Books, 1975.

Francome, Colin. *Unsafe Abortion and Women's Health: Change and Liberalization*. London, UK: Routledge, 2016.

Fraser, Arvonne S. "Becoming Human: The Origins and Development of Women's Human Rights." *Human Rights Quarterly* 21, no. 4 (November 1999): 853–906.

Fraser, Arvonne S. *UN Decade for Women: The Power of Words and Organizations*. Alexandria, VA: Alexander Street, 2012.

Folguera Crespo, Pilar. "El Franquismo. El Retorno a la Esfera Privada (1939–1975)." In Garrido González.

Friedman, Elisabeth Jay. "Gendering the Agenda: The Impact of the Transnational Women's Rights Movement at the UN Conferences of the 1990s." *Women's Studies International Forum* 26, no. 4 (July–August 2003): 313–31.

Garrido González, Elisa, ed. *Historia de las Mujeres en España*. Madrid: Editorial Síntesis, S.A., 1997.

Ghodsee, Kristen. "Revisiting the United Nations Decade for Women: Brief Reflections on Feminism, Capitalism and Cold War Politics in the Early Years of the International Women's Movement." *Women's Studies International Forum* 33, no. 1 (2010): 3–12.

Gibernau, Montserrat. "Spain: a Federation in the Making?" In Smith, 245–54.

Glenn, Kathleen, ed. *Women's Narrative and Film in 20th Century Spain*. New York: Routledge, 2017.

Gómez Del Moral, Alejandro J. *Buying Into Change: Mass Consumption, Dictatorship, and Democratization in Franco's Spain, 1939–1982*. Lincoln, Neb.: University of Nebraska Press, 2021.

Gottlieb, Julie V. *Feminine Fascism: Women in Britain's Fascist Movement, 1923–1945*. London: I.B. Taurus, 2000.

Gottlieb, Julie V. "Women and British Fascism Revisited: Gender, the Far-Right, and Resistance." *Journal of Women's History* 16, no. 3 (Fall 2004): 108–23.

Gunther, Richard, Giacomo Sani, and Goldie Shabad, eds. *Spain after Franco: The Making of a Competitive Party System*. Los Angeles: University of California Press, 1988.

Gunther, Richard, José Ramón Montero Gilbert, and José Ignacio Wert. *The Media and Politics in Spain: From Dictatorship to Democracy*. Barcelona, Spain: Institut de Ciències Polítiques i Socials, 1999.

Gunther, Richard. "Spain: the very model of the modern elite settlement." In Hingley and Gunther, 38–80.

Higley, John and Richard Gunther, eds. *Elites and Democratic Consolidation in Latin American and Southern Europe*. New York: Cambridge University Press, 1992.

Hudson-Richards, Julia. "'Women Want to Work': Shifting Ideologies of Women's Work in Franco's Spain, 1939–1962." *Journal of Women's History* 27, no. 2 (2015): 87–109.

Holguín, Sandie. "'National Spain Invites You': Battlefield Tourism during the Spanish Civil War." *American Historical Review* 110, no. 5 (December 2005): 1399–426.

Hooper, John. *The New Spaniards*. New York: Penguin Books, 2006.

International Commission of Historians Designated to Establish the Military Service of Lt. Kurt Waldheim. *The Waldheim Report: Submitted February 8, 1988, to Federal Chancellor Dr. Franz Vranitzky*. Oxford: The Alden Press, 1993.

Jacques, Hylah M. "Spain: Systematic Torture in a Democratic State." *Monthly Review* 37 (November 1985): 57–63.

Janse, Ronald. "The Evolution of the Political Criteria for Accession to the European Community, 1957–1973." *European Law Journal* 24, no. 1 (2018): 66–8.

Jenson, Jane. "Writing Women Out, Folding Gender in: The European Union 'Modernises' Social Policy." *Social Politics: International Studies in Gender, State & Society* 15, no. 2 (Summer 2008): 131–53.

Jones, Anny Brooksbank. *Women in Contemporary Spain*. New York: Manchester University Press, 1997.

Juste, Antonio Moreno. "The European Economic Community and the End of the Franco Regime: the September 1975 Crisis." *Cahiers de la Méditerranée*, no. 90 (June 2015): 25–45.

Kaplan, Gisela T. *Contemporary Western European Feminism*. New York, NY: New York University Press, 1992.

Kaplan, Temma. "Female Consciousness and Collective Action: The Case of Barcelona, 1910–1918." *Signs* 7, no. 3 (Spring 1982): 545–66.

Kaplan, Temma. *Taking Back the Streets: Women, Youth, and Direct Democracy*. Los Angeles: University of California Press, 2004.

Kaplan, Temma. "Women's Rights as Human Rights: Women as Agents of Social Change." In Agosín, 191–204.

Keene, Judith. "Review Article: Turning Memories into History in the Spanish Year of Historical Memory." *Journal of Contemporary History* 42, no. 4 (October 2007): 661–71.

Klimke, Martin and Joachim Scharloth. *1968 in Europe: A History of Protest and Activism, 1956–1977*. New York: Palgrave Macmillan, 2008.

Koonz, Claudia. *Mothers in the Fatherland: Women, the Family, and Nazi Politics*. New York: St. Martin's Press, 1986.

Labanyi, Jo. "Memory and Modernity in Democratic Spain: The Difficulty of Coming to Terms with the Spanish Civil War." *Poetics Today* 28, no. 1 (Spring 2007): 89–116.

Labanyi, Jo. "Resemanticizing Feminine Surrender: Cross-Gender Identifications in the Writings of Spanish Female Fascist Activists." In Glenn, 75–92.

Landau, Eve C. and Yves Beigbeder. *From ILO Standards to EU Law: The Case of Equality between Men and Women at Work*. Boston: Martinus Nijhoff Publishers, 2008.

Linz, Juan J. "Church and State in Spain from the Civil War to the Return of Democracy." *Daedalus* 120, no. 3 (Summer 1991): 159–78.

Lombardo, Emanuela. "The Influence of the Catholic Church on Spanish Political Debates on Gender Policy (1996–2004)." In Børresen and Cabibbo.

Lombardo, Emanuela and Maxime Forest. eds. *The Europeanization of Gender Equality Policies: A Sociological-Discursive Approach*. New York, NY: Palgrave Macmillan, 2012.

López-Basaguren, Alberto and Leire Escajedo San Epifano, eds. *The Ways of Federalism in Western Countries and the Horizons of Territorial Autonomy in Spain*. Berlin: Springer, 2013.

Lovenduski, Joni, ed. *State Feminism and Political Representation*. New York: Cambridge University Press, 2005.

MacLennan, Julio Crespo. *Spain and the Process of European Integration, 1957–85*. New York: Palgrave Macmillan, 2000.

Martín, Irene and Ignacio Urquizu-Sancho. "The 2011 General Election in Spain: The Collapse of the Socialist Party." *South European Society and Politics* 17, no. 2 (2012): 347–63.

Martín Gaite, Carmen. *Courtship Customs in Postwar Spain (Usos amorosos de la postguerra española)*. Translated by Margaret E. W. Jones. Lewisburg, PA: Bucknell University Press, 2004.

Medina-Ariza, Juanjo and Rosemary Barberet. "Intimate Partner Violence in Spain: Findings from a National Survey." *Violence against Women* 9, no. 3 (March 2003): 302–22.

Moghadam, Valentine M. *Globalizing Women: Transnational Feminist Networks*. Baltimore, MD: Johns Hopkins University Press, 2005.

Moraga García, María Ángeles. "Notas sobre la Situacion Jurídica de la Mujer en el Franquismo." *Feminismo/s* 12 (2008): 229–52.

Morcillo, Aurora G. *The Seduction of Modern Spain: The Female Body and the Francoist Body Politic*. Lewisburg, PA: Bucknell University Press, 2010.

Morcillo, Aurora G. *True Catholic Womanhood: Gender Ideology in Franco's Spain*. DeKalb, IL: Northern Illinois University Press, 1999.

Nash, Mary. *Defying Male Civilization: Women in the Spanish Civil War*. Denver: Arden Press, 1995.

Nielfa Cristóbal, Gloria, ed. *Mujeres y Hombres en la España Franquista: Sociedad, Economía, Política, Cultura*. Madrid: Complutense, 2003.

Ofer, Inbal. "La Guerra de Agua: Notions of Morality, Respectability, and Community in a Madrid Neighborhood." *Journal of Urban History* 35, no. 2 (January 2009): 220–35.

Ofer, Inbal. *Señoritas in Blue: The Making of a Female Political Elite in Franco's Spain*. Toronto: Sussex Academic Press, 2010.

Ortiz-Gómez, Teresa and Agata Ignaciuk, "The Family Planning movement in Spain during the democractic transition," unpublished paper presented at the Health Activist Symposium, Yale University, October 22–3, 2010.

Ortiz-Gómez, Teresa and Agata Ignaciuk. "'Pregnancy and Labour Cause More Deaths than Oral Contraceptives': The Debate on the Pill in the Spanish Press in the 1960s and 1970s." *Public Understanding of Science* 24, no. 6 (August 2015): 658–71.

Pack, Sasha D. *Tourism and Dictatorship: Europe's Peaceful Invasion of Franco's Spain*. New York: Palgrave Macmillan, 2006.

Palomares, Cristina. *The Quest for Survival After Franco: Moderate Francoism and the Slow Journey to the Polls, 1964–1977*. Portland, OR: Sussex Academic Press, 2006.

Payne, Stanley G. *Fascism in Spain, 1923–1977*. Madison, WI: University of Wisconsin Press, 1999.

Payne, Stanley G. *The Franco Regime, 1936–1975*. Madison, WI: University of Wisconsin Press, 1987.

Pereira, Ana Maria Prata Amaral. "Women's Movements, the State, and the Struggle for Abortion Rights: Comparing Spain and Portugal in Times of Democratic Expansion" (*1974–1988*). Ph.D. Diss., University of Minnesota, 2007. ProQuest Dissertations and Theses Global.

Pérez Díaz, Víctor. *The Return of Civil Society: The Emergence of Democratic Spain*. Cambridge, MA: Harvard University Press, 1993.

Portela, M. Edurne. "Writing (in) Prison: The Discourse of Confinement in Lidia Falcón's En El Infierno." *Arizona Journal of Hispanic Cultural Studies* 11 (2007): 121–36.

Powell, Charles. "International Aspects of Democratization: The Case of Spain." In Whitehead, 285–314.

Preston, Paul. *Juan Carlos: Steering Spain from Dictatorship to Democracy*. New York: W.W. Norton & Company, 2004.

Preston, Paul. *The Politics of Revenge: Fascism and the Military in 20th-Century Spain*. New York: Routledge, 2003.

Radcliff, Pamela Beth. "Imagining Female Citizenship in the 'New Spain': Gendering the Democratic Transition, 1975–1978." *Gender and History* 13, no. 4 (November 2001): 498–523.

Radcliff, Pamela Beth. *Making Democratic Citizens in Spain: Civil Society and the Popular Origins of the Transition, 1960–1978*. New York: Palgrave Macmillan, 2011.

Radcliff, Pamela Beth. *Modern Spain: 1808 to the Present*. Hoboken, NJ: Wiley-Blackwell, 2017.

Richmond, Kathleen. *Women and Spanish Fascism: The Women's Section of the Falange 1934–1959*. New York: Routledge, 2003.

Richmond, Kathleen. "The Yoke of Isabella: The Women's Section of the Spanish Falange 1934–1959." Ph.D. Diss., University of Southampton, 1999.

Roggeband, Conny. "'Immediately I Thought We Should Do the Same Thing' International Inspiration and Exchange in Feminist Action against Sexual Violence." *European Journal of Women's Studies* 11, no. 2 (May 2004): 159–75.

Romero, Ana. *Carmen, Suárez, y El Rey: El Triángulo de la Transición*. Barcelona: Planeta, 2013.

Romero, Ana. *Historia de Carmen: memorias de Carmen Díez de Rivera.* Barcelona: Planeta, 2002.

Rosendorf, Neal M. *Franco Sells Spain to America: Hollywood, Tourism and Public Relations as Postwar Spanish Soft Power.* New York: Palgrave Macmillan, 2014.

Rossilli, Mariagrazia, ed. *Gender Policies in the European Union.* New York: Peter Lang Publishing, 2000.

Roth, Silke, ed. *Gender Politics in the Expanding European Union: Mobilization, Inclusion, Exclusion.* New York: Berghahn, 2008.

Royo, Sebastián. "The Experience of Spain and Portugal in the European Union: Lessons for Latin America." Working Paper Series 2, no. 2, Florida International University, EU Center (2002).

Savery, Lynn. *Engendering the State: The International Diffusion of Women's Human Rights.* New York: Routledge, 2007.

Saz Campos, Ismael. "Fascism, Fascistization and Developmentalism in Franco's Dictatorship." *Social History* 29, no. 3 (August 2004): 342–57.

Skard, Torild. "Gender in the Malestream—Acceptance of Women and Gender Equality in Different United Nations Organisations." *Forum for Development Studies* 36, no. 1 (2009).

Smith, Graham, ed. *Federalism: The Multiethnic Challenge.* New York: Routledge, 1995.

Stetson, Dorothy McBride, ed. *Abortion Politics, Women's Movements, and the Democratic State.* New York: Oxford University Press, 2001.

Strid, Sofia. *Gendered Interests in the European Union: The European Women's Lobby and the Organisation and Representation of Women's Interests.* Örebro, Sweden: Örebro University, 2009.

Suárez Fernández, Luis. *Cronica de la Sección Femenina y su tiempo.* Madrid: Asocición Nueva Andadura, 1992.

Sullivan, Donna J. "Women's Human Rights and the 1993 World Conference on Human Rights." *American Journal of International Law* 88, no. 1 (January 1994): 152–67.

Tejada, Luis Alonso. *La represión sexual en la España de Franco.* Barcelona: Luis de Caralt, 1978.

Threlfall, Monica. "Explaining Gender Parity Representation in Spain: The Internal Dynamics of Parties." *West European Politics* 30, no. 5 (November 2007): 1068–95.

Threlfall, Monica. "Feminist Politics and Social Change in Spain." In Threlfall, *Mapping the Women's Movement,* 115–51.

Threlfall, Monica. "Gendering the transition to democracy: reassessing the impact of women's activism." In Threlfall, Cousins, and Valiente, 11–54.

Threlfall, Monica. *Mapping the Women's Movement: Feminist Politics and Social Transformation in the North.* New York: Verso, 1996.

Threlfall, Monica. "The Women's Movement in Spain." *New Left Review* 151 (May–June 1985): 44–73.

Threlfall, Monica, Christine Cousins, and Celia Valiente, eds. *Gendering Spanish Democracy.* New York: Routledge, 2004.

Townson, Nigel, ed. *Spain Transformed: The Late Franco Dictatorship, 1959–1975*. New York: Palgrave Macmillan, 2007.
Tusell, Javier. *Spain: From Dictatorship to Democracy, 1939 to the Present*. Translated by Rosemary Clark. Malden, MA: Wiley-Blackwell, 2011.
United Nations Department of Public Information. *The United Nations and the Advancement of Women, 1945–1996*. The United Nations Blue Books Series, vol. 6. New York: Department of Public Information, 1995.
Valiente, Celia. "But Where Are the Men?: Central-State Public Policies to Combat Violence against Women in Post-Authoritarian Spain (1975–1999)." Paper presented at the Council of Europe Seminar on Men and Violence against Women, Strasbourg, October 7–8, 1999, accessed April 16, 2018, http://www.europrofem.org/White-Ribbon/13.institutions/3.coe/en-violence-coe/16.en-coe-oct99.htm.
Valiente, Celia. "Combating Violence against Women." In Threlfall, Cousins, and Valiente, 101–24.
Valiente, Celia. "Gendering Abortion Debates: State Feminism in Spain." In Stetson, 229–46.
Valiente, Celia. "Spain at the Vanguard in European Gender Equality Policies." In Roth, 101–17.
Valiente, Celia. "The Women's Movement, Gender Equality Agencies and Central-State Debates on Political Representation in Spain." In Lovenduski, 174–94.
van der Vleuten, Anna. *The Price of Gender Equality: Member States and Governance in the European Union*. Burlington, VT: Ashgate Publishing Company, 2007.
Villena, Amalia Morales. "Género, Mujeres, Trabajo Social y Sección Femenina. Historia de una Profesión Feminizada y con Vocación Feminista." Ph.D. Diss., Universidad de Granada, 2010.
Whitehead, Laurence, ed. *The International Dimensions of Democratization: Europe and the Americas*, 2nd ed. Oxford: Oxford University Press, 1996.
Whitfield, Teresa. *Endgame for ETA: Elusive Peace in the Basque Country*. New York: Oxford University Press, 2014.
Wilcox, Clyde. "The Causes and Consequences of Feminist Consciousness among Western European Women." *Comparative Political Studies* 23, no. 4 (January 1991): 519–45.

Index

ABC 8–9, 65, 107, 141
abortion/abortion regulations 12–14, 37,
    76–81, 135, 145–6
    Catholic Church's influence on 59,
        71–2, 74, 77–8
    Cortes's debates 74–5, 77–9
    effects of 146
    hardships in procuring 73, 79–80
    Instituto de la Mujer on 76–9
    machista solution 135
    media on 75
    PSOE's approach to 75–81
    public health campaign 71–2, 74
    restrictions/legalization 1–2, 38, 54,
        70–1, 73–5, 145–8
    Spanish Episcopal Council 74
    Stimezo organization 94
Action Plan Against Intimate Partner
    Violence 1998–2000 122–3, 144
adultery 61–3, 65
Alianza Popular (Popular Alliance/
    AP) 77–8
Alonso, Alba 110
Álvarez, Ángeles 148
Álvarez, Lili 9
Amat Roca, Montserrat 64–5
anti-abortion activists 2, 144–6
anti-rape campaigns 119–20
Antonio, José 38
Arsuaga, Ignacio 2–3
Art Against Domestic Violence 148
Asamblea de Mujeres de Barcelona (AMB)
    46–7
Association of Support to the European
    Lobby of Women (ASEWL) 101
Ayúcar, Ángel Ruiz 21, 25–7, 29

backwardness 6, 12, 17–18, 46, 117
Bando Nacional 21
Barrobes, Karmele Marchante 104
Bayo, Regina 51–2, 91

birth control 71–3, 93. See also abortion/
    abortion regulations
Blanco, Benigno 135
Blanco y Negro 66, 107, 183 n.67
boyish feminists 8
British National Abortion Campaign 94
Bustelo, Carlota 64, 69

Calleja, José Luis 65
Campo de Alange, Maria 37
Carlism 166 n.3
Carlist Party 51–2
Carlos, Juan 52–3, 65, 170 n.51
Carmena, Manuela 141
Carter, Jimmy 44
Catholic Church 2, 4, 59, 74, 77,
    127–8, 135, 141. *See also* National-
    Catholicism
Cazorla, Antonio 6
*Centre de Recherches de reflexion et
    d'information féministe* (CRIF) 92
Checa, Carmen Olmeda 99
Christian feminism 9
Ciudadanos/Citizens (C's) party 151
coeducation 4, 19, 37, 99–100, 109
Coeducation Advisory Boards (CAB) 109
Colau, Ada 141
Cold War 5, 18, 42
Common Market 6, 27, 32
Congreso Internacional de la Mujer
    (*Congreso*) 33–9, 45–6
Constitution 7, 10–12, 19–20, 51–2, 54–5,
    61–9, 77, 132
contraception 38, 54, 62, 72, 74
Convention on the Elimination of All
    Forms of Discrimination Against
    Women (CEDAW) 120, 126, 133,
    136
Cortes 21, 23, 25, 31, 54, 67–9, 74–5,
    77–80, 85, 120, 122–6, 130
Cosmopolitan 31

Cott, Nancy F. 16
Council of Europe 1949 32, 126
Cruz, Manuel 146

DeMille, Cecil B., *Samson and Delilah* 4
democracy 11–21, 53–4, 61–3, 73, 76, 79, 82, 117–18, 143
Diez de Rivera, Carmen 18, 65–6, 68, 170 nn.50–1
dissident groups 56
División Azul 21
divorce 12–14, 37–8, 114, 118–20
   legalization of 80
   PSOE and feminists on 128
domestic terrorism 129–30
domestic violence. *See* intimate partner violence (IPV)
Donaire, Isabel 107
dones en lluita 57–9, 63, 68–71, 90–1, 93
double militants 10, 53–4, 60–3, 69, 75–6, 78, 86, 89, 103–4, 111
Duchen, Claire 16
Dutch wage regulations 30

economic development 15, 17–18
8M 139–40, 142, 148, 150–1
Eisenhower, Dwight D. 5–6
El Colective "Consulterios" del Movimente Italiano de Liberación de la Mujer (MLD) 93–4
El Mundo 1, 66, 129, 134
El País 65, 73, 75, 140, 148, 169 n.46
Equality Act 130
Equal Pay Act 1963 31
equal payment/labor rights 21, 25–8, 30–1
Equal Remuneration Convention 1951 30
Equal Rights Amendment 44
European Court of Human Rights (ECHR) 145
European Economic Community (EEC) 5–7, 15, 21–2, 31–2, 52, 55, 68, 85
   on intimate partner violence 120
   UN and 85, 87, 96
European Political Community 1953 31–2
European Union 15, 20, 86–7, 96–102, 105, 110, 127, 134, 136, 144
European Women's Lobby (EWL) 101
Euskadi ta Askatasuna (ETA) 17

Fagoaga, Concha 105
Falange Española 3, 14
Falcón, Lidia 58–9, 69, 104, 163 n.49
family violence/domestic violence 127–8
fascism 88–90, 136
Federación de Mujeres Progresistas (FMP) 129
Federation of Feminist Organizations 61
Feijóo, Alberto Núñez 142
feminism/feminists 7–11
   Christian 9
   Constitution 64–5, 68–9
   independent/institutional 10–11, 80, 85–8
   international media's view 59
   male politicians and 55, 65, 68
   Moncloa Pacts and 54, 62–3, 69–70
   organizational efforts 7, 13, 37 (*see also* women's organizations)
   policy positions 7
   post-Franco feminism 55–64, 86
   professionalization of 115
   self-identified 9, 60, 88
   single/double militants 10, 60–3, 69 (*see also* double militants; single militants)
   through journalism 59
   of transition era 54–5, 60, 63, 69, 77
   transnational links/internationalism 15, 17, 87–95 (*see also* international feminism)
Femme Força 148
First Conference for Women's Liberation 56, 60
first-wave feminism 15
Forest, Eva 163 n.49
Formica, Mercedes 28
Franco, Francisco 3, 6, 12–13, 16, 28, 33, 53, 88, 114, 116, 118, 163 n.49
   dictatorship 3, 5–6, 21–2, 28, 32, 143, 149
   EEC membership 6, 28, 32
   international engagement 33
   neighborhood and housewives' associations 36–7, 55–6, 60
   opposition to 38
   post-Franco era 7, 53, 114–15
   systemic discrimination 54
   as UN member 5

Fraser, Arvonne 41–5
French feminism 16, 90–2
Friedan, Betty 59
Friedman, Elizabeth 96
Fuero del Trabajo 4

gender discrimination 19, 62, 66, 96, 98, 151
gender equality 1, 7, 18–19, 42, 85–6, 96–7, 115, 123, 144, 147
Gender Equality Law 144
gender mainstreaming 96–7, 100, 102, 105–6, 109, 111, 133, 136
gender quota system 67–9, 130, 133
gender violence 1, 20, 115, 126–7. *See also* intimate partner violence (IPV)
Generalitat de Catalunya 74
Ghodsee, Kristen 42–5
Gómez Del Moral, Alejandro J. 17
Gonzalez, Felipe 81, 107, 120
Gora Iruñea 149
Grupo Parlamentario de Unión de Centro Democrático (GUCD) 67
Gunther, Richard 175 n.106

Hazte Oir 2–3, 144, 146
Holguín, Sandie 3
human rights 2, 19, 31–2, 96, 98, 180 n.34
hunger years 23, 26

Ibarrola, Begoña 61
illegal abortions 1, 74, 144. *See also* abortion/abortion regulations
independent feminists 10–11, 80–1, 85–8, 96, 98
 gender mainstreaming 100, 105–6
 vs. institutional feminists 102–10
 of intimate partner violence 114
 Mujeres para Democracía 134
Industrial Revolution 90
institutional feminists 10–11, 85–8
 equality policies 100–1
 independent *vs.* 102–10
 integration into state's power 104–5
 international feminist networks 96, 100
 of intimate partner violence 115–16
 LOMPIVG and 131, 134–5
 structural challenges 98–9

Instituto de la Mujer 10, 19, 54, 76–9, 85, 87–8, 101, 111, 120, 131, 141, 144, 147, 153, 159 n.37
 Action Plan Against Intimate Partner Violence 122–5, 144
 autonomous communities 99–100
 double militant/institutional feminists 103
 in international events 101–2
 Partido Popular and 147
Intereconomía 1
International Congress of Women 34
international feminism 15, 17, 42, 87–95
International Labor Organization (ILO) 30–1, 140
International Women's Day 20, 80, 93, 109, 139–40, 148, 150, 178 n.21
International Women's Year (IWY) 39–48
Interviú (¡Hola!) 57
intimate partner violence (IPV) 115, 117–18, 148
 assaults of 121
 Consejo General del Poder Judicial study on 184 n.3
 criminalization of 116, 120, 130
 domestic terrorism 129–30
 EEC statistics on 120
 family violence 127–8
 fighting machismo 122
 gender-based violence 126–7
 gender equality 123, 125
 Instituto's Action Plan 122–5
 laws 121, 126
 LOMPIVG and 128–31
 physical violence 125
 Popular Party's attempts to 123–4
 PSOE on 126
Italian feminist activity 92–3

Jenson, Jane 98
Jones, Anny Brooksbank 56
Joya, Gádor 2, 145–6

Kaplan, Gisela T. 15
Kaplan, Temma 13–14, 16, 180 n.34

labor rights 21, 25–8
La Manada (the wolfpack) 149–50
Lanbroa 104–5

La Razón 1
La Vanguardia 64
Law for the Effective Equality of Men and Women/Equality Act 130
Law of Political and Professional Rights for Women 14
legal equality 9, 40, 183 n.67
L'eix Violeta 71–2
Ley de Derechos 18, 24–9
Ley Orgánica de Medidas de Protección Integral contra la Violencia de Género (LOMPIVG) 1, 114–16, 129–35, 143
Ley sobre derechos políticos, profesionales y de trabajo de la mujer (LsD) 21–2, 24–9, 35
Llorente, David 141
Lombardo, Emanuela 127
Lovenduski, Joni 15
Luna, Lola G. 104

MacLennan, Julio Crespo 17
magazines/pamphlets 57–60, 89–93
male chauvinist violence 139
Marino i Serra, Maria Luisa 104
marital abuse 114
marital rape 119, 125
marital status and professions 4, 21
Martín, Areceli 141
Martínez Ten, Carmen 107–8
media 59–60, 64, 68, 72–3, 82, 92, 118, 121–5, 149–50
Meridiana 99–100
Moghadam, Valentine M. 17
Moncloa Pacts 54, 62–3, 69–70
Morcillo, Aurora 8, 13–14, 23
Movimento Democratico de Mujeres (MDM) 14, 37, 47, 56
to women's rights 60
Movimiento Nacional 3–4
Mujeres Democraticas de España (MDE) 38
Mujeres Libres 13
Mujeres para Democracía (MD) 134
Mujer y Socialismo 68

Nash, Mary 13
National-Catholicism 4–5, 14, 21, 23, 25, 38, 49, 54, 114

National Organization of Women 59
National Security Council 42
Navarro, Carlos Arias 41
neighborhood and housewives' associations 36–8, 56–7, 60
Newsweek 66, 170 n.50
New York Times 16, 118–19, 178 n.21
NGO Tribune 41, 44, 102, 145

OCE Bandera pamphlet 64, 69
Ofer, Inbal 6, 13–14
Opción 57, 71, 90–1
Orantes, Ana 113–14, 117–19, 121–3, 125, 127–9
Order for the Protection of Victims of Intimate Partner Violence 126
Organizaciones de Mujeres de Madrid (OMM) 46–7
Organization for European Economic Co-operation (OEEC) 32

Pack, Sasha D. 17
Parejo Avivar, José 113–14, 117
Partido Popular (PP) 1, 20, 124, 126–8, 131, 135, 141–2, 146–8, 150–1
Partido Socialista Obrera Español (PSOE) 1–2, 54, 68, 85, 141
abortion legislation 75–81, 144
creation of *Instituto de la Mujer* 85, 87, 95, 98
on divorce 128
on intimate partner violence 126
Podemos and 141
and *Unidos Podemos* coalition 151
Patriotic Anti-Fascist Revolutionary Front's Popular Union of Women (FRAP-UPM) 51
Paul VI, Pope 9
peace agenda 42
Pepa-García, Paloma Cruz 63, 69
President's Commission on the Status of Women (PCSW) 31
Primo de Rivera, Pilar 8, 21–5, 28–9, 32, 38, 55–6
head of Spanish National Committee 39
women's participation in civic life 24–5

Radcliff, Pamela Beth 12–14, 54, 68, 182 n.63
  on female associational life 14
  on feminists struggles 59–60
  study of housewives' associations 55–6
radical feminism 44, 48, 106–9, 176 n.111
Rajoy, Mariano 143, 147–8, 150
rape/rape laws 70, 79, 118–21, 125, 137, 146, 149–50, 180 n.34
Ray, Dixie Lee 91
Reagan, Ronald 91
Red Magazine 88–9
Revuelta, Raquel 107–8
Ribed de Valcárcel, Carola 39, 45
Richmond, Kathleen 13–14, 56–7
Romero, Carmen 107–8
Ruiz-Gallardón, Alberto 146–8

Saavedra, Paloma 51–2, 91
Sainz Garcia, Maria Jesus 124, 183 n.67
Salinas, Carmen 39, 40, 43–6
Savery, Lynn 5
Schlafly, Phyllis 44
Sección Femenina (SF) 4–6, 18, 56–7, 79
  assertions 21–2
  capitalism and industrialization 43
  and *Congreso* 33–9
  conservative/transformative activism 22–3, 44
  feminists' criticisms of 102
  international leadership 22, 33–6
  labor and financial rights 40
  Ley sobre derechos and 24–9
  magazines 57
  MDE and 38
  neighborhood associations 38
  policy successes 36
  political access 67
  in post-Civil War period 23
  social reforms 16
  WCOW and 40–1, 43–5, 52, 102
  women's rights 8–9, 13–14, 24, 33, 52
Second Republic 3, 13, 64, 143
second-wave feminism 15, 41
Seneca Falls Conference 90
Servicio Social 5
sexual violence 70, 119, 121, 125, 137, 180 n.34

single militants 10, 53, 60–2, 69, 76, 86, 89, 103, 111
Skard, Torild 106
social harmonization 31
social inequalities 130, 141
Solsona i Piñol, Maria Carme 123–4
Spanish Civil War 3, 13, 23, 29
Spanish Communist Party (PCE) 51
Stabilization Plan 6, 23, 26
Stimezo organization 94
Suárez, Adolfo 64–6, 75, 77

TeleCinco television channel 113, 117
Tellado, Miguel 142
Telva 57
Teresa 21, 24–9, 34, 39–40, 45, 57
Thomas, Dolores 94–5
Threlfall, Monica 12–13, 68
Torrús, Alejandro 163 n.49
transitional moment 39–48
Treaty of Rome 24, 27, 32
Tribuna Feminista 71, 80, 91–2, 102
Triunfo 63
true Catholic womanhood 23, 33

Umbral, Francisco 65
Unión de Centro Democrático (Union of the Democratic Center/UCD) 77
United Nations 5, 15, 30, 39, 46–7, 87, 96–7, 100–5, 110, 127, 131, 133, 136

Valiente, Celia 60
Valle de los Caídos (Valley of the Fallen) 129
Verge, Tánia 110
Villacís, Begoña 142
Vindicación Feminista 51–2, 57–9, 69, 71, 90–1
violence 118, 126–7. *See also* gender violence; intimate partner violence (IPV)

Waldheim, Kurt 6
West German Federal Labor Court 30
Wilcox, Clyde 15
Wolf, Naomi, *The Beauty Myth* 107
Woman's Council (*Consejo de la Mujer*) 109

Women's Bureau 31, 67, 85. *See also Instituto de la Mujer*
women's organizations 13–14, 16–17, 37, 60, 76, 80, 85, 101
  abortion law and 80
  and economic development 17–18
  political organizations 55
women's politics 43–4, 54–5, 67–8
  quota system 67–9, 130, 133
women's rights 1, 12, 51–4, 142
  Constitutional ratification 64–70
  in *Cortes* 67
  First Catalan Women's Conference 62
  gender mainstreaming 97–8
  human rights and 96
  international leadership/movement 33–6, 52, 60
  and liberalization 18
  maternity/paternity leave 40
  MDM and 60
  older/younger branch 35–6, 38, 41
  political change and 60
  professional and labor rights. 25–8, 30–1, 40, 144
  protections for 103–4
  renegotiation of 143
  and *Sección Femenina* 6–8, 13–14, 33, 52
World Conference on Women (WCOW) 39–40, 42, 52, 86, 96, 101, 120
  in Beijing 86, 96, 101
  cultures and traditions 41
  Equal Rights Amendment 44
  international political issues 42
  legal equality 40, 86
  in Mexico City 39–40, 42–4, 102
  in Nairobi 102
  NGO involvement 41, 44
  as paternalism 46
  resolutions 45
  United Nations 47
  women in government delegations 42–3
  on women's rights issues 45–6

Yanes, Elias 121–2

Zapatero, José Luis Rodríguez 1–2, 130–1, 143–5
Zionism 42

www.ingramcontent.com/pod-product-compliance
Lightning Source LLC
Chambersburg PA
CBHW052111300426
44116CB00010B/1622